A CHILD'S
HISTORY OF IRELAND

P. W. JOYCE

Facsimile of one page of the *Book of Mac Durnan,* Irish scribe, A.D. 850. The words, which are much contracted, are the beginning of the Gospel of St. Mark, in Latin.—From Westwood's Fac.-sim. of Ang.-Sax. and Irish MSS.

A CHILD'S

HISTORY OF IRELAND

BY

P. W. JOYCE, LL.D., M.R.I.A.

One of the Commissioners for the Publication of the Ancient Laws of Ireland

AUTHOR OF
A Social History of Ancient Ireland
A Short History of Ireland
Irish Names of Places, Old Celtic Romances
Ancient Irish Music
AND OTHER WORKS RELATING TO IRELAND

Great Tower, Clonmacnoise. From Petrie's *Round Towers*.

Sandycroft Publishing

A Child's History of Ireland

By P. W. Joyce

First published 1910

This edition ©2017

Sandycroft Publishing
http://sandycroftpublishing.com

Sculpture over a doorway, Cormac's Chapel, Cashel: Centaur shooting at a lion. From Petrie's *Round Towers,* p. 296.

PREFACE

IN writing this book I have generally followed the plan of weaving the narrative round important events and leading personages. This method, while in no degree interfering with the continuity of the History, has enabled me to divide the whole book into short chapters, each forming a distinct narrative or story more or less complete and it has aided me in my endeavour to make the History of Ireland interesting and attractive.

Without descending to childish phraseology, I have done my best to make the language so simple and plain that any child can understand it who is able to read English with facility. My constant aim has been to make the book easy to read and easy to understand.

Above all I have tried to write soberly and moderately, avoiding exaggeration and bitterness, pointing out extenuating circumstances where it was just and right to do so, giving credit where credit is due, and showing fair play all round. A writer may accomplish all this while sympathising heartily, as I do, with Ireland and her people. Perhaps this book, written as it is in such a broad and just spirit, may help to foster mutual feelings of respect and toleration among Irish people of different parties, and may teach them to love and admire what is great and noble in their history, no matter where found. This indeed was one of the objects I kept steadily in view while writing it. When a young citizen of Limerick and another of Derry read the account given here of the two memorable sieges, I hope it is not too much to expect that the reader in each case, while feeling a natural pride in the part played by his own ancestors, will be moved to a just and generous admiration for those of the other side who so valiantly defended their homes. And the History of Ireland, though on the whole a very sad history, abounds in records of heroic deeds and heroic endurance, like those of Derry and Limerick, which all Irish people of the present day ought to look back to with pride, and which all young persons should be taught to reverence and admire.

Though the book has been written for children, I venture to express a hope that it may be found sufficiently interesting and instructive for the perusal of older people.

The illustrations, all of which relate to the several parts of the text where they occur, and all of which have been selected with great care, will be found, I trust, to add to the interest of the book.

No effort has been spared to secure truthfulness and accuracy of statement; the utmost care has been taken throughout to consult and compare original authorities; and nothing has been accepted on second-hand evidence.

It may not be unnecessary to say that, except in the few places where I quote, the narrative all through this book is original, and not made up by adapting or copying the texts of other modern Irish Histories. For good or for bad I preferred my own way of telling the story.

P. W. J.

Lyre-na-Grena Leinster Road,
Rathmines, Dublin,
November, 1897.

It gives me great pleasure to acknowledge the courtesy of those to whom I applied for permission to reproduce illustrations from copyright books.[1] My thanks are especially due to the following:

To the Council of the Royal Irish Academy, for the use of electrotypes of illustrations in Wilde's *Catalogue of Irish Antiquities.*

To the Council of the Royal Society of Antiquaries of Ireland, for many illustrations from their Journal.

To the Cork Historical and Archaeological Society, through their Secretary, Mr. Denham Franklin, for the use of some illustrations in their Journal.

To the Cambrian Archaeological Association, through their Secretary, the Rev. R. Trevor Owen, for the picture of Dun Aengus.

---

[1] Under each illustration in the book the source from which it is derived is mentioned.

To the Controller of Her Majesty's Stationery Office, London, for the use of many illustrations from *Facsimiles of Irish National Manuscripts,* by Sir John T. Gilbert, LL.D., F.S.A.: a work containing a great amount of original information on the History of Ireland. Before applying to the Controller, I consulted Sir John T. Gilbert himself, who at once gave his consent.

To Miss Margaret Stokes, for many illustrations from her two valuable and beautiful books, *Early Christian Art in Ireland,* and *Early Christian Architecture in Ireland.* I had Miss Stokes's permission also to apply to the Council of the Royal Society of Antiquaries of Ireland for the use of the illustrations in her admirable edition of Dr. Petrie's *Christian Inscriptions in the Irish Language.*

To Lord Walter Fitzgerald, for permission to use the illustrations in the *Journal of the County Kildare Archaeological Society.*

To the Right Hon. The O'Conor Don, who lent me the brass plate engraved from the original portrait of Charles O'Conor of Bellanagar.

To Dr. Richard Garnet, C.B., Keeper of Printed Books in the British Museum, for permission to photograph the engraving of Hugh O'Neill.

To Colonel Wood-Martin, for some of the excellent illustrations from his book on *Pagan Ireland.*

To Mr. Bernard Quaritch, Publisher and Bookseller, London, for permission to copy from Westwood's magnificent work, *Facsimiles of Anglo-Saxon and Irish Manuscripts,* the illuminated page from the Book of Mac Durnan.

To Mr. John Murray, Publisher, London, for an illustration from one of the books published by him.

To Messrs. A. & C. Black, for the use of the illustrations in their reprint of Derrick's *Image of Ireland.*

To the Rev. T. Lee, Adm., St. John's, Limerick, I am indebted for photograph of St. John's Gate, and for some important information about Limerick.

Mr. W. G. Strickland, Registrar, National Gallery, Dublin, was ever ready to help me in my search for portraits, and obtained for me permission to have those I wanted photographed.

Besides the above, a number of illustrations have been taken from books having no copyright, and others have been purchased from the proprietors of copyright works: all of which are acknowledged in the proper places. Among the non-copyright books I am specially indebted to Dr. Petrie's great work on the Round Towers of Ireland, from which I have reproduced many of the exquisite engravings, all drawn originally by

Petrie himself; and lastly, I have used several photographs, most of which were taken for me by a friend, who went specially to the places.

Most of the ornamental capitals at the beginnings of the chapters are taken from a very ancient Irish manuscript called the *Book of Hymns,* but some few are from other old Irish books.

It would be an injustice if I failed to acknowledge the skill and taste with which the Dublin artist, Mr. A. McGoogan, reproduced the beautiful illuminated page of the Book of Mac Durnan, with all its delicate outlines and brilliant colours: the same artist who made the copy of the Map of Ireland that illustrates this book, from my own rudely-drawn though vary carefully-constructed sketch.

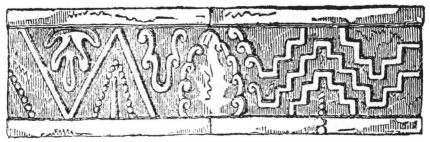

Sculpture on a Column, Church of the Monastery, Glendalough.
From Petrie's *Round Towers,* 260.

CONTENTS

LIST OF ILLUSTRATIONS

HISTORY OF IRELAND

CHAPTER I
THE FACE OF THE COUNTRY IN THE OLDEN TIME

ORDER that the Story of Ireland, as set forth in this book, may be clearly understood, it is necessary, at the outset, to describe how the country looked in early ages, and to give some information about the daily life of the people. This will be done in the first six chapters. The state of things pictured here existed in Ireland from a period beyond the reach of history down to about three hundred years ago, and partially much later: but with many changes from time to time during the long interval.

In old times the appearance of Ireland was very different from what it is at present. The country was everywhere covered with vast forests; and the hillsides, now generally so bare, were then clothed with woods looking down on the pleasant valleys beneath. There were great and dangerous marshes, quagmires, and bogs, covered with reeds, moss, and grass. But though bogs existed from the beginning, many districts where we now find them lying broad and deep were once forest land; and the bog grew after the surface had in some manner become bare of trees. Buried down at a depth of many feet in some of our present bogs, great tree trunks are often found, the relics of the primeval forest.

In those days, as the land of the country was so much encumbered with trees, it was justly regarded as a praiseworthy deed to help to clear spaces for tillage; and accordingly the Annals often record the clearing of certain plains by ancient kings. This work of clearing for tillage always went on; but in later times the forests were cut down quickly enough for

1

another purpose, to supply fuel for smelting iron, which was a common industry in Ireland three or four hundred years ago. Besides all this, there was a regular export trade in Irish oak; and we know that a king of Ireland, Murkertagh O'Brien, presented William Rufus with a number of great oak trees cut down in a spot now covered by a part of Dublin city, with which Westminster Hall was roofed. From all these causes combined the great forests of Ireland were gradually cleared off and finally disappeared about two centuries ago.

At intervals through the country there were open grassy plains, but they were everywhere surrounded by forest land, and broken up and dotted over with clumps of trees and brushwood.

The same sparkling streamlets without number that still delight us tumbled down from the uplands; and there too were the same stately rivers and resounding waterfalls. But the streams and rivers were under little or no restraint: they were not artificially banked in and confined, as in many places they are now; and in times of flood they broke through their banks, overflowed the flat lands, made new beds for themselves, and altogether did very much as they pleased. In many of the rivers the pearl mussel was found, so that Ireland was well known for producing pearls, unusually large and of very fine quality; and in some of these same rivers pearls are still found.[1]

There were the same broad lakes, like inland seas, that we see at the present day; but they were generally larger, and were surrounded with miles of reedy morasses.

Solid gold article (often called a *fibula*) found in Ireland, now in Trinity College Museum, Dublin. 8⅜ inches long; weight 33 oz. From Wilde's Catalogue. Gold articles this shape very numerous in National Museum.

---

[1] See this subject of Irish pearls discussed in my *Irish Names of Places,* Vol. II., p. 375.

Minerals there were too, which, though not nearly so abundant as in the neighbouring island of Great Britain, were yet in sufficient quantity to give rise to many industries. That the mines were worked we know, partly from our historical records, and partly from the Brehon Laws, which lay down many regulations regarding them. The remains of ancient mines, of copper, coal, and other minerals, with many rude antique mining tools, have been found in recent times in some parts of Ireland. Chief among the metals were gold, iron, and copper. From the very earliest times gold has been smelted—or "boiled" as the old Irish records express it: and that it was obtained in considerable quantities is proved by the great number of gold ornaments found from time to time buried in the ground, and now preserved in our museums. The chief gold district lay east of the river Liffey in the present county Wicklow, where gold is found to this day.

Wild animals abounded everywhere. Packs of foxes and savage dogs scoured the country at night, howling and yelping for prey. Otters were in great plenty near rivers and lakes, so that in later times their skins formed an important article of commerce; and so recently as the beginning of the fifteenth century rents were sometimes paid in otter skins. Wolves lurked in glens and coverts, and at last became so numerous and dangerous that the people kept a special breed of dogs to hunt them down, Irish wolf-dogs—great, fierce, shaggy animals—one of them quite a match for a wolf. These dogs were celebrated all over Europe, so that they were often sent as presents to Continental sovereigns, and were sometimes exhibited at the Roman games, to the great astonishment of the people, who had never before seen such large dogs. They have only very recently become extinct; and their savage antagonists, the wolves, were finally exterminated about two centuries ago. There were plenty of wild cats, large, wicked rough looking creatures, very strong and very dangerous; and the race is not yet quite extinct, for wild cats, nearly twice the size of our domestic animals, are still found in some solitary places. Droves of swine roamed through the forests feeding on acorns and beechmast. In the neighbourhood of the inhabited districts these were domestic animals, owned by rich people and tended by swineherds: but in remote parts there were plenty of wild hogs. We know that in the olden time hunting the wild boar was a favourite amusement, though a very dangerous one, for the old Irish boar had formidable tusks and knew well how to use them. The open pasture lands were grazed by herds of cows, sheep, and goats, which at a very ancient period were all wild; but the domesticated animals gradually took their place as the population increased and extended.

Then lived the Irish elk, a gigantic deer with great branching solid antlers, compared with which the largest of our present deer are mere

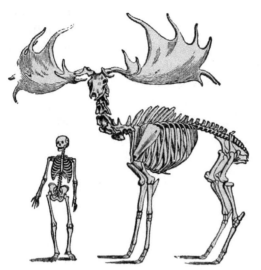

Skeleton of Elk in National Museum, Dublin. From plate of Royal Dublin Society. Human skeleton put in for comparison.

dwarfs. We shall never see such deer alive again, though we often find their bones buried deep down in clay: in one place not far from Dublin, the remains of a whole herd of more than a hundred were dug up some years ago from beneath a bog. Complete skeletons are preserved in Dublin, with antlers standing twice the height of a man and twelve feet across from tip to tip. Great herds of these stately creatures roamed over the plains or crashed their way through brake and forest, tossing proudly their mighty antlers. We know that bears were there too, for we still find their bones in caverns. Although both elks and bears became extinct very early, we have good reason to believe that they continued to live in the country for some time after its occupation by man.

Myriads of noisy sea-fowl circled and screamed and fished all round the coasts and swarmed on the cliffs, among them the strong and graceful sea-eagle; for the sea, as well as the lakes and rivers, teemed with fish. Vast flocks of cranes, wild geese, wild swans, and other fowl tenanted the lakes and marshes; the woods were alive with birds of various kinds; and hawks, kites, and golden eagles skimmed over the plains peering down for prey. The goshawks, or falcons, used in the old game of hawking, were found in great abundance; and those of Ulster were reckoned the best in the world; so that, like wolf-dogs, they were valued everywhere on the Continent, and were often sent as presents to kings. The country, from the earliest times, was noted for its abundance of honey, for bees, both wild and domestic, swarmed everywhere. But there were no snakes or toads. We have now plenty of frogs; but the first ever seen in Ireland, of which there is any record, was found near Waterford towards the close of the twelfth century. As the population of the country increased, the cultivated land increased in proportion. But until a late time, there were few inhabited districts that were not within view, or within easy reach, of unreclaimed waste lands— forest, or bog, or moorland: so that the people had much ado to protect their crops and flocks from the inroads of wild animals.

All round near the coast ran, then as now, the principal mountain ranges, with a great plain in the middle. The air was soft and moist, perhaps even more moist than at present, on account of the great extent of forest. The cleared land was exceedingly fertile, and was well watered with springs, streamlets, and rivers, not only among the mountainous districts, but all over the central plain. Pasture lands were luxuriant and evergreen, inviting flocks and herds without limit. Some of the pleasing features of the country have been well pictured by Denis Florence M'Carthy in his poem of "The Bell Founder":

"O Erin! thou broad-spreading valley,[1] thou well-watered land of
     fresh streams,
When I gaze on thy hills greenly sloping, where the light of such
     loveliness beams,
When I rest on the rim of thy fountains, or stray where thy streams
     disembogue,
Then I think that the fairies have brought me to dwell in the bright
     Tirnanogue."

From the foregoing sketch it will be seen that Ireland, so far as it was brought under cultivation and pasture in those early days, was—as the Venerable Bede calls it—a land flowing with milk and honey, a pleasant, healthful, and fruitful land, well fitted to maintain a prosperous and contented people.

Ancient Irish Bronze Vessel in National Museum, Dublin. From Wilde's Catalogue.

---

[1]"Broad-spreading valley" because it is generally flat in the middle, with mountains all round.

Composed from the Book of Kells.

CHAPTER II
LITERATURE, ART, AND MUSIC

EARNING of all kinds was held in great estimation by the ancient Irish, especially History, Poetry, and Romantic Tales. Most of their lore was written down in books; for after the time of St. Patrick, everything that was considered worthy of being preserved was committed to writing, so that manuscripts gradually accumulated all through the country. But in the dark time of the Danish ravages, and during the troubled centuries that followed the Anglo-Norman invasion, the manuscript collections were gradually dispersed, and a large proportion lost or destroyed. Yet we have remaining—rescued from the general wreck—a great body of manuscript literature. The two most important collections are those in Trinity College and in the Royal Irish Academy, Dublin, where there are manuscripts of various ages, from the sixth down to the present century. There are also many important Irish manuscripts in the British Museum in London, and in the Bodleian Library at Oxford. Great numbers, too, are preserved in Continental libraries, where they were written, or to which they were brought from Ireland, by those Irish missionaries who frequented the Continent in early ages.

A favourite occupation of some of the monks of old was copying the Gospels or other portions of the Holy Scriptures, always in Latin, for the use of the inmates of monasteries or of other persons who could read and understand the language: and many devoted their whole lives to this good work. Books of this kind are the oldest, as well as the most beautiful, we possess, many having been written from the sixth to the ninth century; and nearly all of them are richly ornamented and illuminated. For those accomplished and devoted old scribes thought no trouble too great to beautify the sacred writings.

6

Before the invention of printing it was customary in Ireland for individuals, or families, or religious communities, to keep large manuscript books of miscellaneous literature. In these were written such literary pieces as were considered worthy of being preserved in writing—tales, poems, biographies, histories, annals, and so forth—all mixed up in one volume, and almost always copied from older books. In those days books, being all written by hand on vellum—a very expensive material—were scarce and dear. The only places where they were to be found were the libraries in monasteries, and in the houses of kings or chiefs, or of some learned men; and the value set on them may be estimated from the fact that one of them was sometimes accepted as ransom for a captive chief.

The oldest of all these books of miscellaneous literature is the Book of the Dun Cow, now in the Royal Irish Academy, Dublin. It was written—copied from older books—by Mailmurry Mac Kelleher, a learned scribe, who died in Clonmacnoise in the year 1106. As it now stands it consists of only 134 large vellum pages, a mere fragment of the original work. It contains sixty-five pieces of various kinds, several of which are imperfect on account of missing leaves. There are a number of romantic tales in prose; and, besides other important pieces, a copy of the celebrated *Amra* or Elegy on St. Columkille, composed about the year 592, which no one can yet wholly understand, the language is so ancient and difficult.

The Book of Leinster, which is kept in the library of Trinity College, Dublin, is the largest, though not the oldest, of all the ancient Irish manuscript volumes. It is an immense book of 410 vellum pages, written in or about the year 1160, containing nearly one thousand pieces of various kinds, some in prose, some in poetry, nearly all about Irish affairs. There are historical narratives, stories and descriptions of places in various parts of the country, genealogies of families, and romantic tales belonging to the old times of legend and tradition. Other old books are the Speckled Book of Mac Egan, almost as large as the Book of Leinster, consisting chiefly of religious pieces, the Book of Ballymote, the Book of Lecan [Leckan], and the Yellow Book of Lecan, which are all in Dublin, and contain a vast amount of ancient Irish lore. Much of the contents of these books has been published and translated: but by far the greatest part still remains locked up in the Irish language, waiting to be dealt with by the loving labour of Irish scholars.

The Irish chroniclers were very careful to record in their Annals remarkable occurrences of their own time, or past events as handed down to them by former chroniclers. The Annals are among the most important of the ancient manuscript writings for the study of Irish history. The most extensive and valuable of all are the Annals of the Four Masters. They were compiled in the Franciscan Monastery of Donegal, from older authorities, by three of the O'Clerys, a learned family of laymen, hereditary ollaves or professors of history to the O'Donnells of Tirconnell, and by a fourth scholar named O'Mulconry. These are now commonly known as the "Four Masters." They began the work in 1632 and completed it in 1636. *The Annals of the Four Masters* was translated, with most elaborate and learned annotations, by Dr. John O'Donovan; and it was published in 1851, Irish text, translation, and notes, in seven large volumes.

We have also preserved a vast body of medical manuscripts, which originated in the following manner. There were professional physicians or leeches in Ireland from the very beginning of society, who, like the Brehons, had to undergo a long course of training, and like them kept books for reference, some in Irish and some in Latin. In Ireland, the professions, as for instance those of History, Poetry, Law, &c., commonly ran in families: and many Irish families were distinguished physicians for generations, such as the O'Shiels, the O'Cassidys, the O'Hickeys, and the O'Lees, of whom the fame of some had reached the Continent. Each family kept a medical book, the collected experience and wisdom of ages, which was handed down reverently from father to son. A vast number of these books are preserved in libraries; and there are probably more old medical manuscripts in existence written by Irish doctors than there are belonging to any other country. Kings and chiefs kept physicians attached to their households, many of whom, in the service of the great kings, had for remuneration castles and estates, and lived like princes. Those not so attached subsisted on their fees, like most doctors of the present day. There were hospitals even in pagan times. In later ages most of them were in connexion with monasteries: but some were secular, and came under the Brehon Law, which laid down regulations for them, especially as regarded cleanliness and ventilation. The poor were received free in all hospitals, but those who could afford it were expected to pay for food, medicine, and the attendance of the doctor.

Of all our manuscript remains Romantic Literature is the most abundant. It consists of stories, some very long, some short, chiefly in prose, but often mixed up with poetry, nearly all of them about Irish historical personages, or founded on Irish historical events. A large proportion have reference to the two great heroic cycles mentioned in chapters VII and VIII—that of the Red Branch Knights in the first century, and that of the Fena of Erin in the third. A great number of these have been translated by O'Donovan, O'Curry, Whitley Stokes, and others; and I have given a free translation of twelve of the most beautiful in my *Old Celtic Romances*.

In Ireland Art was practised in four different branches:—Ornamentation and illumination of manuscript books; metal work; sculpture; and building.

Art of every kind reached its highest perfection in the period between the end of the ninth and the beginning of the twelfth century; after which all cultivation degenerated on account of the Danish irruptions and the Anglo-Norman invasion.

As all the books were written by hand, penmanship as an art was carefully cultivated, and was brought to great perfection. The old scribes of Ireland, who were generally, but not always, monks, and were held in great honour, had a method of ornamentation not used by scribes of other countries. It is chiefly a sort of beautiful interlaced work formed of bands, ribbons, and cords, which are curved and twisted and interwoven in the most intricate way, mixed up with waves and spirals; and sometimes you see the faces or forms of dragons, serpents, or other strange-looking animals, their tails, or ears, or tongues lengthened out and woven, till they become mixed up with the general design; and sometimes odd-looking human faces or full figures of men or of angels. The pattern is often so minute as to require the aid of a magnifying glass to examine it. The scribes usually made the capital letters very large, so as sometimes to fill almost an entire page; and on these they exerted their utmost skill. They also painted the open spaces of the letters and ornaments in brilliant colours, like the scribes of other countries; which art was called Illumination.

Several of the highly ornamented books are still preserved, of which the most remarkable is the Book of Kells, now in Trinity College, Dublin, written on vellum, probably in the seventh century. It is a copy of the Four Gospels in Latin; and for beauty of execution no other book in any part of the world can compare with it. The Book of Armagh, containing, among many other pieces, a Life of St. Patrick and a complete copy of the New Testament in Latin, is almost as beautifully written as the Book of Kells. It was finished A.D. 807 by the skilful scribe Ferdomnach of Armagh, and is now in Trinity College, Dublin. Another book, scarcely inferior in beauty of execution to the Book of Kells, is preserved in the Archbishop's Library at Lambeth. It is a copy of the Gospels, now known as the Book of Mac Durnan, written in Ireland some time from A.D. 800 to 850. I have given, as frontispiece, an exact reproduction of one page of this book; and a glance at it will give a better idea of what those accomplished old Irish scribes could do than any amount of description. The Book of Durrow in Trinity College, and the "Stowe Missal" in the Royal Irish Academy, are on a level with most of the preceding. All these books are illuminated in five or six different colours.

The Irish artists in metal work were quite as skilful as the scribes were in penmanship. The ornamental patterns were generally similar to those used in manuscripts, consisting of the same beautiful curves with interlacements; and the materials employed were gold, silver, bronze of a whitish colour, gems, and enamel. A great number of the lovely articles made by those accomplished artists have been found from time to time, of which the most remarkable and beautiful are the Cross of Cong, the Ardagh Chalice, and the Tara Brooch, all now to be seen in the National Museum in Dublin. The Cross of Cong (which will be found figured in this book at p. 86) is 2 feet 6 inches high, covered all over with delicate Celtic designs in gold, silver, enamel, and precious stones, with a series of inscriptions in the Irish language along the sides giving its full history. It was made by order of Turlogh O'Conor, king of Connaught; and the artist, who finished his work in 1123, and who deserves to be remembered to all time for this most beautiful piece of work, was Mailisa MacBraddan O'Hechan. The Chalice was found a few years ago buried in the ground under a stone in an old *lis,* at Ardagh in the county Limerick. It is elaborately ornamented with designs in metal and enamel; and was probably made some time before the tenth century. The Tara Brooch is ornamented all over with amber, glass, enamel, and with the Irish interlaced work in metal. Many old brooches are preserved (one of which is shown here); but the Tara Brooch is the most beautiful and perfect of all.

From very early times the Irish were celebrated for their skill in music; and Irish professors and teachers of music were almost as much in request

The Ardagh Chalice (7 inches in height). From Miss Stokes's
Early Christian Art in Ireland.

in foreign countries as those of literature. In the middle of the seventh century, Gertrude, abbess of Nivelle in Belgium, daughter of Pepin, mayor

The Tara Brooch. Diam. 3¾ in.: length of pin 9 in.

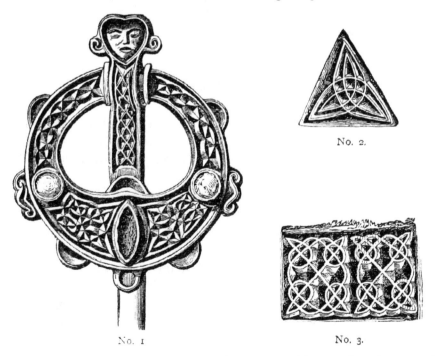

No. 1.—Ancient Ornamented Brooch. Nos. 2 and 3.—Ancient Ornamental Patterns engraved on bone. All in National Museum, Dublin. From Wilde's Catalogue.

11

of the palace, engaged saints Foillan and Ultan, brothers of the Irish saint Fursa, to instruct her nuns in psalmody. In the latter half of the ninth century the cloister schools of St. Gall in Switzerland were conducted by an Irishman, Maengal or Marcellus, under whose teaching the music school there attained its highest fame. Giraldus Cambrensis, who seldom had a good word for anything Irish, speaks of the Irish harpers of his time—the twelfth century—as follows: "They are incomparably more skilful than any other nation I have ever seen. It is astonishing that in so complex and rapid a movement of the fingers the musical proportions [as to time] can be preserved; and that the harmony is completed with such a sweet rapidity." For centuries after the time of Giraldus music continued to be cultivated uninterruptedly; and there was an unbroken succession of great professional harpers, who maintained their ancient pre-eminence till a comparatively recent time. Down to the middle of the last century, Ireland continued to be the school for Welsh and Scotch harpers, who were never considered finished players till

Irish Piper playing at the head of a band marching to battle. From Derrick's *Image of Ireland,* 1578.

they had spent some time under the instruction of the skilled Irish harpers. We still possess great numbers of the lovely airs composed by the old Irish musicians; and many songs have been written to them, the best of which are those by Thomas Moore.

We know the authors of many of the airs composed within the last 200 years: but these form the smallest portion of the whole body of Irish music. All the rest have come down from old times, scattered fragments of exquisite beauty, that remind us of the refined musical culture of our forefathers. Of about 120 Irish airs in all Moore's Melodies, we know the authors of less than a dozen: as to the rest, nothing is known either of the persons who composed them or of the times of their composition.

The harp was the favourite instrument among the higher classes of people, many of whom played on it, merely for pleasure. But the lower classes loved the bagpipes better. Soldiers commonly marched to battle inspirited by the martial strains of one or more pipers marching at their head, a custom retained to this day, especially among the Scotch.

Composed from the Book of Kells.

CHAPTER III
DWELLINGS, FORTRESSES, AND TOMBS

WELLING HOUSES were mostly of a round shape, generally made of wood, very seldom of stone. The wall was very high, and was formed of long peeled poles standing pretty near each other, with their ends fixed deep in the ground; and the spaces between were closed in with wickerwork of peeled rods and twigs. The whole was smoothly plastered and made brilliantly white with lime on the outside: though some houses were fancifully painted all over in bands of bright colours; and in some again the white wickerwork was left uncovered on the outside. The top was cone-shaped, and, like English houses of corresponding periods, thatched with straw or rushes, with an opening to serve as chimney The fire was kept burning in the middle of the floor: but in all large houses there was a special kitchen for cooking. When Henry II was in Dublin in 1171, he had a splendid house of this kind erected, in which he spent the Christmas in great state. Families in good circumstances had two or three of these round structures beside each other, forming several rooms: but the poorer people had only one. In large houses, the doorjambs, bedposts, &c., were often of yew-wood, curiously carved. The family commonly lived, ate, and slept in one large apartment, the beds being placed round the wall, and separated by boarded partitions; but we often find mention of separate bedrooms for different members of the family, and for guests. A bath in a special bathroom was quite usual. In houses of the better class the women had one apartment for themselves called a greenan, that is, a "sunny-house," in the most lightsome part of the building.

As a defence against wild beasts or robbers, each house was surrounded with a high embankment of earth, having a strong close hedge of thorns or a palisade of stakes on top, outside of which was a deep trench often filled

13

with water. This enclosure with its surrounding rampart was called a rath or lis. Sometimes a whole group of houses stood within one large rath. For greater security, dwellings were often constructed on artificial islands made with stakes, trees, and bushes, in shallow lakes: these were called crannoges. Communication with the shore was carried on by means of a small boat kept on the island. Crannoge dwellings were in pretty general use in the time of Queen Elizabeth; and the remains of many of them are still to be seen in our lakes.

The dwelling of a king, which was commonly called a Dun [doon], was fortified with two or three sets of surrounding ramparts and trenches, and there was often a high mound in the centre, flat on top for the house or fortress of the king. The remains of these old palaces may still be seen at most of the ancient royal residences; as for instance at Tara, Emain, and Rathcroghan.[1]

The great "Moat of Kilfinnane," Co. Limerick, believed to be Treda-na-Ree, *the triple-fossed fort of the kings, one of the seats of the kings of Munster. Total diameter 320 feet. From a drawing by the author, 1854.*

Sometimes the rampart surrounding the dwellings was a wall of stone without mortar: for the use of mortar was not known in Ireland till after the time of St. Patrick; and they built in dry masonry like the very early

[1]The following are the most important of the ancient royal residences of Ireland—
Of the kings of Ireland: Tara in Meath (before its abandonment in 6th century): Tailltenn on the river Blackwater, midway between Navan and Kells: Tlachtga, now the Hill of Ward near Athboy in Meath: Ushnagh in Westmeath.
Of the kings of Ulster: Emain near Armagh: Greenan-Ely: Dun-Keltair beside Downpatrick.
Of the kings of Leinster: Naas: Dunlavin in Wicklow: Dinnree: Dun Aillinne near Kilcullen, Co. Kildare.
Of the kings of Munster: Cashel: Bruree in Limerick: Caher in Tipperary: Treda-na-Ree: Kincora at Killaloe.
Of the kings of Connaught: Croghan, near the village of Rathcroghan in the north of Roscommon.
At nearly all of these places, the mounds, entrenchments, and circumvallations of the old palaces, mostly of earth, but sometimes of stone, are still to be seen.

Greeks. These circular stone fortresses, which are built with much rude art—the stones fitting all through with great exactness—are called cahers and sometimes cashels. The palace of the northern Hy Neill, now called Greenan-Ely, situated in Donegal within four miles of Derry, is a caher, very like Staigue Fort in Kerry which is figured here. Another magnificent caher is Dun-Aengus in Aran, which will be found represented at page 35.

Staigue Fort, halfway between Sneem and Darrynane in Kerry. Diameter 114 feet.

There are now no traces left of the wooden houses erected in any of these old forts; but the raths, lisses, duns, cahers, cashels, and mounds are still to be seen in every part of Ireland, and are called by these names. Circular houses within circular forts gradually gave place to the four-cornered houses that we have at present: but they continued in use till the thirteenth or fourteenth century.

The ancient Irish buried their dead in three different ways, of which the most usual was depositing the body in the grave as

Cinerary Urn, found in a pagan grave. From Wilde's Catalogue.

at present. Sometimes the body of a king, or great warrior, or other notable person, was placed standing up in the grave, fully dressed in battle array, with sword in hand, and with his face turned towards the territory of his enemies: King Laegaire [Leary] was buried in this manner in one of the ramparts of Tara. The pagan Irish believed that while the body of their king

15

Cromlech at Tawnatruffaun, Sligo: 7 feet high. From Wood-Martin's Pagan Ireland. *N.B.—Cromlech, are now sometimes called Dolmens.*

remained in this position it exercised a malign influence on their enemies, who were thereby always defeated in battle. Owen Bel, king of Connaught, when dying of a wound received in a battle fought near Sligo against the Ulstermen in A.D. 537, said to his people: "Bury me with my red javelin in my hand on the side of the hill by which the Northerns pass when fleeing before the army of Connaught, and place me with my face turned towards them in my grave." And this was done, and the Ulstermen were always routed after that; till at last they came and removed the body to another grave, placing it head downwards: which broke the baleful spell.

Very often the body was burned, and the ashes were placed in an ornamental urn of baked clay, which was deposited in the ground in a sort of chest formed of flags. Our histories do not tell us about this, for the custom

Burial Mound on the Boyne near Clonard in Meath. Circumference 433 feet; height 50 feet. From Wilde's Boyne and Blackwater.

16

had ceased before history began: but we know it was very general in Ireland, because urns containing ashes and half-burned human bones are very often found in old graves. Sometimes the body or urn was placed in what we now call a cromlech, formed of several large upright stones supporting on top one immense flat stone, so as to enclose a rude chamber. A cromlech was much the same as the flat tombs in churchyards of the present day, except that the stones were much larger, and were in their rough state, without being hammered or chiselled into shape. Many of these cromlechs still remain, and are often called by the people "Giants' Graves."

Often a great mound of stones called a cairn was heaped over the grave. In old times people had a fancy for burying on the tops of hills, so that cairns are still to be seen on many hilltops, under every one of which sleeps some person of consequence in the days of old. On the level lowlands, the mound was sometimes of stones, or of stones and clay; and many of these also remain. In every mound, whether on hill or plain, there was a chamber formed of flags deep down in the centre, in which the body or urn was placed. A burial mound has no ramparts round it; and by this it may generally be distinguished from the mound of a dun or fortress.

CHAPTER IV
FOOD, DRESS, AND DAILY LIFE

t the regular meals the whole household sat in one large room, the chief and his family and distinguished guests at the head, and the rest of the company ranged downwards in order of rank.

For food, the higher classes used the flesh of wild and domestic animals, boiled or roast, much as at the present day, with wheaten bread. The main food of the general body of the people consisted of various kinds of bread baked on a griddle; milk, curds, cheese, butter; fish and fruit; and, for those who could afford it, pork and bacon. Pork was a favourite food among all classes. Oatmeal porridge, or stirabout, as it is called in Ireland, was in very general use, especially for children, and was eaten with milk, butter, or honey. The Irish rivers abounded then as now in salmon, a food which was in great request.

There was then no sugar, and honey was greatly valued: beehives were kept everywhere; and the management of bees was considered

No. 1.   No. 2.

1.—The "Kavanagh Horn," in Museum of Trinity College, Dublin; of ivory, ornamented with gilt metal plates and bands: 16 inches high. 2.—Mether in National Museum: 8½ inches high. Both from Wilde's Catalogue.

such an important industry that a special section of the Brehon Laws is devoted to it. The people used honey in a great many different ways: they basted roasting meat with it; it was used on salmon while cooking, and as a seasoning with all sorts of dishes. Often at meals each person had a little dish, sometimes of silver, filled with honey, beside his plate, and each morsel, whether meat, fish, or bread, was dipped into it before being

Ancient Bronze Caldron: 12 inches deep. From Wilde's Catalogue.

conveyed to the mouth. For drink, they had—besides plain water and milk—ale, mead, and frequently wine brought from the Continent: for in those early days there was frequent communication, as well as considerable trade, with France and other continental countries. The people often mixed honey with milk, either sweet or sour, for drinking. From honey also was made a kind of liquor called mead, very sweet and slightly intoxicating. This was considered a delicacy; and a visitor was often treated to a drink of mead immediately on arrival. People of the higher classes often drank from a beautiful horn of elaborate and costly workmanship. A much more common drinking vessel was what was called a *mether* (from *mead*), made of wood, with one, two, or four handles, which circulated from hand to hand, each passing it to his neighbour after taking a drink

In every great house there was at least one large-sized caldron which was kept in continual use boiling food, so that guests might be hospitably entertained whenever they happened to arrive. Of the many ancient caldrons preserved in the National Museum, Dublin, the gracefully shaped one here figured is made of bronze plates beautifully riveted together.

At intervals through the country there were houses of public hospitality—open *brudins* or hostels—where all travellers who called, and also certain important persons, such as kings, chiefs, bishops, brehons, &c. when on their circuits, were entertained free of expense. The keeper of one of these houses was called a brugaid [broo-ee], *i.e.* a public hostel-keeper: and sometimes a beetagh. He was held in great honour; and he had a tract of land, besides other large allowances, to enable him to maintain his expensive establishment.

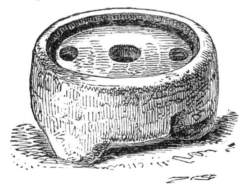

Quern in National Museum. Axis through centre opening. Wooden handles in other two holes, by which the upper stone was turned round. Corn ground between. From Wilde's Catalogue.

Small corn mills driven by water were used in Ireland from very remote ages. In early Christian times almost every monastery had a mill attached to it for the use of the community. In most houses there was a quern or hand mill, which was commonly worked by women, who each evening ground corn enough for next day. Querns continued in use down to our time in remote parts of Ireland.

For light they had dipped candles, which were held in candlesticks, sometimes with branches. The poorer classes used peeled rushes soaked in grease, as we sometimes see at the present day. As bees were so abundant, bees-wax, as might be expected, was turned to account.

19

In some of our old records we find wax candles mentioned as being used in the houses of the richer classes (in Dinnree for instance) long before the fifth century. For a king, it was customary to make an immense candle, sometimes as thick as a man's body, with a great bushy wick, which was always kept burning in his presence at night:—in the palace it was placed high over his head; during war it blazed outside his tent door; and on night marches it was borne before him. As there were forests and thickets everywhere, wood was the most usual fuel; but dried peat cut from bogs was also burned; and coal and charcoal were used by smiths and other metal-workers.

In ordinary outdoor life, the men wore a large loose frieze-mantle or overall, which was often so long as to cover them down to the ankles: among the rich it was usually of fine cloth, often variegated with scarlet and other brilliant colours, and fastened at the throat with a beautiful brooch.

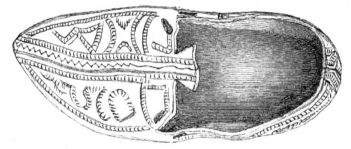

Ancient Irish Ornamented Shoe in National Museum. From Wilde's Catalogue.

Well-dressed people wore inside this a shorter tight-fitting garment, generally reaching to the middle of the thigh, but often below the knee, plaited up and down and fastened at the waist by a belt. This was some-times dyed in colour: the inner coat is a bright red in the original picture of Art Mac Murrogh Kavanagh from which the illustration on page 119 has been copied. In active life the outer mantle was thrown off, as may be seen in the two archers in the illustration, page 29. A single short mantle, al-ways dyed in colour, and sometimes furnished with a hood, was also much worn. This is seen in some of the figures on pages 93 and 129. It should be remarked here that the Irish were very fond of bright colours, and well understood the art of dyeing. The trousers were tight fitting; the cap was usually cone-shaped and without a leaf: as shown in the horseman, p. 32. But the common people generally went bareheaded, wearing the hair long, hanging down behind, and clipped in front just above the eyes, as men-tioned by Camden when describing Shane O'Neill's galloglasses, and as we see in the figures on page 129, and elsewhere in this book. Perhaps the oldest extant representations of Irish costume are those shown in the figures on page 68, from the Book of Kells—seventh century. The shoes or sandals were mostly of untanned hide stitched with thongs, but sometimes of tanned leather curiously stamped or engraved. Occasionally the ladies of high families wore sandals of whitish bronze highly ornamented. In early times gloves were common among the higher classes.

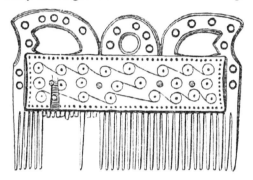

The women generally wore variously-coloured tunics down to the very feet, with many folds and much material—twenty or thirty yards—under which was a long gown or kirtle. Linen, whether used by men or women, was dyed saffron. The married women had a kerchief on the bead: the unmarried girls went bareheaded, with the hair

Ancient Irish Ornamental Comb of bone, in National Museum. From Wilde's Catalogue.

either folded up neatly or hanging down on the back. They took much care of the hair, and used combs, some of them very ornamental. The higher classes were fond of gold ornaments; such as brooches, bracelets for the arms, rings, necklaces, twisted torques or collars to be worn round the neck, or bright rich-looking clasps to confine the hair. Other ornamental articles were made of silver or white bronze, enamelled in various colours, and set with gems. A great number of these, many of most beautiful workmanship, are preserved in the National Museum in Dublin. One torque of pure gold (figured here) found near Tara, measures five and a half feet in length, and weighs twenty-seven and a half ounces.

It was the custom to hold fair-meetings in various places for the transaction of important business, sometimes once a year, sometimes once in three years. The most important of all was the Fes of Tara. Very important yearly meetings were held at the Hill of Ward (*Tlachtga*) near

Gold Torque. From Petrie's Tara.

21

Athboy in Meath; at the Hill of Ushnagh in Westmeath; and at Tailltenn, now Teltown, on the Blackwater between Navan and Kells in Meath. This last was the great national assembly for horse races and all kinds of athletic games and exercises.

A triennial meeting was held at Wexford; and there were fair-meetings in numberless other places. At these assemblies laws were proclaimed to keep them before the minds of the people, taxes were arranged, pastimes and athletic sports were carried on, as well as buying and selling as we see at fairs of the present day.

Bone Chessman, King, full size; found in a bog in Meath about 1817. Drawn by Petrie: Book of Rights, *page lxii.*

In those times, so very few were able to read, that for all information and amusement to be derived from books the people had to depend on professional storytellers and poets, who had great numbers of tales and poems by heart, the very tales and poems contained in the Book of Leinster and the other volumes described in chapter II. There were many such men, who often travelled from place to place and earned a good livelihood by their profession. At every festive gathering, among the lowest as well as the highest, one of these storytellers was sure to be present, who was now and then called upon to repeat a tale or a poem for the amusement of the company. And as soon as he stood up, these rough men ceased their noisy revels, and listened with rapt delight to some tale of the heroes of old. A harper was also present, who charmed the company with his beautiful Irish airs: or if it was a gathering of the lower classes, more likely a piper.

Chess-playing was a favourite pastime of kings and chiefs; and in every great house there were sure to be a chessboard and a set of chessmen for the amusement of the family and their guests. The chessmen were kept in a bag often of woven brass wire. Chess is mentioned in the very oldest of the Irish romantic tales; and it was considered a necessary accomplishment of every hero to be a good player. In the National Museum in Dublin there is one chessman, which is figured here; but many have been found in Scotland.

Fosterage prevailed from the remotest period, and was practised by persons of all classes, but more especially by those of the higher ranks. A man sent his child to be reared and educated in the home and with the family of another member of the tribe, who then became foster-father, and his sons and daughters the foster-brothers and foster-sisters of the child. Fosterage, which was the closest tie between families, was subject to strict regulations, which were carefully set forth in the Brehon Law.

When a man stood sponsor for a child at baptism, he became the child's godfather, and gossip to the parents: this was called gossipred. It was regarded as a sort of religious relationship between families, and created mutual obligations of regard and friendship.

There were five great highways leading in five different directions through Ireland from Tara: and besides these there were numerous others; so that the country seems to have been very fairly provided with roads. The Brehon Law laid down arrangements for keeping them in repair; and every man whose land lay for any distance next a road had to help in cleaning and repairing that part of it. But the roads then were not near so smooth and good as those we have at the present time. When the road came to a bog or marsh, a causeway of bushes and clay was constructed across. Stone bridges were not then used in Ireland; but there were many constructed of timber planks or rough tree trunks. Rivers however were very generally crossed by wading through fords where the stream spread out broad and shallow, and often by swimming; for most young persons were taught to swim as a regular part of their education.

Chariots were used both in private life and in war. The early Irish saints commonly travelled in chariots when on their long missionary journeys. Chariots were often covered in; and those used by persons of high rank were luxuriously furnished with cushions and furs. It was usual to yoke two horses; but sometimes there were four. The battle chariots were open, and were furnished with spikes and scythe-blades for driving through the ranks of the enemy.

Horses were used a good deal by the higher classes. The men rode without saddle or stirrup; and were trained to vault into their seat from either side, right or left. Mac Murrogh Kavanagh rode downhill in this manner when coming to confer with the Earl of Gloucester. Low benches were common on the roadsides to enable old or infirm persons to mount.

The Irish had three kinds of boats:—small sailing vessels, with which oars were employed when the wind failed; canoes of one piece hollowed

Ancient Irish Chariots on base of Cross at Clonmacnoise 9th century. From Wood-Martin, Pagan Ireland, *page 247. It is also figured in Miss Stokes's* Christian Inscriptions, *I., Pl. xxxiii.*

out from the trunks of trees, which were chiefly used on lakes; and *currachs,* that is, wickerwork boats covered with hides.

The single-piece canoes are now often found deep down in bogs, where there were, or are, lakes or crannoges. Currachs are still used on the western coast, as for instance at Kilkee in Co. Clare; but instead of hides, they are now covered with a cheaper material, tarred canvas.

Group on ancient engraved book cover of bone, showing costume: one with cymbals; and all engaged in some kind of dance: 14th or 15th century. From Wilde's Catalogue.

Composed from the Book of Kells.

CHAPTER V
IRISH PAGANISM

T is commonly understood that the religion of the pagan Irish was Druidism. But although our old books speak very often of this Druidism, they do not give us any clear idea of what sort of religion it was. There were persons called Druids, who were learned men, the only men of those times that had any learning: and as all learned professions were then usually combined in the one person, every druid was also a physician, a poet, a historian, and a brehon. But later on, after the people had become Christian, and there were no longer any druids, the professions became divided, and one man was a brehon, another a poet, another a physician, and so on.

The druids had the reputation of being great magicians, and this indeed is the character in which they principally figure in old Irish writings. The people believed that they could do many wonderful things by their spells:—that they could raise clouds and mists, and bring down showers of snow, of fire, or of blood; that they could give a person a "cloak of darkness" to make him invisible; that they could drive a man mad or make him an idiot by flinging in his face a "magic wisp" of straw over which they had pronounced some dreadful words; with many other marvellous things. They professed also to be able to foretell future events by casting lots, by dreams, by listening to the croaking of ravens or the chirping of wrens, or by looking at the clouds or stars. The druids were employed to educate the children of kings and chiefs; so that they were persons of high position and great influence, held in respect by all, and much dreaded by the common people. Some writers think that they were also a sort of pagan priests like those of Greece and Rome. No doubt the druidic systems of Gaul, Britain, and Ireland were originally one and the same, as being derived from some common Eastern source; but druidism seems to have become greatly modified in Ireland: and the descriptions of the Gaulish and British druids by Caesar and others, give us no information regarding those of Ireland. The short account of Irish druids given here is derived from purely native sources, beyond which we cannot go, as we have no information from outside.

The pagan Irish had gods and goddesses, many of whom are named in the old writings: but there was no one of them at the head of all the others, like Jupiter among the Greeks and Romans. The Irish sea god was Mannanan Mac Lir, a Dedannan chief who became deified after his death; and the people thought that when they looked out from shore over the sea, on a stormy night, they could see dimly through the gloom thousands of Mannanan's white-maned steeds careering along on the crests of the waves. The people also worshipped the *shee* or fairies. The belief was that the Dedannans (who are described at pages 36 and 37), after they had been conquered by the Milesians, went to live underground and became fairies. Each Dedannan chief selected a green mound, called in the Irish language a *shee* or fairy hill, under which he took up his residence with his followers, in a glorious palace brilliantly lighted up, and all sparkling with gems and gold. These *shees,* which are scattered over the country, are usually old burial mounds, or natural hills having on top a *rath,* a mound, a great natural rock, or a cairn. The fairies themselves were also called *shee;* and they were believed to issue forth from the hills at night and roam over the country, doing harm much oftener than good. The people did not love the *shee,* but dreaded them very much, and whatever worship they paid them was merely intended to keep them from inflicting injury.

In some places idols were worshipped. There were idols of some kind in the king's palace at Cashel, which were all destroyed when St. Patrick visited the place and converted the king in the present county Cavan, on a plain anciently called by an Irish name signifying the "Plain of Adoration," there stood an idol called Crom Cruach, covered all over with gold, surrounded by twelve smaller idols, all of which were destroyed by St. Patrick. Crom Cruach was adored by King Laegaire [Leary] and by other kings, for it was the chief idol of all Ireland. These thirteen idols were nothing but rough pillar stones; and there is good reason to believe that many others of the idols of Ireland were pillar stones also. There is no good evidence to show that the pagan Irish offered human sacrifices: though some writers, on insufficient authority, have asserted that they did.

Natural objects were worshipped by many. We are told of a druid of the time of St. Patrick who had a certain spring well called *Slan [i.e. Health:* pron. slaun] for a god, but who regarded fire as an evil spirit; and when he was dying, he ordered that his body should be buried deep under the well, to keep his bones cool from the fire that he dreaded. Well-worship was pretty general: while some few worshipped fire, and others the sun and moon. The custom of worshipping such objects was probably the reason that the pagan Irish, when putting people on oath, made them swear by the sun and moon, the earth and sky, the sea and colours, and all the elements: for this was the old Irish form of oath; and it was believed that whoever violated such an oath was sure to suffer some great calamity.

The pagan Irish had a dim sort of belief in a land of everlasting youth and peace, called by various names, such as Moy-Mell, the land of pleasure; *Tirnanoge,* the land of perpetual youth; *I Brazil* or *O Brazil,*

TRANSLATION.—"The adventures of Connla the Comely, son of Conn the Hundred-Fighter, here. Whence the name of Art the Lone One? [Art the son of Conn, who was called 'Art the Lone One' after his brother Connla had been taken away by the fairy.] Not difficult to answer. On a certain day as Connla of the Golden Hair, son of Conn the Hundred-Fighter, stood beside his father on the Hill of Ushnagh, he saw a lady in strange attire coming towards him. Connla spoke: 'Whence hast thou come, O lady?' he says. 'I have come,' replied the lady, from the land of the ever-living, a place where there is neither death, nor sin, nor transgression. We have continual feasts: we practise every benevolent work without contention. We dwell in a large *Shee;* and hence we are called the People of the Fairy-Mound.' 'To whom art thou speaking, my boy?' says Conn to his son: for no one saw the lady save Connla only." This story will be found fully translated in my *Old Celtic Romances.*

27

&c. As to where it was situated, the accounts vary: or perhaps it would be more correct to say that there were many such happy lands. Sometimes it was deep underground in some glittering sparry cave, and sometimes beneath the sea, or down under a lake. I Brazil was out in the Atlantic Ocean; and people thought that it could be seen from the cliffs of the west, lying like a cloud far out on the verge of the sea. This dim western island was also called *Moy-Mell*. It was always fairies who inhabited these happy lands; and sometimes they carried off mortals to them. There is a pretty story, more than a thousand years old, in the Book of the Dun Cow, which relates how Prince Connla of the Golden Hair, son of Conn the Hundred-Fighter, was carried off by a fairy from the western shore in a crystal boat out to Moy-Mell, and was never seen again. In the note below is given the opening of this tale exactly as it came from the pen of the old scribe MacKelleher, who copied it into the Book of the Dun Cow, from some older book, about the year 1100 [see excerpt on previous page].

Mortals who were brought to Fairyland never grew older; and they passed the time there so pleasantly, that perhaps a whole century passed away when they thought it was only about a year.

These were the beliefs and practices that passed for religion among the pagan Irish. But so far as we can judge from the information that has come down to us, it hardly deserved the name of a religion at all; for it was without any settled general form of worship, it did not lay down any rules of duty or conduct, and it had no influence in making people lead better lives.

——————◆◇◆——————

Chapter VI
Government and Law

HE Clan or Tribe System prevailed in Ireland, as it did in all other countries of Europe in early ages. A Clan or Sept consisted of a number of families all of one kindred, living in the same district, and generally bearing the same family name, such as O'Donnell or MacCarthy. A Tribe was a larger group, consisting of several clans or septs, all more or less distantly related to each other. A tribe occupied a territory, of which each sept had a separate district, without interference by other septs of the same tribe. Over each tribe, as well as over each sept, there was a chief, and the chief of the tribe had authority over those of the several septs under him. If the territory occupied by a tribe was very large, the chief was a ri,[1] or king. Sometimes a king ruled over two or more tribes.

From a very early time, Ireland was partitioned into five provinces:— Ulster, Leinster, Munster, Connaught, and Meath. Ulster, in its coastline, extended from the Boyne round northwards to the little river Drowes, which issues from Lough Melvin, and flows between the counties of Donegal and Leitrim: Leinster from the Boyne to the mouth of the Suir: Munster from the Suir round southwards to the Shannon: Connaught from the Shannon to the Drowes. The province of Meath, which was the last formed, was much larger than the present two counties of Meath and Westmeath: it extended from the Shannon eastward to the sea; and from the confines of the present King's County and county Kildare on the south, to the confines of Fermanagh and Armagh on the north. Subsequently there were some changes. Clare was wrested from Connaught and added to Munster; and Louth was transferred from Ulster to Leinster. Finally, in the later subdivisions of the country, Meath disappeared altogether as a province, and the four older provinces still remain.

Irish Kings and Archers, 13th century. From frescoes in Abbey Knockmoy, Galway.
Dublin Penny Journal, *1832, pp. 228, 229. Drawn by Petrie.*

Over each province there was a ri or king; and there was a king over all Ireland who was called the Ard-ri, *i.e.* the "over-king" or supreme monarch. The Ard-ri lived at Tara till its abandonment in the sixth century, and the province of Meath always belonged to him, to enable him to maintain his court with due dignity. Besides this, he received—or was supposed

---

[1]Pronounced *ree*. Henceforward the pronunciation of Irish words will be given in brackets whenever necessary.

to receive—tribute from the provincial kings to support his armies and defray other expenses of government. The kings of the provinces were in like manner paid tribute by the kings or chiefs of their several tribes, or sub-kingdoms; and these again were partly supported by payments from their subordinate chiefs and heads of households. As the Ard-ri had Meath, as "Mensal land," for his personal expenses, so each king and chief, from the highest grade to the lowest, had a tract of land for life, or as long as he continued chief, for the support of his household, along with the payments he received from those under him. This land, on his death, went, not to his family, but to his successor in the chiefship; a custom which was called Tanistry. A king sat on a throne and wore a crown on state occasions: he was richly dressed, and had great numbers of attendants.

Every tenant of land, and most heads of homesteads of whatever business, had to pay contributions to the chief. These were not in money, for there was little or no coined money in those times, but in kind, viz. cattle, corn, pigs, butter, wine, clothing, handmade articles, &c., and sometimes gold and silver weighed out by the ounce. Some of the land tenants were independent and well to do; and some, on the other hand, were dependent and bound down by hard conditions to their chief. Many of these latter tenants had to receive the chief and his attendants on visitation, and to supply them with food and drink during the time they stayed. Food and drink given in this way was called coiney; and the number of followers, the time, and the kind of food, were carefully regulated by the Brehon Law. But it was a bad and a dangerous custom.

In later times the Anglo-Irish lords imitated and abused this regulation by what was called coyne and livery. A military leader, when he had no money to pay his soldiers, turned them out with arms in their hands among the English colonists (seldom among the old Irish) to pay themselves in money and food. This was Coyne and Livery. There were here no rules laid down, as there were for *coiney;* and the soldiers, being under no restraint, plundered and oppressed the people, and committed many other crimes. Bad as the Irish *coiney* was, Coyne and Livery was much worse: and at one time it was so constantly carried on that it almost ruined the English settlement of the Pale round Dublin.

The king or chief was always taken from the members of one ruling family of the tribe or clan, that member being chosen who was considered best able to govern and lead, in peace and war (which would of course exclude children): and he should be free from bodily deformity or any well-marked personal blemish. He might be son, brother, cousin, or any other relative of the last chief; and he was elected by the votes of the principal men. Very often, during the life of a king or chief, a person was elected to succeed him, in order to prevent quarrels whenever a vacancy should occur. This person was called the Tanist, and he stood next to the king in rank. The king, of whatever grade, was not absolute: he could not decide on any important matter concerning the tribe or territory without consulting and obtaining the consent of the principal men; which was usually done at one of the meetings.

The Irish kings seldom kept standing armies; but the men of the tribe were called on, as occasions arose, to serve in war; and when the campaign or expedition was over, they returned to their homes. They did not use cavalry in war; but on marches the chief leaders rode at the head of their men. We do not find cavalry mentioned on either side at the battle of Clontarf. The Irish had, however, horse soldiers for special services, each of whom had two attendants:—a man to look after his arms and accoutrements, and a boy to attend to the horse; as shown at the end of this chapter.

Galloglass. Painted figure on a Charter of Queen Elizabeth to City of Dublin, 1582. From Gilbert's "Fac-Sim. Nat. MSS."

Two kinds of foot-soldiers were employed:—Galloglasses and Kern. The galloglasses were heavy-armed soldiers. They wore a coat of mail and an iron helmet; a long sword hung by the side, and in the hand was carried a broad, heavy, keen-edged axe. They are described as large-limbed, tall, and fierce looking, and were noted for their dexterity in the use of the battleaxe, against which neither armour nor helmet was a sufficient protection. Besides the broad axe used by the galloglasses, another kind of axe called a *sparth* was in use, long, narrow, and very sharp. Dermot Mac Murrogh, as figured at p. 89, has a sparth, and so has the soldier shown at p. 93.

The Irish never took to armour very generally, but preferred to fight in saffron linen tunics, which lost them many a battle when contending against the Danes and Anglo-Normans. The Kern were light-armed: they wore head-pieces, and fought with a *skean, i.e.* a dagger or short sword, a small bow, and a javelin attached to a thong.

The gradation of authority among the kings and chiefs seemed perfect:—The monarch of Ireland ruled over the provincial kings; the provincial kings over the kings of tribes; and these over the chiefs of clans. But it was perfect only in name. The supreme monarch was never able to enforce his authority over the provincial kings, who in their turn were often defied by their sub-kings. The several kings and chiefs were seldom under proper control; and they were continually quarrelling and fighting. This constant state of warfare kept the people in misery wherever it went on. The kings and chiefs could seldom be brought to unite heartily for any common purpose; so that invaders from over sea were able to make lodgements without meeting with any serious opposition. It should be remarked however that in this respect the people of Ireland were not worse than those of other countries at the corresponding period: the minor kings and chiefs of England were just as bad in the time of the Heptarchy. But in England it so happened that the kings of one particular state grew so powerful that they at length mastered all the others, and became the undisputed kings of all England. In Ireland no doubt something of the same kind would in the end have come to pass; but before things had time to work themselves out in this manner, the Danish incursions and the Anglo-Norman invasion came and changed the whole fortunes of the country.

We have seen that the people belonging to each sept of a tribe had a tract of land set apart for themselves. A small part of this land was the

Horse Soldier with attendant and horseboy. From Derrick's
Image of Ireland: 1578.

private property of individuals: all the rest was Tribe-land or Sept-land, that is, it belonged not to individuals but to the sept in general. Each head of a family had a farm for the time being; but every three or four years there was a new distribution of the sept-land (without disturbing that of the neighbouring septs), when the people had to give up their farms and take others: which generally happened on the death of one of the householders who had land. This custom was called Gavelkind: but it was not a good plan: it prevented improvements; for no man will drain, or fence, or subsoil land that he may have to give up in a few years. A somewhat different sort of Gavelkind prevailed in Wales and England, and exists in a modified form at the present time in Kent. Another part of the land occupied by the sept was Commons, that is, waste land, such as mountain, bog, or wood, which was not assigned to any individuals in particular, but which every householder of the sept had a right to use for grazing, fuel, hunting, and such like purposes.

The ancient law of Ireland, which grew up gradually in the course of ages, is now commonly called the Brehon Law; and the judges who tried and decided cases were called Brehons. To become a brehon a person had to undergo a long and carefully arranged course of training, under masters who were themselves skilled brehons. Injuries of all kinds as between man and man were atoned for by a compensation payment. Homicide, or bodily injury of any kind, whether by intent or by misadventure, was atoned for by a money fine, called an eric [er'rick]: the amount was adjudged by a brehon. The brehons had collections of laws in volumes, in the Irish language, by which they regulated their judgments. Many of these old volumes, all in beautiful handwriting, are still preserved, and several of them have lately been published with English translations. The Brehon Law came down from a time beyond the reach of history; and it continued to be used pretty generally till the beginning of the seventeenth century, when it was abolished by act of parliament, and English law was extended to the whole of Ireland.

Composed from the Book of Kells.

CHAPTER VII
THE LEGENDS

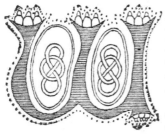 E have no means of finding out for a certainty how Ireland was first peopled. It is highly probable that part at least of its earliest colonists came across the narrow sea from Great Britain, which had been itself colonised by some of the Celtic tribes that in those days occupied a large part of the west of Europe. There is good reason to believe that other colonies came hither direct from the Continent, some from Spain and some from Greece. All these movements however took place long before the time when our regular history began. But, though those far distant ages are beyond the ken of History, we have in our old books—the manuscript books already spoken of—plenty of legends about them, that is to say, stories partly or wholly fabulous, handed down by word of mouth in the beginning for many generations, and at last committed to writing. It is more than a thousand years ago since these old stories began to be written down, though all are not so old as that. Some of them have doubtless a foundation of truth at bottom; for in most of the places where they tell us that battles were fought, or that other remarkable events took place, there are to this day old graves, cairns, pillar-stones, burial mounds, raths, and other monuments of earth and stone: just such marks and tokens as might be expected.

The Legends relate at great length how five successive colonies arrived in Ireland many centuries before the Christian Era; and in the Book of Leinster and other ancient manuscripts there are great numbers of beautiful stories about the people of these colonies, their wanderings and adventures before their arrival in Ireland, and the mighty deeds of their heroes. No person can understand ancient Irish literature who does not know something of these legends.

The First Colony.—The leader of the first was Parthalon, who came hither from Greece with a thousand followers. He took up his abode at first on the little island of Inish-Samer in the river Erne, just below the waterfall of Assaroe at Ballyshannon (see p. 40). But after some time he and his people left this place and made their way south-east through forest and bog till they reached the east coast. At that time the plain on which Dublin now stands, extending from Tallaght to Ben-Edar or Howth, was open and free from the dense forests that clothed the country all round. And it was so sunny and pleasant that immense flocks of birds used to come every day from the neighbouring forests to bask in the bright warm sunshine; so that it came to be known by the name of Moy-Elta, the Plain of the Bird-flocks. On this plain the Parthalonians took up their abode; and here they increased and multiplied; till at the end of three hundred years they were all carried off in one week by a plague.

The legend goes on to tell that they were buried at Tallaght; and here we come upon some solid facts that seem to lend an air of reality to parts of this shadowy old story. We know that the name Tallaght, or, as it is written in Irish, *Tamlacht,* signifies *plague-grave;* and on the slope of Tallaght Hill there are still to be seen a number of rude stone graves and burial mounds.

The Second Colony.—After the destruction of Parthalon's people Ireland remained a solitude for thirty years, till the Nemedians came hither from Scythia, under the leadership of Nemed. These people were harassed by a race of fierce sea-robbers from Scandinavia called Fomorians; and so many battles were fought between them that very few of either party survived. One ship's crew of Nemedians fled over the sea to Greece, whence after a lapse of several hundred years, their descendants under the names of Firbolgs and Dedannans, made their way back to Ireland.

Dun-Aengus on the Great Island of Aran, on the edge of a cliff overhanging the sea: circular Firbolg caher: without mortar: the standing stones were intended to prevent a rush of a body of enemies. Drawn for Dr. Wilde: published in *Arch. Cambr.,* 1858 and subsequently in Wilde's *Lough Corrib.*

The Third Colony.—The Firbolgs, who sprang from one branch of the Nemedians, came first, fleeing from the oppression of the Greeks in a number of the king's ships they had seized: and having landed in Ireland, their leaders, the five sons of Dela, partitioned the country into five provinces.[1] This ancient division has survived with some alterations to the present day. The Firbolgs held sway for only thirty-six years, when they were conquered by the next colony. After their defeat at Moytura, they retreated to the remote parts of Connaught, where they erected those immense stone forts, some on the Aran Islands and some on the adjacent mainland, many of which still remain and excite the wonder of all that see them. The descendants of these Firbolgs, who are described as a small, dark-haired, swarthy race, were distinguishable in Connaught down to comparatively recent times.

Cromlech on Moytirra; near north-east shore of Lough Arrow, Sligo. From Wood-Martin's Pagan Ireland.

The Fourth Colony.—The Dedannans, who were the descendants of another branch of the Nemedians, dwelt near Athens in Greece for many generations; and they learned magic from the Greeks till they became better magicians than their masters. They were forced to flee from Greece, fearing the vengeance of some on whom they had exercised their wonderful

---

[1]These five were, Leinster, Ulster, Connaught, and the two Munsters (East and West: meeting at Cork). The two Munsters soon merged into one; and in the second century the province of Meath was created, still making five. A better known subdivision of Munster was into Thomond or North Munster (roughly including Limerick, Clare, and Tipperary), and Desmond or South Munster (Kerry, Cork, and Waterford).

spells; and faring slowly for generations through the north of Europe, they at length arrived on the north coast of Ireland, under the command of their mighty chief Nuada of the Silver Hand. As soon as they had landed they burned their ships; and shrouding themselves in a magic fog, so that the Firbolgs could not see them, they marched unperceived to Slieve-an-Ierin, a mountain in the present county Leitrim. And they sent one of their champions to the Firbolgs with a demand either to yield up the sovereignty of the country or fight for it. The Firbolgs chose battle; and the two armies fought for four successive days on the plain of South Moytura near Cong. The Firbolgs were defeated, their king was slain, and the Dedannans remained masters of the island.

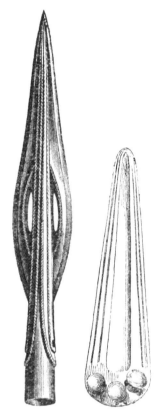

No. 1.   No. 2.

1.—Supposed Dedannan Spearhead.   2.—Supposed Firbolg Spearhead. Both of bronze, and in the National Museum. From Wilde's Catalogue.

The Fomorians still continued to plague the country; and twenty-seven years after the battle of South Moytura, a battle was fought between them and the Dedannans at North Moytura near Sligo, where the Fomorians were defeated and all their chief men slain. The two plains of Moytura are well known, and both are covered all over with cairns, cromlechs, and other sepulchral monuments, the relics of two great battles. Moreover, the northern battlefield still retains its old name in the form of Moytirra.

These mysterious Dedannans were celebrated not only as magicians, but also as skilled artisans in metal, wood, and stone. Many beautifully-formed bronze spearheads, thought to be of their workmanship, are preserved in the National Museum, Dublin; they are long and slender: while those ascribed by tradition to the Firbolgs are less graceful, and are rounded at the point.

The chief burial place of these people was along the Boyne between Drogheda and Slane, where many monuments still remain, the principal of which are the three great mounds of Newgrange, Dowth, and Knowth. In subsequent ages the Dedannans were deified and became *Shee* or fairies whom the pagan Irish worshipped.

The Fifth Colony.—The legends dwell with fond minuteness on the origin, the wanderings, and the adventures of this last and greatest of the Irish colonies. From Scythia, their original home, began their long pilgrimage: and having wandered from one country to another for many generations, seeking for Inisfail—the "Isle of Destiny"—their final home, of which one of their druids had told them, they settled in Spain, from which, after a long sojourn, they migrated to Ireland. They were led by the eight sons of the hero *Miled* of Spain [Mee-lĕ], or Milesius, whence they were called Milesians.

Sailing into the mouth of the Slaney, they were driven to sea by the spells of the Dedannans, and finally landed at Inver-Skena or Kenmare Bay. Marching northwards to Tara, they there met the three kings of the Dedannans, and demanded from them the surrender of the country or battle. But the cunning Dedannans pretended that they had been taken unawares and treated unfairly, and demanded judgment in the matter. The dispute was referred to Amergin, one of the eight brothers, who was the chief druid or brehon of the Milesians. Now this druid delivered what he believed to be a just judgment even against his own people: namely, that the Milesians should re-embark at Inver-Skena and retire nine waves from shore; and if after this they could make good their landing, the country should be given up to them. And to this both parties agreed. But no sooner had the ships got nine waves out than the Dedannans raised a furious tempest by their magical spells, which wrecked the fleet and drowned five of the brothers. The remaining three, Eremon, Eber-Finn, and Amergin, landed with their crews, and having defeated the Dedannans in two great battles, took possession of the country. Eremon was their first king; and thenceforward Ireland was ruled by a succession of Milesian kings till the reign of Roderick O'Conor who was the last native over-king. From these Milesian people descend all those of the modern Irish who have or had an "O" or a "Mac" to their surname.

In the legendary pages of our old records, the first kings of those dim ages pass indistinctly in review before us, and we hardly know whether to regard them as mere shadows or real personages. Tigernmas [Teernmas] was the first to have gold regularly mined and worked; chiefly in the gold district near the Liffey. He distinguished his people by the number of colours in their garments, from the slave who had only one colour, to the king who had six. King Tigernmas was suddenly destroyed on *Samin* eve—the eve of the first of November—in some mysterious way, with a multitude of his people, while worshipping the great idol Crom Cruach.

From the earliest times of which we have any record, it was the custom to hold a *Fes* or meeting at Tara, the residence of the Ard-ri, where the nobles and learned men of the whole country met; with the Ard-ri at their head, to examine the laws and records of the kingdom, and to transact other important business. The proceedings were written down in a book called the Psalter of Tara; but this book, if it ever existed, was lost or destroyed ages ago. According to the legend, the *Fes* was instituted by the mighty King *Ollamh Fodla* [Ollav Fōla], who reigned two or three centuries after Tigernmas. It was held for some days before and after *Samin* or the first of November; and the intention was to summon it every third year. But this intention was not carried out, for in reality it was held only at irregular intervals: generally at the beginning of each king's reign, and occasionally at other times, when any important business required it. It is necessary to observe that the holding of the *Fes* of Tara is not mere legend, but a historical fact. Tara was abandoned as a royal residence in the sixth century; but extensive remains of mounds and raths are still to be seen on and around the hill, one of which is figured here.

The Mound called the Forra, at Tara. From Mrs. Hall's Ireland.
Drawn by Wakeman.

About three centuries before the Christian era, Macha of the Golden Hair, queen of *Cimbaeth* [Kimbay] king of Ulster, built the palace of *Emain* or Emania, which continued to be the residence of the kings of Ulster for more than six hundred years. The remains of this palace, consisting of a great mound surrounded by earthen ramparts, now called the Navan Fort, are to be seen two miles from Armagh. At the beginning of the Christian era, when Conary I was king of Ireland, the Red Branch Knights of Ulster, a sort of heroic militia, mighty men all, came every year to Emain to be trained in military science and feats of arms, residing for the time in a separate palace called Creeveroe or the Red Branch. Their greatest commander was Cuculainn, the mightiest of all the Irish heroes of antiquity, whose residence was Dundalgan, now called the Fort of Castletown near Dundalk. They were in the service of Concobar or Conor Mac Nessa, king of Ulster, who feasted the leading heroes every day in his own palace. The finest of the Romantic Stories in the Book of the Dun Cow, the Book of Leinster, and other old manuscripts, are about those Red Branch Knights.

Inish-Samer. House on top modern.

Chapter VIII
The Dawn of History
A.D. 130–463.

LTHOUGH our narrative is not yet free from legend, the matters related in this chapter may for the most part be taken as fact.

Several very important events took place during the reign of Tuathal [Too'hal] the Legitimate, a powerful king of Ireland, who reigned from A.D. 130 to 160. About twenty years before his accession, the plebeian races, consisting chiefly of the people of the older colonies who had been reduced to slavery by the Milesians, rose up in rebellion and seized the throne, murdering or banishing the members of the reigning family, and a great part of the nobles of the country. But the Milesian monarchy was restored in the person of Tuathal, who from this circumstance was surnamed "the Legitimate."

Hitherto the Ard-ri had for his land allowance only a small tract round Tara; but Tuathal formed the province of Meath to be the special estate or mensal land of the kings of Ireland forever. At that time the four older provinces, Leinster, Ulster, Connaught, and Munster, met at a great stone called the "Stone of the Divisions," which was considered the centre of Ireland, and which is still to be seen on the side of the hill of Ushnagh in Westmeath: and the new province was made by cutting off a portion of each of the other four round this stone.

Aill-na-meeran, *the Stone of the Divisions. Now often called the Cat's Rock.*

One of Tuathal's daughters was married to the king of Leinster, who, however, growing tired of her, hid her in a remote part of his palace and gave out that she was dead. And after due time he went to Tara and obtained from the king his other daughter in marriage. But one day, soon after the return of the newly married couple, the two sisters met by accident, and were so overwhelmed with astonishment, grief, and shame, that they both died immediately. To punish this wicked crime, Tuathal imposed on Leinster a heavy tribute to be paid every second year—many times heavier than the ordinary tribute due from a provincial king. Whether we believe this half-legendary account of its origin or not, one thing is certain beyond all doubt: that from a very remote period the kings of Ireland claimed from Leinster an enormous tribute called the Boruma or Boru, consisting of cows, sheep, hogs, mantles, brazen caldrons, and ounces of silver: a tribute that brought great disaster on the country, and in the end indeed helped to break up the monarchy. Every householder in the province had to contribute; and the tax was so distressing on all, that it was hardly ever paid without a battle: so that the kings of Leinster were always at enmity with the kings of Ireland, and were ever ready to takes sides against them.

We know that one of them joined the Danes and was the chief agent in bringing on the battle of Clontarf; and it is notorious how another—Dermot Mac Murrogh—brought over the Anglo-Normans to invade Ireland.

Dinnree, the most ancient residence of the kings of Leinster. Now Ballyknockan Fort on the west bank of the Barrow, half a mile below Leighlinbridge, Carlow. From Mrs. Hall's Ireland.

Conn the Hundred-Fighter, or as he is often called, Conn of the Hundred Battles, who became king, A.D. 177, was a great, warlike, and active king, as may be judged from his name. But he had a formidable antagonist, a man just as able and as fond of fighting as himself: Owen-More king of Munster, otherwise called *Mogh-Nuadat* [Mow-Nooat]. Between these two there was constant warfare for many years: and Owen defeated his great rival in ten battles, till at last he forced him to divide Ireland equally between them. The boundary line agreed on was a low slender ridge of natural sand hills called *Esker-Riada* [Reeda], which still remains, running across Ireland from Dublin to Galway. This division is very often referred to in Irish writings: the northern half was called Leth-Conn [Leh Conn], that is, Conn's half; and the southern Leth-Mow, Mow's half. But Owen, becoming discontented with his share, renewed the quarrel; and a decisive battle was fought between them at a place called Moylena, near Tullamore in the present King's County, in which the Munster king was defeated and slain.

Conn was succeeded by his son Conary II, A.D. 212, whose son Riada [Reeda] led a colony to Scotland, as will be related in chapter XIII.

The most illustrious of all the pagan kings of Ireland was Cormac Mac Art, grandson of Conn the Hundred-Fighter. He was a great warrior, scholar, and lawmaker, as well as an encourager of learning: and the legendary accounts describe him as a model of majesty, magnificence, and manly beauty. We are told that he founded three colleges at Tara; one for the teaching of law; one for history and literature; and the third for military science. After a prosperous reign he retired from the throne on account of the accidental loss of an eye, and took up his residence in a beautiful cottage called Cletta on the south bank of the Boyne near Newgrange, where for the rest of his life he devoted himself to learning. Here he composed a number of law books, of some of which we still have copies in the old Brehon Law volumes. The legend says that Cormac became a Christian; and that his death was brought about by the druids, who practised their wicked spells against him, and caused him to be choked by the bone of a salmon.

In the time of Cormac flourished the "Fena of Erin," a body of militia kept for the defence of the throne, very like the Red Branch Knights of an earlier period. Their most celebrated leader was King Cormac's son-in-law, Finn the son of Cumal [Coole], who of all the ancient heroes of Ireland is at the present day best remembered in tradition. We have in our old manuscripts many beautiful stories of these Fena, like those of the Red Branch Knights.

Niall of the Nine Hostages, who reigned from A.D. 379 to 405, was the most warlike and adventurous of all the pagan kings. Four of his sons settled in Meath, near Tara, and four others conquered a territory for themselves in Ulster, where they settled down. The posterity of this great king are called Hy Neill, meaning "descendants of Niall"; the brothers who settled in Meath, and their descendants, were the "Southern Hy Neill"; those who went to Ulster, and their descendants, the "Northern Hy Neill." With two exceptions (Dathi and Olioll Molt) all the over-kings of Ireland from the time of Niall down to the accession of Brian Boru belonged to this illustrious family of Hy Neill, who in later ages took the name of O'Neill.

Those who have read the early history of England will remember that the Picts and Scots, marching southwards from the Scottish Highlands, gave much trouble, year after year for a long period, to the Romans and Britons. The Picts were the people of Scotland at the time; and the Scots were the Irish, who, crossing over to Alban or Scotland, joined the Picts in their formidable raids southwards. We know all this, not only from our own native historians, but also from Roman writers, who tell us how the Romans had often to fight in Britain against the Scots from Ireland. For at that time Ireland was called (among other names) Scotia; and the Irish people were known as Scots. When, subsequently, the Irish made settlements and founded a kingdom in Scotland—as will be told farther on—Ireland was usually called Scotia Major, while Scotland, whose old name was *Alban,* began to be known as Scotia Minor. This continued till the eleventh or twelfth century, when our own country dropped the name Scotia and was called *Eirè-land,* or Ireland, from the old native name *Eirè* or Erin; and Alban came to be known by its present name Scotland, that is, the land of the Scots or Irish.

In those early ages the Irish were very much in the habit of crossing the sea on warlike expeditions; and they did not confine their excursions to Scotland. Long before the time of Niall, they had conquered the Isle of Man and a large part of Wales, and many traces of their occupation remain in both places to this day, such as old place-names, old forts, and other monuments. The most formidable of all the invaders was Niall; and when the power of the Romans began to wane in Britain, he led several expeditions against them. He also invaded Gaul; and in one of his incursions to that country, while marching at the head of his troops, according to the old legendary account, he was shot dead with an arrow across the river Loire by one of his chiefs, the king of Leinster (A.D. 405).

Niall's nephew *Dathi* [Dauhy] succeeded, and was the last king of pagan Ireland. He too led expeditious into foreign lands and we read in the old legend that he was struck dead by a flash of lightning at the foot of the Alps, after he had wantonly destroyed the cell of a holy hermit named Parmenius (A.D. 428). His followers brought his body all the way home and buried it in the old cemetery at the palace of Croghan, beside Rathcroghan, in Roscommon, under a great red pillar-stone which stands there to this day.

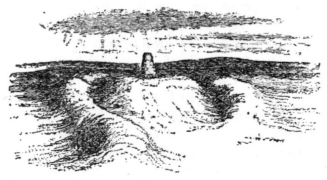

King Dathi's Grave. From Proceedings, *Royal Irish Academy, 1872, page 117.*

The next king was Laegaire [Leary] son of Niall of the Nine Hostages: the first of the Hy Neill kings (A.D. 428). It was in the fifth year of his reign that St. Patrick arrived in Ireland to begin his mission, as will be told in the next chapter. In an attempt to levy the Boruma, Laegaire was defeated and taken prisoner by the Leinster men: but they set him free after he had sworn the old pagan oath, by the sun and wind and by all the elements, that he would never more demand the tribute. Yet in less than two years he again led his army against them, determined this time to exact it, but died suddenly on his march. The legend says that it was the sun and wind that killed him for having violated his oath. As he lived and died a pagan, he was buried, in pagan fashion, under one of the ramparts of his own rath at Tara, standing up fully armed in his grave, with his face towards Leinster. His grave was made at the south-east of the outer rampart; and as the rath is still well known, we can point out, almost with certainty, the exact spot.

We have now arrived at the fifth century and shall have little more to do with legend: we have, as it were, emerged from twilight into the open day. Henceforward the narrative is historical, and may be generally accepted as truth.

The history of pagan Ireland ends here: and so far we have drawn our information regarding those ancient times almost entirely from the native records. In those days of imperfect navigation, Ireland was so remote that foreign writers knew very little about it; but the few notices of it they have left us are very important. It was known to the Phoenicians, who probably visited it: and Greek writers mention it under the names of *Iernis* and *Ierne* [I-er-nè], and as the "Sacred Island" thickly inhabited by the *Hiberni*. The Greek geographer Ptolemy, writing in the second century, who drew his information from Phoenician authorities, has given us a description of Ireland much more accurate than the account he has left us of Great Britain. And that the people of Ireland carried on a considerable trade with foreign countries in those early ages we know from the statement of the Roman historian Tacitus, that in his time—the end of the first century—the harbours of Ireland were better known to trading nations than those of Britain. People that carry on commerce cannot be altogether barbarous: and these few notices show that the country had some settled institutions and a certain degree of civilisation as early at least as the beginning of the Christian era. So that the native writers, with all their legends and overdrawn pictures of ancient Ireland, have some truth on their side.

The next four chapters will be devoted to a sketch of the progress of Christianity and learning from the time of the arrival of St. Patrick: the secular History will be resumed in chapter XIII.

Composed from the Book of Kells.

Chapter IX
St. Patrick—Part I
A.D. 431–433.

EADERS of our early history know that there were Christians in Ireland before the time of St. Patrick; and they must have grown to be pretty numerous by the beginning of the fifth century: for in the year 431, as we are told by a writer who lived at the time, Pope Celestine sent Palladius "to the Scots believing in Christ to be their first bishop." Nevertheless the great body of the Irish were at this time pagans; but Palladius was not the man destined for their conversion. He landed on the coast of Wicklow; but after a short sojourn, during which he visited some Christians scattered through that district, and founded three little churches, he was expelled by the chief of the place, and died soon afterwards in Scotland.

The next mission had a very different result. No nation in the world was converted to Christianity in so short a time as the Irish; and no missionary, after the age of the apostles, preached the Gospel with more success than St. Patrick. He was a man of strong will and great courage, with much tact and good sense; and wherever he went, the people he addressed were all the more willing to hearken to his preaching on account of the noble simplicity and purity of his life. He cared nothing for riches and honours: but he loved the people of Ireland, and his whole anxiety was to make them good Christians. We do not know for certain his birthplace; but the best authorities believe he was born near Dumbarton in Alban or Scotland, though others think in the west of Gaul. At that time both Gaul and Britain were under the Romans, and there is evidence that his family, whichever of the two places they belonged to, were Christians, and that they were in a respectable station of life; for his father Calpurn was a magistrate in the Roman service.

When Patrick was a boy of sixteen, he was, as we are told by himself in his writings, taken captive and brought to Ireland. This was about the year 403. He was sold as a slave to a certain rich man named Milcho, who employed him to herd sheep and swine on the slopes of Slemish Mountain in the present county Antrim. Here he spent six years of his life. If he felt at first heartbroken and miserably lonely, as no doubt he did, he soon recovered himself, and made nothing of the hardships he endured on the bleak hillside; for in his solitude his mind was turned to God, and every spare moment was given up to devotions. He tells us in his own earnest and beautiful words:—"I was daily employed tending flocks; and I prayed frequently during the day, and the love of God was more and more enkindled in my heart, my fear and faith were increased, and my spirit was stirred; so much so that in a single day I poured out my prayers a hundred times, and nearly as often in the night. Nay even in the woods and mountains I remained, and rose before the dawn to my prayer, in frost and snow and rain; neither did I suffer any injury from it, nor did I yield to any slothfulness, such as I now experience; for the spirit of the Lord was fervent within me." But he stood alone in the little world of light and holiness; for his master was a pagan; and though the people he mixed with were bright and lovable, they too were all pagans, grossly superstitious, but beyond that, with little idea of religion of any kind.

At the end of six years of slavery Patrick escaped and made his way through many hardships and dangers to his home and family. During his residence in Ireland he had become familiar with the language of the people; and the memory of the pagan darkness in which they lived haunted him night and day, so that he formed the resolution to devote his life to their conversion. His steadfast will was shown even at this early period by the manner in which he set about preparing himself for his noble work. He first studied with great diligence for about four years in the great monastic school of St. Martin of Tours; and subsequently under St. Germain of Auxerre for about the same length of time; after which he continued his preparation in an island near the Italian coast, and elsewhere, till he was ready to begin his mission. During all this time his thoughts were ever turned lovingly to Ireland; and he had dreams and visions about it. Once he dreamed, as he tells us, that a man from Ireland came to him and gave him a letter, which began with the words "The Voice of the Irish." "Whilst I was reading the letter"—he goes on to say—"I imagined at the moment that I heard the voices of many, who were near the wood of Foclut which is [in Ireland] beside the Western Ocean: crying out as if with one voice, 'we entreat thee, O holy youth, to come and still walk amongst us.' And I was exceedingly afflicted in my heart and could read no more, but quickly awoke."

Having received authority and benediction from Pope Celestine,[1] he set out for Ireland. On his way through Gaul news came of the death of Palladius; and as this left Ireland without a bishop, Patrick was consecrated bishop in Gaul by a certain holy prelate named Amator. Embarking for Ireland, he landed on the Wicklow coast; but having been expelled, like his predecessor, he sailed northwards, and finally disembarked with his companions at Lecale in the present county Down. Dicho, the chief of the district, thinking they were pirates, hastily armed his followers and sallied forth to expel them: but when they appeared in view, he was so struck by their calm and dignified demeanour, that instead of attacking, he saluted them respectfully and invited them to his house. Here Patrick announced his mission and explained his doctrine; and Dicho and his whole family became Christians and were baptised: the first of the Irish converted by St. Patrick. As there was no church; the chief presented him with a *sabhall* [saul] or barn for Divine Service, on the site of which a monastery was subsequently erected in honour of the saint, which for many ages was held in great veneration. And the memory of the happy event is preserved to this day in the name of the little village of Saul near Downpatrick. He remained in this neighbourhood for some time; and the people, following the example of their chief, listened to his preaching, and were baptised in great numbers.

Chapter X
St. Patrick—Part II
A.D. 433–465.

т. Patrick adopted, from the very beginning, a bold and courageous plan of preaching the Gospel in Ireland:—He always made straight for the palaces and other great houses, and began by attempting to convert the kings and chiefs. He was well aware of the veneration of the clansmen for their ruling families; and he knew that once the king had become a Christian the people would soon follow. He had experienced the success

---

[1] So we find it stated by several ancient authorities, the oldest of whom is an Irish saint who lived a century and a half after the time of St. Patrick. Celestine was the same pope who had commissioned Palladius about a year before Patrick's arrival. But although there is unquestionable contemporary evidence that this pope sent Palladius to Ireland, some writers dispute the statement that Patrick received his commission from him.

of this plan in Saul; and now he came to the bold resolution to go to Tara, and present himself before King Laegaire [Leary] and his court. Bidding farewell to his friend Dicho, he sailed southward to the mouth of the Boyne; whence he set out on foot for Tara with his companions. Soon after leaving the boat, night fell on them; and they were hospitably entertained at the house of a chief, whom the saint converted, with his whole family. One of the children, a youth to whom Patrick gave the name of Benen or Benignus from his gentle disposition, became so attached to him that he insisted on going along with him next morning. Thenceforward Benen was Patrick's constant companion and beloved disciple; and after the death of his master he succeeded him as archbishop of Armagh.

The saint and his little company arrived at the hill of Slane on Easter Eve, A.D. 433. Here he prepared to celebrate the festival; and towards nightfall, as was then the custom, he lighted the Paschal fire on the top of the hill. It so happened that at this very time the king and his nobles were celebrating a festival of some kind at Tara; and the attendants were about to light a great fire on the hill, which was part of the ceremonial. Now there was a law that while this fire was burning no other should be kindled in the country all round on pain of death; and accordingly, when the king and his courtiers saw the fire ablaze on the hill of Slane, nine miles off, they were much astonished at such an open violation of the law. The monarch instantly called his druids and questioned them about it; and they said:—"If that fire which we now see be not extinguished tonight, it will never be extinguished, but will overtop all our fires: and he that has kindled it will overturn thy kingdom." Whereupon the king, in great wrath, instantly set out in his chariot with a small

St. Erc's Hermitage. From Wilde's Boyne and Blackwater. *Wakeman.*

retinue, nine chariots in all; and having arrived near Slane, he summoned the strangers to his presence. He had commanded that none should rise up to show them respect; but when they presented themselves, one of the courtiers, Erc the son of Dego, struck with the saint's commanding appearance, rose from his seat and saluted him. This Erc was converted, and became afterwards bishop of Slane; and to this day there is, on the bank of the Boyne near Slane, a little ruined oratory called from him St. Erc's Hermitage. The result of this interview was what St. Patrick most earnestly desired: he was directed to appear next day at Tara and give an account of his proceedings before the assembled court. On the summit of the hill of Slane, at the spot where Patrick lighted his Paschal fire, there are still the ruins of a monastery erected in commemoration of the event.

Slane Monastery. From Wilde's Boyne and Blackwater. *Wakeman.*

The next day was Easter Sunday. Early in the morning Patrick and his companions set out for the palace, and on their way they chanted a hymn in the native tongue—an invocation for protection against the dangers and treachery by which they were beset; for they had heard that persons were lying in wait to slay them. This noble and beautiful hymn was long held in great veneration by the people of this country, and we still possess copies of it in a very old dialect of the Irish language. In the history of the spread of Christianity, it would be difficult to find a more singular and impressive scene than was presented at the court of King Laegaire on that memorable Easter morning. Patrick was robed in white, as were also his companions; he wore his mitre, and carried his crosier in his hand; and when he presented himself before the assembly, Dubthach [Duffa], Laegaire's chief poet, rose to welcome him, contrary to the express commands of the king. The saint, all aflame with zeal and unawed by the presence of king and court, explained to the assembly the leading points of the Christian doctrine, and silenced the king's druids in argument. Dubthach became a convert, and thenceforward devoted his poetical talents to the service of God; and Laegaire gave permission to the strange missionaries to preach their doctrines throughout his dominions. The king himself however was not converted; and for the remaining thirty years of his life he remained an unbeliever, while the paganism of the whole country was rapidly going down before the fiery energy of the great missionary.

Patrick next proceeded to Tailltenn where, during the celebration of the national games, he preached for a week to the assembled multitudes, making many converts, among whom was Conall Gulban, brother to King Laegaire, the ancestor of the O'Donnells of Tir*connell*. We find him soon afterwards making for the plain where stood the great national idol Crom Cruach with the twelve lesser idols, all of which he destroyed.

About the year 438, with the concurrence of King Laegaire, he undertook the task of revising the Brehon Law. He was aided by eight others, among them King Laegaire himself, and at the end of three years, this Committee of Nine produced a new code, free from all pagan customs and ordinances, which was ever after known as "Cain Patrick" or Patrick's Law. This Law Book, which is also called the *Senchus Mór* [Shan'ahus More], has been lately translated and published.

In his journey through Connaught he met the two daughters of King Laegaire—Ethnea the fair and Fedelma the ruddy—near the palace of Croghan, where they lived at that time in fosterage with their two druid tutors. They had come out one morning at sunrise to wash their hands in a certain spring well, as was their custom, and were greatly astonished to find Patrick and his companions at the well with books in their hands, chanting a hymn. Having never seen persons in that garb before, the virgins thought at first that they were beings from the *shee* or fairy hills; but when the first surprise was over they fell into conversation with them, and inquired whence they had come. And Patrick gently replied:—"It were better for you to confess to our true God than to inquire concerning our race." They eagerly asked many questions about God, his dwelling-place—whether in the sea, in rivers, in mountainous places, or in valleys—how knowledge of him was to be obtained, how he was to be found, seen, and loved, with other inquiries of a like nature. The saint answered all their questions, and explained the leading points of the faith; and the virgins were immediately baptised and consecrated to the service of religion.

On the approach of Lent he retired to the mountain which has ever since borne his name—Croagh Patrick or Patrick's hill—where he spent some time in fasting and prayer. About this time, A.D. 449, the seven sons of Amalgaid [Awley] king of Connaught were holding a meeting in Tirawley, to which Patrick repaired. He expounded his doctrines to the wondering assembly; and the seven princes with twelve thousand persons were baptised. After spending seven years in Connaught, he visited successively Ulster, Leinster, and Munster, in each of which he preached for several years. Soon after entering Leinster, he converted, at the palace beside Naas where the Leinster kings then resided, the two princes Illann and Olioll, sons of King Dunlang, who both afterwards succeeded to the throne of their father. And at Cashel, the seat of the kings of Munster, he was met by the king, Aengus the son of Natfree, who conducted him into the palace on the rock with the greatest reverence, and was at once baptised.

North Moat, Naas: remains of ancient palace. (House on top modern.)
From a drawing by the author, 1857.

Wherever St. Patrick went he founded churches, and left them in charge of his disciples. In his various journeys, he encountered many dangers and met with numerous temporary repulses; but his courage and resolution never wavered, and success attended his efforts in almost every part of his wonderful career. He founded the see of Armagh about the year 455, and made it the head see of all Ireland. The greater part of the country was now filled with Christians and with churches; and the mission of the venerable apostle was drawing to a close. He was seized with his death illness in Saul, the scene of his first triumph; and he breathed his last on the seventeenth of March, in or about the year 465, in the seventy-eighth year of his age.[1]

[1]There is much uncertainty both as to St. Patrick's age and as to the year of his death. I have given the age and the year that seem to me most probable.

The news of his death was the signal for universal mourning. From the remotest districts of the island, clergy and laity turned their steps towards the little village of Saul, to pay the last tribute of love and respect to their great master. They celebrated the obsequies for twelve days and nights without interruption, joining in the ceremonies as they arrived in succession; and in the language of one of his biographers, the blaze of myriads of torches made the whole time appear like one continuous day. He was buried with great solemnity at Dun-da-leth-glas, the old residence of the princes of Ulidia; and the name in the altered form of Downpatrick, commemorates to all time the saint's place of interment.

CHAPTER XI
PROGRESS OF RELIGION

URING the lifetime of St. Patrick there was extraordinary religious fervour in Ireland which lasted on for several centuries, such as, probably, has never been witnessed in any other country. There gathered round the great apostle a crowd of holy and earnest men, who, when they passed away, were succeeded by others as holy and as earnest: and the long succession continued unbroken for centuries. We have the lives of those men pictured in minute detail in our old writings: and it is impossible to look on them without feelings of wonder and admiration. They were wholly indifferent to bodily comfort or to worldly advancement. They traversed the country on foot, and endured without flinching privations and dangers of every kind for the one object of their lives—to spread religion and civilisation among their rude countrymen; and when at home in their monasteries, many lived and slept in poor comfortless little houses, the remains of which may be seen to this day—places we should now hesitate to house our animals in. The lot of the poorest and hardest-worked labouring man of our time is luxury itself compared with the life led by many of those noble old missionaries. But even these were surpassed by those resolute Irishmen who went in crowds, in the seventh and eighth centuries, to preach the Gospel to the half-savage, ferocious, and vicious people who then inhabited Gaul, North Italy, and Germany.

It must not be supposed that all the people of Ireland were converted by St. Patrick and his companions. There were large districts never visited by them; and in many others the Christianity of the people was merely on the surface. Much pagan superstition remained; the druids still retained great influence; and for more than a century after St. Patrick's death Christianity had a hard struggle with paganism; so that there was plenty of work for his successors. Of these the two most illustrious were St. Brigit and St. Columkille, who of all the Irish saints, with the single exception of St. Patrick himself, are most venerated by the Irish people.

The Church called "St. Columb's house," Kells, Co. Meath (in 1840).
From Petrie's Round Towers.

St. Brigit of Kildare was born about the year 455 at Faughart near Dundalk; but her father, who was a powerful chief, belonged to Leinster. She became a nun when very young; and soon the fame of her sanctity spread through the whole country. Having founded convents in various parts of Ireland, she finally settled—about the year 480—at a place in Leinster, where she built her little wooden cell under the shade of a great oak tree, whence it got the name of *Killdara,* the church of the oak, now Kildare. This became the greatest and most famous nunnery ever established in Ireland. St. Brigit died on the 1st of February, 523. She is affectionately revered in every part of Ireland; and there are places all through the country still called Kilbride, and Kilbreedy (Brigit's church) which received their names from churches founded by or in commemoration of her.

St. Columba or Columkille was born in 521 at Gartan in Donegal. He belonged to the Northern Hy Neill, his father being great-grandson of Niall of the Nine Hostages; but he gave up all the worldly advantages of his princely birth for religion. In the year 546 he built the church of Derry on a spot presented to him by prince Aed Mac Ainmirè [An'mĭra], afterwards king of Ireland. During the next sixteen years, he travelled and preached and founded a great number of churches and monasteries all over the country, among others those of Kells, Swords, Tory Island, Lambay near Dublin, and Burrow in King's County, the last of which was his chief establishment in Ireland. All these places were venerated for centuries after the saint's death, and in all there are interesting ruins to this day.

Inishcaltra or Holy Island in Lough Derg on the Shannon. Island Monastery founded by St. Camin, died 653. From Kilkenny Archaeological Journal: *1889, page 162. Wakeman.*

In the year 563 Columba went with twelve companions to the little island of Iona on the west coast of Scotland, which had been granted to him by his relative the king of that part of Scotland. Here he settled, and founded the monastery which afterwards became so illustrious. He converted the Picts; and he traversed the Hebrides, preaching to the people and founding churches wherever he went. After a life of incessant activity in the service of religion, his death sickness came upon him at Iona in the year 597, when he was seventy-six years of age. His biographer St. Adamnan has left us a full account of the manner of his death. Though feeling his end approaching, he continued, as long as he was able, working at his favourite occupation, copying the Scriptures, with one of his disciples, Baithen, constantly beside him. When at last he could write no more, he laid down the pen and said, "Let Baithen write the rest." At the toll of the midnight bell he rose from his bed, which was nothing but a bare flagstone, and went to the church hard by, followed immediately after by his attendant Dermot. He arrived there before the others had time to bring in the lights; and Dermot losing sight of him in the darkness, called out "Where are you, father?" Receiving no reply, he felt his way, till he found his master before the altar kneeling and leaning forward on the steps: and raising him up a little, supported his head on his breast. The monks now came up with the lights; and seeing their beloved old master dying, they began to weep. He looked at them with his face lighted up with joy, and tried to utter a blessing; but being unable to speak, he raised his hand a little to bless them, and in the very act of doing so he died in Dermot's arms. The funeral services lasted three days and three nights, and he was buried within the monastery.[1]

---

[1]Besides Patrick, Brigit, and Columkille, the following are a few of the most eminent of the Irish saints:—

St. Ailbè of Emly in Limerick, who was ordained bishop of Cashel by St. Patrick: he was ecclesiastical head of Munster.

St. Enna or Endeus of Aran in Galway Bay; died about 542. This island was afterwards called *Ara-na-Naemh* [naive], Aran of the saints, from the number of holy men who lived in it.

St. Finnen of Clonard, the founder of the great school there: called "The Tutor of the Saints of Ireland": died 549.

St. Ciaran [Kieran] of Clonmacnoise, which became one of the greatest of all the Irish monasteries: died 549.

St. Ciaran or Kieran, the patron of Ossory: born in the island of Cape Clear; but his father belonged to Ossory: died about 550.

St. Ita, Ida, or Mida, virgin saint, of Killeedy in Limerick; often called the Brigit of Munster: died 569.

St. Brendan of Clonfert in Galway, or "Brendan the Navigator": born in Kerry: died 577.

St. Senan of Scattery Island in the Shannon: died about 560.

St. Comgall, the founder of the celebrated school of Bangor in Down, which rivalled Clonard: died 602.

St. Kevin, the founder of Glendalough in Wicklow: died 618.

St. Carrthach or Mochuda of Lismore, where he founded one of Ireland's greatest schools: died 637.

St. Adamnan the biographer of St. Columkille; ninth abbot of Iona: born in Donegal: died 703.

Among the vast number of Irish men and women who became illustrious on the Continent, the following may be named:—

The early monastic clergy of Ireland may be said to have been mainly of two classes. Those of the one class settled in the inhabited districts, and concerned themselves with the functions of education and religious ministration. They went freely among chiefs and people, restrained their quarrels so far as they could, and instructed, assisted, and encouraged them by advice and example. Those of the other class gave themselves up to a life of prayer, contemplation, and work; and these took up their abode in remote islands or mountain valleys, places generally hard to reach, and often almost inaccessible. Here the little communities lived in huts, built by themselves, one for each individual, while nearby was the little church for common worship. There was a very general inclination among religious men for this monastic hermit life in the early Christian ages—from about the middle of the sixth century; and on almost all the islands round the coast, as well as on those in the lakes and rivers, the remains of churches and primitive establishments are found to this day.

The churches which began to be built after the arrival of St. Patrick were generally of wood, but often of stone and mortar. For hundreds of years they continued very simple and small, for the congregations were small: but in the twelfth century large and splendid churches began to be erected, both by the Anglo-Norman lords, and by the native chiefs. The ruins of numbers of the little stone churches of the early Christian times (of

St. Fursa of Peronne and his brothers Foillan and Ultan; Fursa died about 650.

St. Dympna or Domnat of Gheel, virgin martyr, to whom the great sanatorium for lunatics at Gheel in Belgium is dedicated: daughter of an Irish pagan king: martyred, seventh century.

St. Columbanus of Bobbio in Italy, a pupil of Bangor, founded the two monasteries of Luxeuil and Fontaines: expelled from Burgundy for denouncing the vices of king Theodoric; preached successfully to the Gauls; wrote learned letters: finally settled at Bobbio, where he died, 615.

St. Gall, a disciple of Columbanus, patron of St. Gall (in Switzerland) which was named from him.

St. Fridolin the Traveller of Seckingen on the Rhine: died in the beginning of the sixth century.

St. Kilian the apostle of Franconia: martyred 689.

St. Cataldus bishop of Tarentum, from the school of Lismore, where he was a professor: seventh century.

Virgil or Virgilius bishop of Salzburg, called Virgil the Geometer, from his eminence in science: taught, probably for the first time, the rotundity of the earth: died 785.

Clement and Albinus, placed by Charlemagne at the head of two great seminaries. John Scotus Erigena, celebrated for his knowledge of Greek: the most distinguished scholar of his time in Europe: taught philosophy with great distinction in Paris: died about 870.

which St. Mac Dara's church, figured below, is a good example), and of the grand churches and monasteries of the twelfth and subsequent centuries, are still to be seen in various parts of the country. Of the latter, Kilmallock Abbey, represented at p. 87, is a fine specimen. In connexion with many of the churches and monasteries were slender round towers, from 60 to 150 feet high, divided into stories and lighted by small windows. The doorway was usually ten or fifteen feet from the ground, and was reached by a small ladder. These towers were erected at various times from the ninth to the thirteenth century: and they had at least a twofold use:—as belfries, and as keeps or fortresses, to which the inmates of the monasteries could retire for the time, with their valuables, in case of sudden attack by the Danes or others: which latter was their most important use. Some were probably also used as beacons and watchtowers. About eighty of the round towers still remain, of which upwards of twenty are perfect.

St. Mac Dara's primitive church on St. Mac Dara's Island off the coast of Galway. Interior measurement 15 feet by 11. From Petrie's Round Towers.

Almost all churches and monasteries were founded on tracts of land granted for the purpose by kings or chiefs; and after their establishment they were supported, partly by donations and bequests, and partly by the labours of their communities, as described below. Many of them became rich, and their wealth was expended in relieving poverty, in entertaining guests, and in the production of those lovely works of art in gold, silver, and gems, which have been already described.

The inmates of these monasteries, whether established in inhabited districts or in solitudes, did not lead an idle life. On the contrary they were kept busily at work; and some of the old records giving an account of how the monks were employed in their various avocations are very pleasant reading. When the founder of a monastery had determined on the neighbourhood in which to settle, and had fixed on the site for his establishment, he brought together those who had agreed to become his disciples and companions, and they set about preparing the place for residence. They did all the work with their own hands, seeking no help from outside. While some levelled and fenced in the ground, others cut down, in the surrounding woods, timber for the houses or for the church, dragging the great logs along, or bringing home on their backs bundles of wattles and twigs for the wickerwork walls. Even the leaders claimed no exemption, but often worked manfully with axe and spade like the rest.

Round Tower (perfect), Devenish Island in Lough Erne near Enniskillen. From Kilkenny Archaeological Journal. *Wakeman.*

When settled down in their new home the inmates supported themselves by the work of their hands, and no one was permitted to be idle. Agriculture formed one of the principal employments; for, as already stated, there was land attached to almost every monastery. Those working in the fields were always under the superintendence of some member deputed by the abbot; and they returned in the evening, bringing on their backs heavy loads of provisions or other necessaries for next day. Some milked the cows and brought home the milk in vessels strapped on their shoulders; while those who had a trade always worked at it, for the use of the community or guests. Others again attended in the evening to the mill, if there was one attached to the monastery, or if not, worked at the querns till they had ground corn enough for next day.

Attached to every monastery, and forming part of it, was what was called the "Guest-house" for the reception of travellers; and some of the inmates were told off for this duty, whose business it was to receive the stranger, to wash his feet, and prepare supper and bed for him. For in those days travellers, whether of high or low rank, were always sure of a hospitable reception free of charge at the monasteries; a function which was continued till their suppression by Henry VIII. Some of the monks too were skilled in simple herb remedies, and the poor people around often came to them for advice and medicine in sickness.

Scribe writing the Book of Kildare. From an illuminated MS. of Giraldus Cambrensis, transcribed about A.D. 1200: now in British Museum. Photographed from reproduction in Gilbert's "Fac.Sim. Nat. MSS."

In the educational establishments teaching afforded abundant employment to the scholarly members of the community. Others again worked at copying and multiplying books for the library, or for presentation outside; and to the industry of these scribes we owe the chief part of the ancient Irish lore, and other learning, that has been preserved to us. St. Columkille devoted every moment of his spare time to this work, writing in a little wooden hut that he had erected for his use at Iona; and it is recorded that he wrote with his own hand three hundred copies of the New Testament, which he presented to the various churches he had founded. Some spent their time in ornamenting and illuminating books—generally of a religious character, such as copies of portions of Scripture: and these men produced the wonderful penwork of the Book of Kells and other such manuscripts. Others were skilled metal-workers, and made crosiers, crosses, bells, brooches, and other articles, of which many are preserved to this day, that show the surpassing taste and skill of the artists.

The cares of governing the household generally gave occupation enough to the abbot or head of the community; yet he is often found working in the fields, attending to the cattle, ploughing or digging, or taking his turn in bringing corn on his back to the mill and grinding it for next day's food. St. Brigit, accompanied by a few of her nuns, often herded her sheep on the level sward round her nunnery in Kildare. With all this the inmates had of course their devotions to attend to; and in most monasteries had to rise at sound of bell in the middle of the night, all the year round, and go to the church to prayers. Thus they led a busy and laborious life, contented and cheerful in the consciousness that they were doing good and useful work.

Church and (imperfect) Round Tower of Dysert-Aengus near Croom in Limerick. From Mrs. Hall's *Ireland.*

Sculpture on a Capital: Priest's House. Glendalough: Beranger, 1779. From Petrie's Round Towers.

CHAPTER XII
PROGRESS OF LEARNING

ANCIENT Ireland, Religion and Education went hand in hand, so that in tracing their history it is impossible to separate them. By far the greatest part of the education of the country was carried on by, or under the direction of, priests and monks, who always combined religious with secular teaching.

From the middle of the sixth century, schools rapidly arose all over the country, most of them in connexion with monasteries. Some had very large numbers of students; for instance we are told that there were 3,000 under St. Finnen at Clonard; and some other schools, such as Bangor, had as many. A few of the students resided in the college, such as sons of kings and chiefs, and those who were literary foster children of the professors; but the most usual arrangement was that each student lived in a little hut of wood and sods, built by himself; or perhaps two or more joined and built a more commodious house for common use. Whole streets of these little houses surrounded the monastery: the huts of the scholars of St. Movi of Glasnevin, near Dublin, extended along the banks of the river Tolka near the present bridge. At stated times the students came forth in crowds to hear the lectures of the professors, which were often given in the open air.

In all the more important schools there were students from foreign lands. The majority were from Great Britain, from which they came in *fleetloads,* as Aldhelm, an English bishop of the year 705, expresses it. Numbers also came from the Continent, among whom were some princes: Aldfrid king of Northumbria, and Dagobert II king of France, both, when in exile in the seventh century, found an asylum and were educated in

Ireland: and others of like rank might be named. We get some idea of the numbers of foreigners from the words of Aengus the Culdee, an Irish writer of the ninth century, who mentions by name many Romans, Gauls, Germans, Britons, and even Egyptians, all of whom died in Ireland. Venerable Bede, describing the ravages of the Yellow Plague in 664, says:—"This pestilence did no less harm in the island of Ireland. Many of the nobility and of the lower ranks of the English nation were there at that time: and some of them devoted themselves to a monastic life: others chose to apply themselves to study. The Scots willingly received them all, and took care to supply them with food, as also to furnish them with [manuscript] books to read, and their teaching, all gratis."

Ancient baptismal font of Clonard: three feet high: still preserved in the church there. From Wilde's Boyne *and* Blackwater. *Not a vestige of any old building remains on the site of this great monastery.*

In the course of three or four centuries from the time of St. Patrick, Ireland became the most learned country in Europe: and it came to be known by the name now so familiar to us—*Insula sanctorum et doctorum,* the Island of saints and scholars.

In these great seminaries all branches of knowledge then known were taught: they were, in fact, the models of our present universities; and besides those persons preparing for a religious life, great numbers of young men, both native and foreign, the sons of kings, chiefs, and others, attended them to get a good general education. Laymen who distinguished themselves as scholars were often employed as professors in the monastic schools. One of the most eminent of the professors in the college of Monasterboice was "Flann of the Monastery," a layman of the eleventh century, several of whose poems, as well as his Book of Annals, are preserved. But some few schools were purely lay and professional:—for Law, Medicine, Poetry, or Literature; and these were taught generally by laymen.

At these colleges, whether clerical or lay, they had various degrees, as there are in modern universities. The highest was that of Ollave or Doctor; and there were ollaves of the several professions; so that a man might be an ollave poet, an ollave historian, an ollave builder, &c.; just as we have now doctors of law, medicine, literature, and music. The full course for an ollave was twelve years: the lower degrees had shorter periods. Men of learning were held in great estimation and much honoured. They had many valuable allowances and privileges: and an ollave sat at table next to the king or chief.

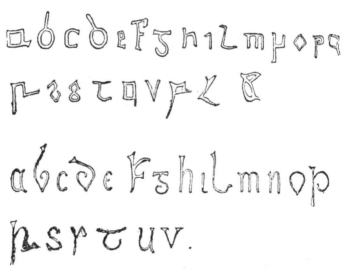

Two Irish alphabets: the upper one of the 7th century: the lower of the 11th. The three last characters of the first alphabet are Y, Z, and &c. (There are two forms of s in each.) From Miss Stokes's Christian Inscriptions, *II, 135.*

Great numbers of Irishmen went to teach and to preach the Gospel in Great Britain, Wales, and Scotland. The Picts of Scotland, who then occupied the greatest part of the country, were converted by St. Columba and his monks from Iona; and the whole western coasts of England and Wales abound in memorials of Irish missionaries. The monastery of Lindisfarne in Northumbria, which became so illustrious in after ages, was founded in 634 by Aidan an Irish monk from Iona; and for thirty years after its foundation it was governed by him and by two other Irish bishops, Finan and Colman, in succession. So we see that Mr. Lecky had good reason for his statement that "England owed a great part of her Christianity to Irish monks who laboured among her people before the arrival of Augustine."

Whole crowds of ardent and learned Irishmen travelled to the Continent, spreading Christianity and general knowledge among people ten times more rude and dangerous in those ages than the inhabitants of these islands. "What," says Eric, a well-known French writer of the ninth century, "what shall I say of Ireland, who despising the dangers of the deep, is migrating with almost her whole train of philosophers to our coasts?" Irish professors and teachers were in those times held in such estimation that they were employed in most of the schools and colleges of Great Britain and the Continent. And Irish teachers of music were quite as eminent and as much sought after as those of literature and philosophy, as has been already stated. We know that Charlemagne, who was crowned emperor of the West, A.D. 800, held the learned men from Ireland in great respect, and often invited them as guests to his table; and half a century later, Johannes Scotus Erigena, *i.e.* John the Irish Scot, the greatest scholar of his day, was on terms of affectionate intimacy with Charles the Bald, king of France. To this day in many towns of France, Germany, Switzerland, and Italy, Irishmen are venerated as patron saints. Nay, they found their way even to Iceland; for we have the best authority for the statement that when the Norwegians first arrived at that island, they found there Irish books, bells, crosiers, and other traces of Irish missionaries.

For four or five hundred years after the time of St. Patrick, the monasteries were unmolested; and learning was cultivated within their walls. In the ninth and tenth and the beginning of the eleventh century, science and art, the Gaelic language, and learning of every kind, were brought to their highest state of perfection. But a change for the worse had set in. The Danish inroads broke up most of the schools and threw everything into disorder. Then the monasteries were no longer the quiet and safe asylums they had been—they became indeed rather more dangerous than other places, so much did the Danes hate them—and learning and art gradually declined in Ireland. There was a revival in the time of Brian Boru; but this too was arrested by the troubles of the Anglo-Norman invasion.

Sculpture on window: Cathedral Church, Glendalough: Beranger, 1779. From Petrie's Round Towers.

CHAPTER XIII
FROM LAEGAIRE TO THE DANES
A.D. 463–637.

AEGAIRE, it will be remembered, was son of Niall of the Nine Hostages. At the time of his sudden death, his son Lewy was only a child and could not be elected king. So the throne was taken by king Dathi's son Olioll Molt, who was at that time the most powerful prince of the reigning family, though he was not of the Hy Neill. But after the lapse of many years, when Lewy grew up to be a man, he was determined to win back the crown for himself and for his own immediate kindred: and collecting a great army he defeated and slew Olioll Molt in a battle fought at a place called Ocha near Tara in Meath, and took possession of the throne. This great battle proved decisive; for, after that date, for five centuries without a break, that is, from Lewy to Malachy II, the Hy Neill gave kings to Ireland, sometimes through the northern branch and sometimes through the southern.

From the cliffs of Antrim, on any clear day, you can see the blue hills and headlands of Scotland, forming a long line on the distant horizon. The Irish, or Gaels, or Scots, of Ulster, from the earliest ages, were in the habit of crossing over in their *currachs* to this lovely-looking coast; and some carried on a regular trade with Alban, as Scotland was then called, and many settled there and made it their home. Scotland was inhabited at that time by a people called the Picts, who often attempted to expel the intruders; but the Irish held their ground, and as time went on they occupied more and more of the western coast and islands. Nearly three hundred years before the time we are now treating of, a leader named Reuda or Riada [Reeda], a grandson of Conn the Hundred-Fighter, and first cousin of Cormac Mac Art, settled among the Picts with a large following of

66

Munster fighting-men and their families. From this Riada all that western district in Scotland was called Dalriada (Riada's portion): and there was an Irish Dalriada, also named from him, comprising the northern part of Antrim. Our own ancient Irish writers tells us all about this colony; but we are not dependent on their testimony only; for the most distinguished of the early English historians, the Venerable Bede, has given the same account of this leader Reuda in his Ecclesiastical History.

The greatest of all these colonisations of which we have any detailed historical account, took place in the reign of the present king Lewy, under the command of three brothers, named Fergus, Angus, and Lorne, from the district of Dalriada in Ulster, sons of a chief named Erc, a direct descendant of Riada. Riada and his followers were pagans; but these three brothers and their people were all Christians. They appear to have met with little or no opposition; and being joined by the previous settlers, they took possession of a large territory; which was formed into a kingdom, of which Fergus, or Fergus Mac Erc, as he is generally called, was the first king. The memory of these three princes is deeply graven on the history of Scotland, so that many Scottish persons and places have been named from them. This colonial kingdom was subject and tributary to the kings of Ireland, and continued so for nearly three-quarters of a century, when King Aedan, who was brother of Branduff, king of Leinster, refused to pay tribute any longer, or to acknowledge, as his sovereign lord, the king of Ireland, who at this time happened to be Aed Mac Ainmirè [An'mirĕ].

In order to bring this dangerous dispute, as well as other important matters, to a settlement by peaceful arbitration, a convention of the chief men, both lay and clerical, of Ireland and of the Scottish colony, was summoned by king Aed. This important meeting, which is much celebrated in early Irish history, was held at a place called Drum-Ketta on the river Roe near Limavady in Derry; for Tara had been abandoned as a royal residence some years previously; otherwise this *Fes* would no doubt have been held there. Among other eminent men, St. Columba, who was nearly related to both the Irish and the Scottish kings (for they all belonged to the Hy Neill), came over from Iona to take part in the deliberations; and mainly through his influence, the king of Ireland wisely agreed that the little Scottish kingdom should be then and for evermore independent of the Irish monarchs. The people of this colony, having now free scope for their energies, ultimately mastered the whole country. Fergus was the ancestor of the subsequent kings of Scotland; and from him, through the Stuarts, descend, in one of their lines of pedigree, our present royal family.

Another important matter considered at this convention was the position of the bards or poets. As learning of every kind was so much respected in

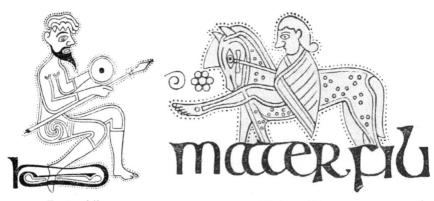

Foot soldier.   Horse soldier.

Grotesque figures from the Book of Kells, 7th century, showing some costumes of the period. Foot Soldier: *headdress yellow; coat green; breeches very tight, light-blue; legs and feet bare; small shield held by the left hand; spear exactly the shape of some of those preserved in the National Museum.* Horse Soldier: *cap yellow; cloak green, with bright red and yellow border; breeches green; leg clothed; foot naked. Horse covered with yellow cloth. From Wilde's Catalogue.*

Ireland, these bards were greatly revered and held in high honour. But they had lately grown very numerous, insolent, and troublesome. The ollave poets were in the habit of going about the country with great companies of pupils and followers, and wherever they came they expected to be entertained—themselves and their retinue—in great style, and well paid by the chiefs they visited, who, for dread of their bitter lampoons, seldom ventured to refuse them. They became at last so overbearing and oppressive that the people rose up in indignation against them: and at this meeting of Drum-Ketta many of the leading men, including the king of Ireland, urged that the whole bardic order should be suppressed, and the worst among them expelled the country. But here again Columkille interposed with a more moderate and a better proposal, which was agreed to. The bards and their followers were greatly reduced in number; strict rules were laid down for the regulation of their conduct in the future; and those who were fit for it, especially the ollaves of learning, were set to work to teach schools, with land for their maintenance, so as to relieve the people from their exactions.

This king, Aed Mac Ainmirè, reigned twenty-six years (572 to 598), and would have reigned longer had he not made an attempt to levy the Boru tribute. His first demand was refused; whereupon, collecting his forces, he marched into the heart of Leinster. But by a skilful stratagem, Branduff, king of the province, with a much smaller force, defeated his army in a night surprise at Dunbolg near Dunlavin in Wicklow; and King Aed himself was slain while retreating.

After several short unimportant reigns, Donall, son of the last-mentioned king Aed Mac Ainmirè, ascended the throne in 627. One of his first acts was to expel from Ireland a powerful Ulster prince named Congal Claen, who had killed Donall's predecessor. Congal fled to Britain where he had many relatives among the kings and chiefs there, who espoused his cause. After an exile of nine years, he returned with a great army, determined to wrest the throne from King Donall; and he was immediately joined by his Ulster partisans. Donall had however been made aware of the projected invasion, so that he was fully prepared: and marching north he confronted his enemies at Moyrath, now Moira in the present county of Down. Here was fought one of the most noted and sanguinary battles recorded in Irish history, which lasted for six successive days, and terminated in the total overthrow of the invaders. Congal fell fiercely fighting at the head of his forces; and few of his great army escaped from the field.

On the accession of Finaghta the Festive in 674, he made the old demand on Leinster, and defeated the Leinster men when they rose in resistance. But the iniquity of the Boru tax and the evils resulting from it seem at last to have created general discontent: for soon after, at the earnest solicitation of St. Moling of Ferns, King Finaghta solemnly renounced the Boru for himself and his successors. This however did not end the trouble. After the lapse of some reigns other kings renewed the claim, and two more destructive battles were fought on account of it; after which this ill-omened tribute gradually fell into disuse, leaving however an evil mark on the country.

CHAPTER XIV
THE DANISH WARS
A.D. 795–1013.

EFORE the close of the eighth century the Danes began to make descents on the coasts of Europe. From Jutland, Norway, Sweden, and in general from the coasts and islands of the Baltic, came forth swarms of daring robbers, who for two centuries kept the whole of western Europe in a state of continual terror. They appeared for the first time on the Irish coast in A.D. 795, when they plundered St. Columkille's church on Rechru or Lambay Island near

Dublin. Once they had found the way, party after party continued to sail to Ireland, plundering and murdering wherever they came. They soon found out that many of the monasteries were rich in works of art: such as crosiers, shrines, books, bells, &c., ornamented with much gold, silver, and precious stones; and as they hated Christianity and learning of all kinds, they had a double motive in seeking out these establishments. Accordingly they plundered churches, monasteries, and libraries, both on the islands and on the mainland, and what they could not bring away they burned or otherwise destroyed, so far as lay in their power. Their movements moreover were so sudden and quick, that they generally made their escape before the people had time to intercept them. About the middle of the ninth century they established themselves permanently in Dublin, Limerick, and Waterford, where they built fortresses.

Clonmacnoise in 1825. From Brewer's Beauties of Ireland. *Drawn by Petrie.*

For some time in the beginning the Danes came in detached bands, each small party plundering on their own account, with no combined action. But at length their scattered forces were united under their most renowned leader, Turgesius, who arrived with a great fleet, and was acknowledged leader by all the Danes then in Ireland. Other fleets soon followed under his direction; and he fixed his headquarters, first at Armagh, and afterwards on Lough Ree, where he had one of his fleets; and from both centres, he plundered the districts all round, murdering the people and destroying a vast number of churches and monasteries. At Clonmacnoise his queen Ota desecrated St. Kieran's venerated church by seating herself daily on the high altar, in derision of the sacred place, and there performing some of her pagan rites, and giving audience to her visitors. At last he was defeated and taken prisoner by Malachi, king of Meath, who caused him to be drowned in Lough Owel in Westmeath. This brave king became Ard-ri, as Malachi I, in the following year (846).

The Danes were often intercepted in their murderous raids and slaughtered without mercy by the Irish kings and chiefs: but this had not much effect in putting a stop to their ravages; for they were bold, and brave, and faced danger and death with the utmost fearlessness. Moreover there was seldom any union among the Irish chiefs, who often fought more bitterly against each other than against the Northmen; and while they were fighting, the Danes were plundering. But there were some chiefs of a more patriotic spirit. Such were Niall Glunduff, of the Northern Hy Neill, king of Ireland (916 to 919), and his heroic son Murkertagh of the Leather Cloaks. They attacked the Northmen at every opportunity, and defeated them in several battles, but in the end both fell fighting against them— Niall in a great battle fought at Kilmashogue near Dublin, Murkertagh at Ardee—both dying bravely as they had lived, in conflict with the enemies of their country.

In the second half of this tenth century the tide commenced to turn when two great men began their career:—Malachi II, or Malachi the Great as he is often called, who became king of Ireland in 980, and Brian Boru king of Munster, the man who was destined to finally crush the power of the Danes in Ireland.

When Brian was a young man, his elder brother Mahon was king of Munster. Both belonged to the Dalgas or Dalcassians, a brave and powerful tribe who occupied Thomond or North Munster, and who subsequently took the family name of O'Brien. At this time the Danes held the chief fortresses of Munster, including Limerick, Cork, and Waterford, from which they constantly issued forth, and committed dreadful ravages all over the province; so that the two brothers, unable to withstand them, had to cross the Shannon and take refuge with their followers in the woods and mountain solitudes of Clare, where they defended themselves as best they could.

The career of young Brian was singularly like that of Alfred the Great who lived only a short time before: at first borne down and driven to hide with a few followers in remote fastnesses by the overwhelming power of the Danes, but gradually gaining ground by never-failing pluck and determination. Even the brave Mahon at one time found it necessary to make peace with them; but the fiery young Brian would have no peace-dealings with the Danes, and at last persuaded his brother to call a general meeting of the tribe to consider what should be done to free the province from their intolerable tyranny. Here the question was put, was it to be peace or war: and the people answered to a man, War, and demanded to be led once more against the pirates. Collecting all their forces, the two brothers attacked the Danish army at Sulcoit or Sollohod near the present Limerick Junction, routed them in a decisive battle, pursued them all the way to Limerick—full twenty miles—and recovered possession of the old city. Mahon followed up this success by defeating the Northmen in seven battles; but in the end he was invited to a conference and assassinated by two base Irish chiefs aided by the Danish king Ivar. Brian was overwhelmed with grief, and the old Irish record represents him as uttering this lament:

> "The death of Mahon is grievous to me—
> The majestic king of Cashel the renowned;
> Alas, alas that he fell not in battle,
> Under cover of his broad shield:
> Alas that in friendship he trusted
> To the treacherous word of his betrayer.
> It was an evil deed for those three chiefs
> To murder the great and majestic king;
> And if my hand retains its power,
> They shall not escape my vengeance
> Either I shall fall—fall without dread, without regret—
> Or they will meet with a dire fate at my hand:
> I feel that my heart will burst
> If I avenge not our noble king."

But this villainous deed only brought a more powerful and dangerous rival to the front, for now Brian became king of Munster; and his first care was to avenge his brother's murder, which he did by defeating and slaying the three assassins one after another. From that time forward, for about twenty-five years, his life was one of incessant warfare, chiefly against the Danes.

Meantime Malachi, in his own part of the country, was struggling against the foreigners bravely and successfully. He defeated them in a great battle at Tara in 979, the year before he was elected king of Ireland; and marching eastwards, he took Dublin and liberated 2,000 captives. Some time afterwards however, the Danes recovered the city; whereupon he again swooped suddenly down, and captured and plundered it. Among the trophies that he brought away on this occasion were two heirlooms greatly prized by the Norsemen, the torque or collar of the Norwegian prince Tomar—who had been killed 148 years before—and the sword of Carlus, who fell in battle in 869: both in Ireland. This is the incident referred to by Moore in the words:—"When Malachi wore the collar of gold which he won from her proud invader."

For many years after Malachi's accession in 980, he and Brian quarrelled and fought: but at length in 998 they agreed to divide Ireland between them: Malachi taking Leth-Conn and Brian Leth-Mow. But Mailmora king of Leinster was not pleased with the terms of this peace, which placed him under the authority of Brian; for Leinster was part of Leth-Mow; and in the very next year he and the Danes of Dublin revolted. Without delay Brian marched northwards, and being joined by Malachi, encamped at Glenmama near Dunlavin in Wicklow. Here they were attacked by Mailmora and Harold the Dane of Dublin; and in the terrible battle that followed, Brian and Malachi defeated them and slew 4,000 of the Danes and Leinster men. To this day the neighbourhood abounds in memorials and traditions of the battle.

About this time Brian came to the determination to depose Malachi; and the better to strengthen himself he made alliance with those who had lately been his enemies. He married Gormlaith, mother of the king of the Dublin Danes (Sitric of the Silken Beard), and sister of Mailmora king of Leinster; he gave his own daughter in marriage to Sitric; and he took Mailmora into favour.

His next proceeding was to invade Malachi's territory, in 1002, in violation of the treaty of four years before; and he sent to him to demand submission or battle. Malachi finding he was not strong enough to resist, rode into Brian's encampment with merely a small retinue, and without any guarantee or promise of safety, depending on Brian's honour: and having told him plainly he would fight if he had been strong enough, he made his submission. From that year, Brian was acknowledged king of Ireland, Malachi going back to his own special kingdom of Meath.

And now after forty years of incessant warfare king Brian devoted his mind to works of peace, like the great Alfred of England. His palace, which was named Kincora, was situated on the high ridge over the Shannon now occupied by the town of Killaloe. He rebuilt the monasteries that had been destroyed by the Danes, and erected bridges and fortresses all over the country. He founded and restored schools and colleges, repressed evil-doers, and caused the laws to be obeyed, so that the country was less disturbed and more prosperous than it had been for a long time before. The bright picture handed down to us of the state of Ireland during the dozen years that elapsed from his accession to the battle of Clontarf, is illustrated by the well-known legend, that a beautiful young lady richly dressed, and bearing a gold ring of great value on her wand, traversed the country alone from north to south without being molested: a fiction which Moore has embalmed in the beautiful song "Rich and rare were the gems she wore."

CHAPTER XV
THE BATTLE OF CLONTARF[1]—PART I
A.D. 1013–1014.

LTHOUGH chafing under Brian Boru's rule, the Danes durst not make any hostile move, for the old king was stern and strong, and while they hated him much they feared him more. It is likely that in the long run they would have taken some opportunity to break out and attempt his overthrow; yet the immediate circumstances that led to the battle of Clontarf were brought about, not by them, but by Mailmora, king of Leinster.

On one occasion while Mailmora was on a visit at Kincora with the king his brother-in-law, some bitter words passed between him and Murrogh, Brian's eldest son, at a game of chess; so that he left the palace in anger and made his way to his own kingdom of Leinster, determined to revolt. He induced some neighbouring chiefs, and also the Dublin Danes, to join him; and they began by attacking Malachi's kingdom of Meath, as he was now one of Brian's adherents. Malachi defended himself successfully for some time, but was at last obliged to call in the aid of Brian; and the war went on without much result till Christmas, when the king returned to Kincora, determined to renew the campaign in the following spring.

Mailmora and the Danish leaders now began actively at the work of mustering forces for the final struggle; and Gormlaith, who was at this time in Dublin among her own people—having been discarded by Brian because she had taken sides against himself and in favour of the Danes—was no less active than her relatives. Her son Sitric of the Silken Beard,

---

[1]The account of the battle given in these two chapters is taken mainly from an ancient Irish chronicle called "The Wars of the Gaels with the Galls" (of the Irish with the Danes), and partly from the Norse *Saga* or story called "Burnt Nial," in which is given the Danish account of the battle.

Danish king of Dublin, acting under her directions, engaged the services of Sigurd, earl of the Orkneys, as well as of Broder and Amlaff of the Isle of Man, the two earls of all the north of England, who promised to be in Dublin on Palm Sunday, the day fixed on for the meeting of all the confederates. Broder had once been a Christian, but now worshipped heathen fiends: "he had a coat of mail on which no steel would bite"; he was both tall and strong, and his black locks were so long that he tucked them under his belt. These two Vikings, Broder and Amlaff, who had a great fleet with 2,000 "Danmarkians" are described as "the chiefs of ships and outlaws and Danes of all the west of Europe, having no reverence for God or for man, for church or for sanctuary." There came also 1,000 men covered with coats of mail from head to foot: a very formidable band, seeing that the Irish fought as usual in tunics. Envoys were despatched in other directions also: and troops of Norsemen sailed towards Dublin from Scotland, from the Isles of Shetland, from the Hebrides, from France and Germany; and from the distant shores of Scandinavia.

While Sitric and others were thus successfully working abroad, Mailmora was equally active at home; and by the time all the foreign auxiliaries had joined muster, and Dublin Bay was crowded with their black ships from the Liffey to Ben Edar, he had collected the forces of Leinster and arranged them in three great battalions within and around the walls of Dublin.

The Irish monarch had now no time to lose. He assembled his army about the 17th of March; and having encamped near Kilmainham, on the "Green of Aha-clee" (Dublin), that is, on the level grassy plain now called the Phoenix Park, he set fire to the Danish districts near Dublin, so that the fierce Norsemen within the city could see the country the whole way from Dublin to Howth smoking and blazing. And brooding vengeance, they raised their standards and sallied forth determined to give battle.

On Thursday evening the king got word that the Danes were making preparations to fight next day—Good Friday. The good king Brian was very unwilling to fight on that solemn day; but he was not able to avoid it. At dawn of day on Friday, 23rd April, the Irish army began their march from their encampment in three divisions. The van consisted of the Dalcassians commanded by Murrogh; next came the men of the rest of Munster under O'Faelan prince of the Decies; and the forces of Connaught formed the third division under O'Hyne and O'Kelly. There were two companies brought by the great Stewards of Mar and Lennox in Scotland, who were related to the southern Irish, and who now came to aid them in their hour of need. The men of Meath, the southern Hy Neill, were also there under Malachi: the northern Hy Neill took no part in the battle. A few days previously, Brian's son Donogh had been sent with a large body of Dalcassians to devastate Leinster, expecting to be back in time for battle. With that exception every living man of the old king's family stood there that day to fight by his side—all his sons and nephews, and his grandson Turlogh, a youth of fifteen, the son of Murrogh. The ranks were in very close order; so solid looking that, in the language of one of the old records, it seemed as if a chariot could be driven along on their heads.

The Danish and Leinster forces also formed three divisions. In the van were the foreign Danes under the command of Broder and Sigurd; behind these were the Danes of Dublin under a chief named Duvgall; and the Leinster men, led by Mailmora, formed the third division. Sitric the king of Dublin was not in the battle: he remained behind to guard the city. We are not told the numbers engaged: but there were probably about 20,000 men on each side.

At that time Dublin city, which was held by the Danes, lay altogether south of the Liffey, the narrow streets crowding round the Danish fortress which crowned the hill where now stands Dublin Castle. All the district on the north bank of the river, from the Phoenix Park to Clontarf, now covered by portions of the city, was open country, with a piece of natural forest called Tomar's Wood stretching from the neighbourhood of Drumcondra, on by Phibsborough, towards the Liffey: and the only way to reach the city from that side was by Duvgall's Bridge, on the site of the present bridge at the foot of Church Street, just above the Four Courts. The Liffey was then unconfined, and spread out widely, and the sea flowed over the space where now stand the Custom House, Amiens Street, the Northern Railway Terminus, and all the adjacent streets lying between them and the sea. The main battleground extended from about the present Upper Sackville Street to the river Tolka, and beyond along the shore towards Clontarf. The Danes stood with their backs to the sea; the Irish on the land side facing them. Malachi and his men stood on the high ground, probably somewhere about Cabra and Phibsborough. The hardest fighting appears to have taken place round the fishing weir on the Tolka, at, or perhaps a little above, the present Ballybough Bridge: and indeed the battle is called in some old Irish authorities "The Battle of the Weir of Clontarf."

In the march from the camping place the venerable monarch rode at the head of the army; but his sons and friends prevailed on him, on account of his age—he was now seventy-three—to leave the chief command to his son Murrogh. When they had come near the place of conflict, the army halted; and the king, holding aloft a crucifix in sight of all, rode from rank to rank and addressed them in a few spirited words. He reminded them that on that day their good Lord had died for them; and he exhorted them to fight bravely for their religion and their country. Then giving the signal for battle, he withdrew to his tent in the rear.

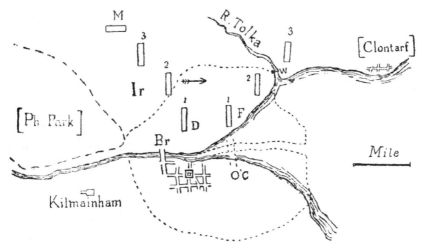

BATTLE OF CLONTARF

Ir. (1, 2, 3.) Irish army on march: in three divisions.
D. Dalcassians.
F. Foreign Danes. 1, 2, 3. Danish army in three divisions.
M. Malachy with his Meathmen.
Br. Duvgall's Bridge: city near it with Danish fortress in centre.
W. Fishing weir, where young Turlogh was found drowned.
O'C. The present O'Connell Bridge.
The dotted lines show the present limits of city and river.

Little or no tactics appear to have been employed. It was simply a fight of man against man, a series of hand-to-hand encounters; and the commanders fought side by side with their men. On the evening before, a Dane named Platt, one of the thousand in armour, had challenged any man of the Irish army to single combat; and he was taken up by Donall, the Great Steward of Mar. Now stepped forth Platt in the middle space, just before the battle began, and called out three times, "Where is Donall?" "Here I am, villain!" answered Donall. And they fought in sight of the two armies till both fell, with the sword of each through the heart of the other, and hands entangled in each other's hair.

The first divisions to meet were the Dalcassians and the foreign Danes; then the men of Connaught and the Danes of Dublin fell on one another; and the battle soon became general. From early morning until sunset they fought without the least intermission. The thousand Danes in coats of mail were marked out for special attack: and they were all cut to pieces; for their armour was no protection against the terrible battleaxes of the Dalcassians. The Danish fortress of Dublin, perched on its hill-summit, overlooked the field; and Sitric and those with him in the city crowded the parapets, straining their eyes to unravel the details of the terrible conflict. They compared the battle to a party of reapers cutting down corn; and once when Sitric thought he observed the Danes prevailing, he said triumphantly to his wife, King Brian's daughter, "Well do the foreigners reap the field: see how they fling the sheaves to the ground!" "The result will be seen at the close of the day," answered she, quietly: for her heart was with her kindred.

The old chronicle describes Murrogh as dealing fearful havoc. Three several times he rushed with his household troops through the thick press of the furious Norsemen, mowing down men to the right and left; for he wielded a heavy sword in each hand, and needed no second blow. At last he came on Earl Sigurd, whom he found slaughtering the Dalcassians; and here we have some interesting legendary details from the Danish account of the battle in the Nial Saga. Sigurd had a banner which was made by his mother with all her dark art of heathen witchcraft. It was in raven's shape; and when the wind blew, then it was as though the raven flapped his wings. It always brought victory to Sigurd, but whoever bore it was doomed to death: now, in the presence of the Christian host, it lost the gift of victory but retained its death-doom for the bearer. Murrogh approached, breaking through the ranks of the Northmen, and slew the standard-bearer: and he and Sigurd fought a hard fight. Sigurd now calls out to Hrafn the Red: "Bear thou the banner!" "Bear thy own demon thyself," replied Hrafn. Then the earl took the banner and put it under his cloak, and again turned on Murrogh. But Murrogh struck off his helmet with a blow of the right-hand sword, bursting straps and buckles; and with the other felled him to the earth—dead.

Towards evening the Irish made a general and determined attack; and the main body of the Danes at last gave way: or as the Danish Saga expresses it: "Then flight broke out throughout all the host." Crowds fled along the level shore towards Dublin, vainly hoping to reach either the ships or the bridge leading to the city. But Malachi, who had stood by till this moment, rushed down with his Meathmen and cut off their retreat. When the battle commenced in the morning there was high tide; and now, after the long day, the tide was again at flood, so that the ships lay beyond reach far out from shore. The flying multitude were caught between the Meathmen on the one side and the sea on the other, with the vengeful pursuers close behind; and most of those who escaped the sword were driven into the sea and drowned. The greatest slaughter of the Danes took place during this rout, on the level space now covered with streets, from Ballybough Bridge to the Four Courts.

The rout was plainly seen by those on the parapets of the Dublin fortress; and Sitric's wife, whose turn of triumph had now come, said to her husband with bitter mockery:—"It seems to me that the foreigners are making fast for their inheritance—the sea: they look like a herd of cows galloping over the plain on a sultry summer day, driven mad by heat and gadflies: but indeed they do not look like cows that wait to be milked!" Sitric's brutal answer was a blow on the mouth which broke one of her teeth.

Chapter XVI
The Battle of Clontarf—Part II

o far we have related the disasters of the Danes. But the Irish had their disasters also; and dearly did they pay for their great victory.

After the rout of the Danish main body, scattered parties of Danes continued to fight for life with despairing fury at various points over the plain. On one of these groups came Morrogh, still fighting, but so fatigued that he could scarce lift his hands. Anrad the leader of the band dashed at him furiously. But Morrogh, who had dropped his sword, closing on him, grasped him in his arms, and by main strength pulled his armour over his head; then getting him under, he seized the Norseman's sword and thrust it three times through his body to the very ground. Anrad, writhing in the death agony, plunged his dagger into the prince's side, inflicting a mortal wound. The Irish hero lived till next morning when he received the solemn rites of the church.

The heroic boy Turlogh, only fifteen years of age, the son of Murrogh, fought valiantly during the day in his father's division, side by side with his elder relatives. After the battle, late in the evening, he was found drowned at the fishing weir of the river Tolka, with his hands entangled in the long hair of a Dane, whom he had pursued into the tide at the time of the great flight.

But the crowning tragedy of the bloody day of Clontarf was yet to come. The aged king remained in his tent engaged in earnest prayer, while he listened anxiously to the din of battle. He had a single attendant, Laiten, who stood at the door to view the field; and close round the tent was a guard. Once, early in the day, the king asked how the battle fared. "The battalions," replied Laiten, "are mixed together in deadly struggle; and I hear their blows as if a multitude were hewing down Tomar's Wood with heavy axes. I see Murrogh's banner standing aloft, with the banners of the Dalgas around it." Then the king's cushion was adjusted and he clasped his hands in prayer.

Again, after a time, he made the same anxious inquiry. "They are now so mingled that no living man could distinguish them, all covered as they are with blood and dust, so that a father could scarce know his own son. Many have fallen, but Murrogh's banner still stands, moving through the battalions." "That is well," replied the king: "as long as the men of Erin see that standard they will fight with courage and valour."

The same question a third time towards evening. "It is now as if Tomar's Wood were on fire, and the flames burning, and the multitudes hewing down the underwood, leaving the tall trees standing. For the ranks are thinned, and only a few great heroes are left to maintain the fight. The foreigners are now defeated; but the standard of Murrogh has fallen."

"Evil are those tidings," said the old warrior king: "if Murrogh is fallen the valour of the men of Erin is fled, and they shall never more look on a champion like him." And again he knelt and prayed.

And now came the great rout; and the guards, thinking all danger past, eagerly joined in the pursuit, so that the king and his attendant were left alone. Then Laiten becoming alarmed, said:—"Many flying parties of foreigners are around us: let us hasten to the camp where we shall be in safety." But the king replied:—"Retreat becomes us not; I know I shall not leave this place alive: and what avails me, now in my old age, to survive Murrogh and the other champions of the Dalgas." He then spoke his last will to the attendant, giving his property to various religious houses, and directing, as a farewell mark of devotion to the church, that his body should be buried at Armagh: and after this he resumed his prayers.

It happened that Broder, who had fled from the battlefield, came with some followers at this very time towards the tent. "I see some people approaching," said Laiten. "What manner of people are they?" asked the king. "Blue and naked people," replied the attendant. "They are Danes in armour," exclaimed the king, and instantly rising from his cushion, he drew his sword. Broder at that instant rushed on him with a double-edged battleaxe, but was met by a blow of the heavy sword that cut off both legs, one from the knee and the other from the ankle. But the furious Viking, even while falling, cleft the king's head with the axe. After a little time the guards, as if struck by a sudden sense of danger, returned in haste: but too late. They found the king dead, and his slayer stretched by his side dying.

As to the numbers killed, the records differ greatly. According to the annals of Ulster 7,000 fell on the Danish side and 4,000 on the Irish, which is probably about the truth. Almost all the leaders on both sides were slain, and among them Mailmora, the direct inciter of the battle.

The battle of Clontarf was the last great struggle between Christianity and heathenism. The news resounded through all Europe, and brought dismay and terror to every Norse household from the Baltic shore to their furthest settlements in the south. The Nial Saga—the Danish chronicle—relates the whole story of the battle as a great defeat, and tells of fearful visions and portents seen by the Scandinavian people in their homes in the north, on that fatal Good Friday. It ought to be remembered that in the very year of this great battle, Sweyn the Dane overran and mastered England; and that after his death three Danish kings ruled the country in succession.

The body of King Brian and that of his son Murrogh were conveyed with great solemnity to Armagh, where they were interred in the cathedral, the archbishop and the clergy celebrating the obsequies for twelve days.

On Easter Sunday Donogh entered the camp to find that all was over. As soon as the dead had been buried, he led his shattered Dalcassian battalions homewards towards Kincora, bearing their wounded on litters. When they had arrived near Athy, Mac Gilla Patrick, prince of Ossory, an old enemy of the Dalcassians, basely marched out to attack them. Donogh, making hasty preparations to meet him, gave orders that all the sick and wounded should be placed in the rear, with one-third of the army to guard them: but these brave men, feeble as they were, insisted on taking part in the fight. "Let stakes from the neighbouring wood be fixed in the ground," said they, "and let us be tied to them for support, with our swords in our hands, having our wounds bound up with moss, and let two unwounded men stand by each of us, on the right and on the left. Thus will we fight; and our companions will fight the better for seeing us." It was done so. And when the Ossorians saw this, they were struck with fear and pity, and refused point blank to attack such resolute and desperate men: so that the Dalcassians were permitted to pass on. This is the incident referred to by Moore in the song, "Remember the glories of Brian the brave":

> "Forget not our wounded companions who stood
> In the day of distress by our side,
> When the moss of the valley grew red with their blood,
> Yet they stirred not but conquered and died."

After the battle of Clontarf and the death of Brian, Malachi, by general consent, took possession of the throne. He reigned for eight years after, and gave evidence of his old energy by crushing some risings of the Danes—feeble expiring imitations of their ancient ferocious raids—and by gaining several victories over the Leinster men. He died in 1022, in the seventy-third year of his age, leaving behind him a noble record of self-denial, public spirit, and kingly dignity.

CHAPTER XVII
THE EVE OF THE INVASION
A.D. 1022–1166.

ETWEEN the death of Malachi II and the Anglo-Norman invasion about a century and a half elapsed, which was a period of great confusion; for the provincial kings waged incessant war with one another, striving who should be Ard-ri. At first the struggle lay between the O'Loghlins or Mac Loghlins of Ulster (who were a branch of the O'Neills) and the O'Briens of Thomond—the descendants of Brian Boru—till at last the O'Briens went down; and next between the O'Loghlins and the O'Conors of Connaught, till the O'Conors finally triumphed. These dissensions so weakened the country that the first Anglo-Norman invaders met with only a fitful and feeble resistance, and gained a foothold without any very great difficulty. Yet amid all this turmoil, the Irish kings continued to patronise and encourage learning and art, as is proved by works still remaining, several of which are figured in this chapter.

During this time there were eight provincial kings who are commonly set down as kings of Ireland; but not one of them made any pretence to rule the whole country: to every one there was opposition—a refusal to acknowledge his authority—from some one or more of the provinces. Hence these eight are known in history as "kings with opposition."

The first was Donogh, king of Munster, son of Brian Boru, who mastered all Ireland except Ulster, on which he never made any attempt. After some years he was deposed by rivals, and went on a pilgrimage to Rome, where he died. At the time of his deposition (1064), the most powerful of the provincial was Dermot Mac Mailnamo, king of Leinster,

The beautiful and costly Shrine here represented was made by order of King Donall O'Loghlin to cover the venerable little iron bell of St. Patrick. Both Shrine and Bell are in the National Museum, Dublin. Shrine 10 ½ inches high. From Miss Stokes's Christian Inscriptions.

who is regarded as the second of the kings with opposition. Immediately on his death (1072), Turlogh O'Brien, king of Munster, grandson of Brian Boru, asserted his claim to the supreme monarchy; and he is reckoned the third "king with opposition." He reduced all Ireland except Ulster: but when he marched north, the Ulstermen routed him at Ardee, so that he had to make a hasty retreat back to Munster. Turlogh's son, Murkertagh O'Brien, succeeded as king of Munster (1086); and in pushing his claim to the throne of Ireland, he was opposed by an equally powerful claimant, Donall O'Loghlin, king of Ulster, of the princely family of O'Neill. For more than a quarter of a century these two distinguished princes contended for supremacy, and the contest remained undecided to the last, so that both are counted kings of Ireland. Both finally retired to monasteries, where they ended their lives, Murkertagh at Lismore in 1119, and Donall at Derry in 1121. With Murkertagh passed away forever the predominance of the O'Brien family.

Church at Killaloe, Murkertagh's burial place. From Petrie's Round Towers.

Down to Murkertagh's time Cashel was the chief seat of the kings of Munster, who had their residence in a great military *dun* on the rock. But this king granted "Cashel of the kings," as it is called in the old records, to the church, and changed his residence to Limerick, which from that time forth continued to be the seat of the Thomond kings. As soon as Cashel had come into the possession of the church, those buildings began to be erected, the remains of which now form one of the most interesting groups of ecclesiastical ruins in the kingdom.

The O'Conors, kings of Connaught, had been all this time gaining power and influence: and after the death of the two last mentioned kings, Turlogh O'Conor claimed to be king of Ireland. He first reduced all Munster, though only after a severe struggle with one of the O'Briens, during which the country was torn by feuds, and more especially the two provinces in

Rock of Cashel (top of Round Tower appears to the right). From Brewer's
Beauties of Ireland. *Drawn by Petrie.*

dispute. His next opponent was Murkertagh O'Loghlin king of Ulster: and these two, who are both reckoned as kings of Ireland, contended till the death of Turlogh which occurred in 1156. It was by Turlogh's order (while king of Connaught) that the Cross of Cong was made.

Turlogh's son Rory, or as he is more commonly called, Roderick O'Conor, took up the quarrel against O'Loghlin, who however defeated and reduced him to submission. But after O'Loghlin's death, Roderick, having now no rival of any consequence, was made Ard-ri. He was the last native king of Ireland; and in his reign occurred the most important events in the long history of the country, which will be related in the following chapters.

During this century and a half we hear little of the Danes. After the battle of Clontarf no attempt was made to expel them, so that they remained in the country; but from that time forward they gave little trouble. Long before the period we have now arrived at they had become Christians, had settled down like the rest of the people, and devoted themselves to industry and commerce. At the time of the invasion they formed a large part of the inhabitants of the seaport towns—Dublin, Carlingford, Larne, Wexford, Waterford, Limerick, Cork, &c., some of which were governed by Danish chiefs, in a great measure or altogether independent of the Irish princes. Their towns were walled and fortified, while those of the natives continued, after the Irish fashion, open and unprotected. Although living very much

The Cross of Cong.

apart, they intermarried a good deal with the natives, stood on the whole on good terms with them, and at first, as we shall see, generally took sides with them against the new invaders.

Though most of the great educational establishments had been broken up during the Danish ravages, many rose from their ruins or held their ground. There was a revival of learning and art in the time of Brian Boru, which continued after the Danes had been crushed at Clontarf. Even to the beginning of the twelfth century Ireland still retained some portion of her ancient fame for learning; and we find the schools of Armagh, Lismore, Clonmacnoise, Monasterboice, and others, still attracting great numbers of students, many of them foreigners. Moreover, some of the greatest scholars and writers the country ever produced flourished at this time, whose works we still have in our old books; and Irishmen still continued to distinguish themselves on the Continent. Art too was successfully cultivated in spite of all discouragements: and we have seen that the exquisitely executed Cross of Cong was made in 1123.

The Anglo-Normans, who are henceforward to play a leading part in our history, were a great race, valiant, high-spirited, full of talents and full of energy. They were great builders, and filled England and Ireland with splendid castles, monasteries, and cathedrals, many of which still remain to bear witness to the grand ideas of their founders. But it is as mighty warriors that they are best known. Besides being personally brave and daring, they were very skilful in the sort of warfare and fighting suited to those times. They wore coats of mail, were celebrated for their skill in archery, using both the long and the cross bow; and what more than all helped to their success in war, they were under perfect discipline on

Dominican Abbey, Kilmallock, Co. Limerick. Founded in 1291 by Gilbert Fitzgerald. From Kilkenny Archaeological Journal, *1879–82, p. 710.*

the field of battle. But with all their noble qualities they were cruel and merciless to those who resisted them.[1]

The Irish mode of going to battle was totally different. They were, man for man, as brave and as expert in the use of their weapons as the Anglo-Normans, quite as tall and muscular, as fearless and valiant. The Irish soldiers, especially the Galloglasses, are praised by many English writers, one of whom, in the 16th century, says of them:—"The Galloglasses are picked and selected men of great and mighty bodies, cruel without compassion. The greatest force of the battle consisteth in their choosing rather to die than to yield, so that

Two Galloglasses depicted on a Map of Ireland of 1567. From State Papers of Henry VIII, *Ireland, vol. ii.*

---

[1]It ought to be observed here that the first of the adventurers to arrive in Ireland were not *Anglo*-Normans but Welsh-Normans. For their ancestors had settled in Wales and had intermarried with the Welsh chiefs and princes, so that Strongbow, the Geraldines, the De Burgos, and others, were half Welsh half Norman. But as time went on, Anglo-Normans came over in great numbers from various parts of England.

when it cometh to handy blows they are quickly slain or win the field."
Another writer, speaking of the Irish soldiers, says:—"No man at arms,
be he ever so well mounted, can overtake them, they are so light of foot.
Sometimes they leap from the ground behind a horseman and embrace the
rider so tightly that he can no way get rid of them." Spenser, writing in
the sixteenth century, says:—"[The Irish soldiers] are very valiaunt, and
hardie, for the most part great indurers of colde, labour, hunger, and all
hardnesse, very active and strong of hand, very swift of foot, very vigilant
and circumspect in their enterprises, very present [*i.e.* having presence of
mind] in perils, very great scorners of death."

But the Irish fighting men lacked the great tactical skill of their
opponents, their discipline was loose, and they fought rather in crowds,
than in regularly arranged ranks. They had no walled cities. Their surest
defence was the nature of the country, full of impassable bogs and forests;
and their best plan of warfare was to hang on the flanks and rear of an
invading army and harass them as opportunity offered, retreating, when
hard pressed, to their fastnesses, whither no enemy could follow. So
long as they kept to this they could, and often did, hold their own, even
against superior numbers. But in open fighting their tunic-clad crowds
were, number for number, no match for the steel-cased Anglo-Norman
battalions. Nevertheless, as time went on they gradually learned the
Anglo-Norman methods of warfare, and often turned them successfully
against the invaders.

CHAPTER XVIII
THE ANGLO-NORMAN INVASION
A.D. 1166–1173.

URING the time that the two O'Conors were struggling
with Murkertagh O'Loghlin, Dermot Mac Murrogh was
king of Leinster. This Dermot, who was afterwards often
called Dermot-na-Gall (of the English), is described by
Cambrensis as "a tall man of stature, and of a large and
great bodie, a valiant and bold warrior in his nation; and
by reason of his continuall halowing and crieng [in battle]
his voice was hoarse: he rather choce to be feared than to be loved: a great
oppressor of his nobilitie, but a great advancer of the poore and weake.

To his owne people he was rough and greevous, and hatefull to strangers; he would be against all men, and all men against him" (old translation). He was a headstrong and passionate man, and was as much hated in his own day as his memory has been hated ever since. Yet with all his evil qualities he founded many churches and encouraged learning. In 1152 he carried off Dervorgilla the wife of Ternan O'Ruarc prince of Brefney, while O'Ruarc himself was absent from home; and she took away all she had brought to her husband as dowry. O'Ruarc appealed for redress to Turlogh O'Conor king of Ireland, who in 1153 marched with an army into Leinster and forced Dermot to restore Dervorgilla and all her rich dowry. This woman retired after a little time to the abbey of Mellifont, where she spent the rest of her days doing works of penitence and charity, and where she died in 1193 at the age of eighty-five.

Dermot Mac Murrogh. From the MS. of Giraldus Cambrensis (A.D. 1200). Reproduced here from Wilde's Catalogue.

At last Dermot's conduct becoming unbearable; he was deposed and banished by King Roderick O'Conor, O'Ruarc, and others (A.D. 1166); whereupon, breathing vengeance, he fled across the sea, resolved to seek the aid of the great King Henry II of England.

Many years before this time, Pope Adrian IV, an Englishman, influenced by an unfair and exaggerated account of the evil state of religion in Ireland given to him by an envoy of King Henry, issued a bull authorising the king to take possession of Ireland. Some writers have questioned the issue of this bull. But the evidence is so strong on the other side as to leave no good reason to doubt that the pope did really issue it, believing that it would be for the advancement of religion and for the good of Ireland.

Dermot presented himself before the king at Aquitaine, and prayed him for help against his enemies, offering to acknowledge him as lord and master. The king eagerly accepted the offer; but being then too busy with the affairs of his own kingdom to go to Ireland himself, he gave permission to any of his British or French subjects that pleased to join the

Mellifont Abbey in 1791. From Grose's Antiquities of Ireland.

Irish king. Dermot immediately proceeded to Bristol, where he engaged the services of Richard de Clare earl of Pembroke, better known by the name of Strongbow; who agreed to help him on condition that he should get Dermot's daughter Eva in marriage, and should succeed him as king of Leinster. At St. David's in Wales he engaged a number of the Geraldines, among them Maurice Fitzgerald and Robert Fitzstephen, to whom he promised the town of Wexford and the adjoining district. After this Dermot returned to Ferns, his capital, where he remained during the winter of 1168, concealed in the Augustinian monastery founded by himself.

In fulfilment of his engagement, Robert Fitzstephen, with a companion adventurer, Maurice Prendergast, landed in the month of May at the harbour of Bannow in Wexford, with a force of 100 knights and 600 archers, with common soldiers and attendants, amounting in all to about 2,000 men: while Maurice Fitzgerald and others made their preparations to follow. Having been joined by Dermot and his son Donall Kavanagh, the united forces marched on the town of Wexford; and Fitzstephen straightway led his troops to scale the walls. But the townsmen resisted so valiantly, hurling down great stones and beams of timber on the assailants' heads, that he was forced to withdraw, leaving many of his men dead beneath the walls; and going to the strand he set fire to all the ships he found lying there. Next morning when he was about to renew the assault, the clergy, wishing to avoid further bloodshed, persuaded the people to yield up the town; and Dermot's subjects very unwillingly placed themselves again under the authority of their hateful old king. After this, Dermot carried out his promise by making large grants of land to Fitzstephen and others—

land which he had no right to give away, for it belonged not to him but to the people. And having an old grudge against his neighbour, Mac Gilla Patrick king of Ossory, he and the strangers ravaged that district with fire and sword, though not without spirited resistance.

Augustinian Monastery, Ferns. From Journal of Royal Society of Antiquaries, *1895, p. 404. Wakeman.*

When King Roderick O'Conor heard of these proceedings, he became alarmed, and collecting a large army he marched to Ferns, where he found Dermot and his allies strongly entrenched. But Roderick was a feebleminded king, having none of the spirit or vigour of Niall Glunduff or Brian Boru of the olden time; and instead of promptly crushing the rebellious king and his small party of foreigners, as he might have done, he made peace with him, and restored him to his kingdom, on condition that he should send home the strangers, and bring hither no more of them. The treacherous Dermot had no intention of keeping to this treaty: he merely wanted to gain time; and when Maurice Fitzgerald landed soon afterwards, the whole party, natives and foreigners, marched on Dublin, and forced the Danish king Hasculf Mac Turkill to submit to them.

At last Dermot resolved to make himself king of Ireland, and sent a pressing message to Strongbow to come over. Strongbow embarked with an army of 3,000 men, and landed, in August, near Waterford. He was immediately joined by Raymond Fitzgerald, better known as Raymond le Gros (the corpulent), the bravest and most distinguished of all his officers—who had come over some time before—by Miles de Cogan, and by Dermot: and with the combined army of about 5,500 men they attacked and captured the city of Waterford, slaughtering great numbers of the inhabitants. The Danish chief Reginald, and O'Faelan prince of the Decies, were taken prisoners and locked up in an old Danish castle, then and still called Reginald's Tower; but as they were about to be executed Dermot interposed and saved them. After the fight, and while the streets still ran red with the blood of the citizens, Strongbow and Eva were married in fulfilment of Dermot's promise.

Reginald's Tower.

Scarcely had the ceremony ended when news came that Hasculf of Dublin had revolted; whereupon Strongbow and Dermot set out for Dublin with an army of 5,000 men; and instead of going round by the level country where they might be intercepted, these men of iron frames marched straight over the Wicklow Mountains, by Glendalough, making their way through difficult passes, bogs, and forests; and the first intelligence the people of Dublin had of their movement was to see the army defiling down the hill slopes towards the city. Terrified beyond measure, the citizens sent their saintly and illustrious archbishop Laurence O'Toole, with conditions of surrender. But even while the conference was going on, and after the conclusion of a truce, Raymond le Gros and Miles de Cogan, with a band of followers, forced their way into the city, and falling on the unresisting citizens, massacred them without mercy. Hasculf escaped, and Dermot and Strongbow remained in possession of the city. Of the arch traitor Dermot Mac Murrogh we shall hear no more in this History: for he died in the following year (1171) at Ferns in the sixty-first year of his age.

Figure in the illuminated MS. copy of Giraldus Cambrensis, showing costume and sparth *or battle-axe of the period (A.D. 1200). Olive-green mantle; light-brown trousers; hair and beard long; head bare. From Wilde's Catalogue.*

The fame of the great conquests made by Strongbow got noised abroad, so that it came to the ears of King Henry. Fearing that Strongbow might make himself king, he issued an edict forbidding further intercourse with Ireland: and at the same time he began to prepare for his own expedition. This reduced Strongbow and his army to great distress in Dublin: for they were unable to procure either men or provisions, as all supplies from over sea were stopped. And a worse danger now threatened them. The patriotic archbishop Laurence O'Toole went through the country and persuaded the kings and chiefs to unite in an attempt to crush the invaders; and a great army was soon encamped in separate detachments round about the city, under King Roderick's command After two months' siege, the garrison, with hunger staring them in the face and no hope of relief, came to the resolution to attempt to cut their way in a body through the enemy, and so escape. About 3 o'clock in the afternoon, the desperate little band, 600 Anglo-Normans with some Irish under Donall Kavanagh, suddenly sallied out and took the Irish completely by surprise; and the king himself, who happened to be in his bath at the time, escaped with much difficulty half naked from the field. The panic spread rapidly, so that the various scattered contingents broke up and fled. And the garrison returned triumphant to the city, laden with booty, and with provisions enough for a whole year.

Meantime King Henry had been busily preparing; and on the 18th October, he landed at Crook a little below Waterford, with many of his nobles, and an army of 4,400 knights and men at arms. Counting common soldiers and attendants, he probably had 10,000 fighting men. To resist such a force was out of the question: and most of the Irish princes and chiefs made their submission to him. He now rewarded his followers by grants of large tracts of country, giving away the lands belonging to the natives without the least scruple. Leinster was granted to Strongbow, with the exception of Dublin and some other maritime towns; the province of Meath to Hugh de Lacy; and Ulster to John de Courcy. In all the chief towns he left governors. He granted Dublin to a colony of Bristol people, with De Lacy as governor, who is generally regarded as the first viceroy of Ireland.[1] Having completed these arrangements, the king embarked at Wexford in April and returned to England. From the moment of his departure his arrangements were all disregarded; and his followers did just as they pleased, plundering and harassing the unfortunate natives without mercy and without restraint. But the natives were now beginning to profit by the skill of their adversaries, and often successfully defended themselves. On one occasion Strongbow, returning from a plundering raid through Offaly, was intercepted by its chief, O'Dempsey, and defeated, a great number of his men, with his son-in-law De Quenci, being slain. As the disturbances continued, the king appointed Strongbow viceroy in the following year—1173—hoping that by increasing his authority he might be able to reduce the country to quietness.

Chapter XIX
The Anglo-Irish Lords
A.D. 1173–1176.—Henry II

OST of the adventurers who settled in Ireland in the time of Henry II belonged to good families of ancient and honourable descent. But nearly all of them were men who had run through their estates by extravagance; and being brave and daring as well as poor, they were ready to engage in any enterprise, however dangerous, that

---

[1]The governors of Ireland at that time, and for centuries after, were designated by various titles, such as viceroy, lieutenant, lord lieutenant, lord justice or justiciary, governor, etc. A person appointed to govern temporarily in place of an absent lord lieutenant or viceroy was designated deputy or lord deputy. The governor, by whatever name he was called, had a number of persons, called a Council, to assist him by their advice: a practice which has continued to the present day.

held out a hope of retrieving their fortunes. After they had settled down in Ireland in the districts granted them by the king, they became great and powerful, and from them the chief Anglo-Irish families were derived. Among these the most distinguished were the Geraldines (Fitzgeralds, Barrys, Cogans, Graces, and others); the Butlers; and the De Burgos (Burkes, Mac Williams, Mac Davids, &c.). Maurice Fitzgerald was the chief founder of the family of the Geraldines, of whom there were two main branches: one in Leinster, whose chiefs became, first, barons of Offaly, then earls of Kildare, and finally dukes of Leinster: the other in Munster, whose heads were earls of Desmond. The Butlers settled in Leinster, and their chiefs became earls, and finally dukes, of Ormond. The family of De Burgo was founded by William de Burgo: they settled chiefly in Connaught, and were of two main branches.

It was related at the end of the last chapter how Strongbow had been appointed viceroy in 1173 by King Henry. No sooner had he entered on his new duties than troubles began to thicken round him. He found most of the Irish princes in revolt, notwithstanding their forced submission to the king; and the money he had brought was soon spent, so that he had no pay for his soldiers. This naturally made the men discontented; and another circumstance that greatly increased their ill humour was that a general whom they hated—Hervey Mountmaurice, Strongbow's uncle—had been placed over them, instead of their favourite leader Raymond le Gros. Raymond was their idol; for he was a brave and dashing officer, and in all his expeditions, had given them full license to plunder. Having now neither pay nor booty, nor any prospect of either, they presented themselves in a body before the viceroy, and threatened to return to England or join the Irish, unless Raymond was placed at their head. Strongbow was not pleased at this; but he had no choice, for the men seemed determined: so he appointed Raymond to the chief command: on which the new general led the men south on a freebooting excursion, and ravaged Offaly and the country round Lismore. Loading a number of boats he had found near the mouth of the Blackwater, with part of the spoils, he sent them on towards Waterford, while he and his army set out in the same direction and marched along near the coast, driving before them 4,000 cows, the property of the poor country people. The boats were attacked by a small fleet from Cork—half Irish, half Danish—and the land army was intercepted by Dermot Mac Carthy prince of Desmond; but both attacks were repulsed; and Raymond and his companions got clear off and made their way with all the plunder to Waterford.

Soon after this, during Raymond's temporary absence in Wales, Strongbow led his army towards Limerick against Donall O'Brien, king of Thomond, one of those who had submitted to the king, but who had lately revolted. But O'Brien and King Roderick intercepted him at Thurles, defeated him, and killed 1,700 of his men—the best part of his army. Strongbow fled to Waterford, and full of grief and rage, shut himself

up there, but was besieged and in great danger, till Raymond returned and rescued him; on which he gave his sister Basilea in marriage to his rescuer, and made him constable or military commander of Leinster. Raymond next made preparation to avenge on Donall O'Brien the defeat of Thurles. He led his troops to Limerick; and in the face of enormous difficulties he forded the deep and rapid river that flowed between him and the stronghold on the island, stormed the city, and gave it up to slaughter and plunder. Then leaving a sufficient garrison under the command of Miles de Cogan he returned to Dublin.

But now Raymond was exposed to a great danger; for his rival Mountmaurice secretly whispered to the king that he aimed at making himself king of Ireland; whereupon Henry ordered that he should be sent to England. But even while Raymond was preparing to obey the command, news came that Donall O'Brien had

Monument (lying flat) of Strongbow and his wife Eva in Christchurch Cathedral, Dublin. From Mrs. Hall's Ireland.

laid siege to Limerick; and when Strongbow ordered out the army for its relief, the men refused point blank to march under Mountmaurice. So Raymond had to be replaced in command, and marching southwards he defeated O'Brien and relieved the city.

One day while he was in the south, a courier arrived posthaste from Dublin with an odd message from his wife Basilea:—"Be it known to you that the great jaw-tooth which used to trouble me so much has fallen out. Wherefore return with all speed." She took this enigmatical way of telling him that her brother the earl was dead; for, knowing well the precarious position of the colony in Dublin, and fearing the Irish might rise if they knew of his death, she determined to keep the matter secret till Raymond should be present. Raymond understood the meaning and returned; and the earl was interred with great pomp in Christchurch Cathedral, archbishop Laurence O'Toole conducting the ceremonies.

As soon as the king heard of Strongbow's death, being still jealous of the brilliant soldier Raymond, he appointed William de Burgo viceroy in this same year, with John de Courcy, Robert Fitzstephen, and Miles de Cogan to assist him. Raymond met them near Wexford, and having given them a most respectful reception, he delivered up all his authority to the new viceroy without a murmur. After this we hear little more of Raymond le Gros in public life. He retired to his estates in Wexford where he resided quietly till his death, which took place in 1182.

Chapter XX
John De Courcy
Henry II (to 1189).
A.D. 1176–1204. Richard I (1189–1199).
John (1199).

E Burgo, the new governor, was from the first disliked by the colonists: for he wished for peace and discouraged outrage on the natives; whereas war was what the colonists most desired, as it brought them plunder and sure increase of territory. Among all his officers not was so discontented as Sir John de Courcy. He was a man of gigantic size and strength, brave and daring; and he now resolved to attempt the conquest of Ulster, which the king had granted to him five years before. So gathering round him a small band of 320 knights and archers, who with their attendants made an army of about 1,000 men, he set out from Dublin for Ulster. Passing northwards with all speed, he arrived on the morning of the fourth day—the 2nd of February—at Downpatrick, then the capital of Ulidia or Eastern Ulster. As there were no walls, the townspeople knew nothing of the expedition till they were startled at dawn by the martial sound of bugles and the clattering of cavalry in the streets. The adventurers were half starved as they entered the town; and they fell upon everything they could lay hands on: they ate and drank, plundered, killed, and destroyed, till half the town was in ruins.

At the end of a week Mac Dunlevy prince of Ulidia came with a large undisciplined army to attack him. De Courcy, nothing daunted, went out to meet them, and chose a favourable position to withstand the assault. The Irish rushed on with tumultuous bravery, but they were not able to break the disciplined ranks of the enemy; and after a furious fight they were repulsed with great loss.

Dundrum Castle, near Newcastle, Co. Down. Built by John de Courcy. From Kilkenny Archaeological Journal, *1833–4, p. 158.*

Still the Ulstermen continued to offer the most determined resistance. The valiant De Courcy battled bravely through all his difficulties, and three several times in the same year, 1177, he defeated in battle the people of the surrounding districts. But as time went on he met with many reverses, and he had quite enough to do to hold his ground. In the following year he was defeated near Newry with a loss of 450 men; and again he was intercepted in one of his terrible raids, and routed by the Dalaradian chief Cumee O'Flynn. He escaped from this battlefield with only eleven companions; and having lost their horses, they fled on foot for two days and two nights closely pursued, without food or sleep, till they reached a place of safety. But in several other battles he was victorious. Other adventurers arrived to join him from time to time; and, as opportunities offered, he built many castles in vantage points all over the province; so that as years went by he strengthened his position in Ulster.

While these events were taking place in the northern province, the country in and around the English settlement in Leinster still continued to be very much disturbed; and the king determined to send over his son prince John, hoping that his presence would restore tranquillity. The prince, then nineteen years of age, landed at Waterford with a splendid retinue and a large body of cavalry. He had the title of Lord of Ireland; and his secretary and tutor was a Welsh priest named Gerald Barry, now better known as Giraldus Cambrensis, or Gerald of Wales, who afterwards wrote in Latin a description of Ireland and a history of the Anglo-Norman invasion. But Prince John soon raised the whole country in revolt by his foolish and vicious conduct; and he even turned the old colonists against him by contemptuous treatment. The Irish chiefs crowded to him in Waterford, both to pay him respect and to acknowledge him as their lord; but his insolent young associates—close-shaven dandies—ridiculed their dress and manners, and insulted them by plucking their beards, which they wore long according to the custom of the country.

Incensed by this treatment the proud Irish nobles withdrew to their homes, brooding mischief. The settlements were attacked at all points; and the most active of the assailants was the valiant Donall O'Brien of Thomond. A great number of the new strongholds were taken, and many of the bravest of the Anglo-Norman chiefs were slain. The colonists were driven to take refuge in the towns; and almost the whole of prince John's army perished in the numerous conflicts.

When the country had been for some time in this state of turmoil, King Henry came to hear how matters stood, and at once recalled the prince, after a stay of about eight months, appointing De Courcy viceroy. The prince, both before and after his return, threw the whole blame of the disturbance on Hugh de Lacy. This De Lacy, though not the greatest warrior, was the wisest and best governor of all the barons who served King Henry in Ireland; he built strong castles all over Meath, and greatly increased his power and influence with the Irish by marrying a daughter of the old king Roderick O'Conor; so that he was accused by the prince of conspiring to make himself king of Ireland. But he never lived to clear himself. One day while with a few attendants he was inspecting his new castle at Durrow, a young Irishman suddenly drew forth a battle-axe from under his cloak, and with one blow struck off the great baron's head: after which he made his escape. This was done to avenge De Lacy's seizure of lands, and his desecration of St. Columbkille's venerated monastery of Durrow, which he had pulled down to get materials for his castle.

But to return to De Courcy. During his vice-royalty he invaded Connaught, plundering, burning, and slaying, after his usual fashion, much like the Danes of old: but before he had advanced far into the province, he was confronted by the two kings of Connaught and Thomond—Conor

Mainmoy and Donall O'Brien—with their united armies. Not venturing to give battle to this formidable force, he retreated northwards, his only anxiety now being to save himself and his army from destruction. But when he had arrived at Ballysadare, on the coast of Sligo, the prince of Tirconnell came marching down on him in front, while his pursuers were pressing on close behind. Setting fire to Ballysadare, he fled south-east; but as he was crossing the Curlieu Rills he was overtaken by Conor Mainmoy and O'Brien, who fell upon him and killed a great number of his men; and it was with much difficulty he escaped with the remnant of his army into Leinster.

Trim Castle, originally built by De Lacy; but afterwards rebuilt.

Two years later he was tempted to try his fortune a second time in Connaught, during a contest for the throne among the O'Conor princes; but with no better result than before. He and Hugh de Lacy the younger (son of the great de Lacy) were both induced by one of the claimants to come to his assistance in the struggle for the throne of Connaught. But the rival O'Conor king caught the allies in an ambuscade in a wood, and inflicted on them a crushing defeat, slaying more than half of the English army. De Courcy had a narrow escape here, being felled from his horse by a stone. Recovering, however, he fled from the battlefield northwards till he reached Rindown Castle on the western shore of Lough Ree, where he proceeded to convey his army in boats across the lake. He had been a week engaged at this, when, on the very last day, the victorious O'Conor pounced down on those that still remained at Rindown and killed and drowned great numbers of them; while De Courcy and the rest, being safe at the far side, made good their escape.

The career of this extraordinary man ended in ruin and disgrace. Hugh de Lacy took every means to poison King John's mind against him. He was proclaimed a rebel and a traitor; and De Lacy, now lord justice, was commissioned to arrest him. After several unsuccessful attempts, De Courcy was at length betrayed by some of his own servants, who led De Lacy's men to his retreat at Downpatrick, where he was taken. Some records relate that his enemies came down on him on Good Friday, when he was barefooted and unarmed, doing penance in the cathedral of Downpatrick, and that he snatched up the nearest weapon—a great wooden cross standing on a grave—with which he dashed out the brains of thirteen of his assailants before he was overpowered. After his arrest history loses sight of him; and we know nothing certain of his subsequent fortunes or how he ended his life. Some Anglo-Irish historians indeed tell several very interesting stories about him, but they are all fabulous.

CHAPTER XXI
TURMOIL
John (to 1216).
A.D. 1204–1307. Henry III (1216–1272).
Edward I (1272–1307).

Y whatever title the governor of Ireland was known, he was supposed to stand in place of the king, and he usually resided in Dublin: but he seldom or never had an army large enough to enable him to enforce his authority. The kings of England took good care not to allow their governors a sufficient army, fearing that some one of them might become strong enough to make himself an independent king of Ireland. This absence of a strong central government, owing to the jealousy of the kings, was the root of most of the evils that afflicted Ireland now and for ages afterwards. The great barons, who were settled all over the country, were well aware of their governor's weakness, and cared very little for his authority; and they generally cared just as little for the authority of the king, who was at too great a distance to reach them, or even to obtain much information of their proceedings. They ruled like independent princes, taxed their people, made war or peace, and raised armies and fought, just as they pleased. Bad as was the state of things before the Invasion, it was much worse now, for there were more people to quarrel, with less means of checking them. The native chiefs continued to wrangle and fight among themselves, the same as before; the barons fought with each other even still more bitterly; and all this time the English were everywhere making inroads on the Irish to win new lands, while the Irish defended their homes as best they could. The king of England came over of an odd time, always with an army; and while he remained in the country, there was quietness; but the moment he re-embarked, or ceased to keep a direct watch on the barons, all was again turmoil and bloodshed. What is related in this chapter will give the reader a good idea of the hard ordeal of suffering the unhappy country had to pass through during this thirteenth and many subsequent centuries.

In the first years of the reign of King John the country was all in confusion, of which he was kept well informed by his agents. Seeing no prospect of improvement so long as things were permitted to go on in their usual course, he came to the resolution to visit Ireland and reduce the turbulent barons and chiefs to submission. He landed at Crook, near Waterford, with a formidable army; and from the very day of his arrival the fighting ceased, the most troublesome of the barons fled, and the country became tranquil. As he had no fighting to do, he employed himself more usefully in making arrangements for the better government of the country. Those parts of Ireland which were under English jurisdiction, he parcelled out into twelve counties or shires, and this was the beginning of the subdivision into counties, such as we now have them.[1] He directed

---

[1]The division of Ireland into shires or counties is of Anglo-Norman and English origin. The counties generally represent the older native territories and sub-kingdoms. The twelve formed by King John are Dublin, Kildare, Meath, Uriel (or Louth), Carlow, Kilkenny, Wexford, Waterford, Cork, Kerry, Limerick, and Tipperary. Queen's County and King's County were formed in the time of Queen Mary, and were so called in honour of the Queen and her husband Philip—after whom also were named the two capitals of the counties—Maryborough and Philipstown. Sir Henry Sydney, about 1565, formed the county Longford from the ancient district of Annaly. He also divided Connaught into six counties:—Galway, Sligo, Mayo, Roscommon, Leitrim, and Clare (but Clare was subsequently annexed to Munster, to which it had in earlier times belonged). Sir John Perrott, about 1584, formed the following seven counties of Ulster:—Armagh, Monaghan, Tyrone, Coleraine (now the county Derry), Donegal, Fermanagh, and Cavan: the

that in these twelve counties English law should be administered, and for this purpose he had courts of justice erected, and appointed magistrates and other officers to hold sessions and decide cases. But it must be borne in mind that all this was for the settlers only, not for the natives, who were then and for long afterwards outside the pale of the law. So far as they went, King John's arrangements were sensible and useful. He returned to England in August, after a stay of about two months; and during the remainder of his reign, Ireland was moderately quiet.

The century that elapsed from the death of John and the accession of Henry III (A.D. 1216) to the invasion of Edward Bruce was a period of strife and bloodshed, a period of woe and misery for the common people: it seemed as if the whole island was abandoned to anarchy. What is sometimes called the "War of Meath," for it was in fact a civil war on a small scale—a destructive feud between William Marshal, the owner of vast estates in Leinster, and Hugh de Lacy the younger—began in 1224, and continued unchecked till the whole of Meath was wasted. Scarcely was this strife ended when another—the "War of Kildare"—broke out in the following manner. After William Marshal's death, his brother Richard, a handsome, valiant, noble-minded knight, inherited his titles and estates. He was in England at the time of his brother's death; and having incurred the anger of King Henry III, fled to Ireland. But Geoffrey Marisco, Maurice Fitzgerald, and Hugh de Lacy conspired to destroy him, hoping to share his vast estates. Marisco pretended friendship, and arranged a meeting on the Curragh of Kildare (in 1234) to discuss certain matters in dispute. Here young Marshal was treacherously attacked by de Lacy and the others, and being betrayed and abandoned by Marisco, he was, though a renowned swordsman, at length wounded, overpowered, and taken prisoner. He soon after died of his wounds; but his assassins gained nothing by their villainy. Marisco was banished by the indignant king, to whom the whole base plot was soon afterwards revealed; and his son, who had espoused his cause, having been captured, was executed.

In these Leinster counties there was at this time a mixed population of English settlers and native Irish, most of them quiet people, who wished for nothing more than to be permitted to till their farms, herd their cattle, and live with their families in peace. But these everlasting feuds of the barons stopped all industry, and brought death and desolation everywhere.

---

other two Ulster counties, Antrim and Down, had been constituted some time before. This makes thirty, so far. In the time of Henry VIII Meath was divided into two: Meath proper, and Westmeath. At first the county Dublin included Wicklow; but in 1605, under Sir Arthur Chichester, Wicklow was formed into a separate county. This makes the present number thirty-two.

While this warfare was going on in Leinster, Connaught was in a state of strife which lasted for many years; and the struggles among the several claimants of the O'Conor family for the throne of Connaught went on unceasingly: battles, skirmishes, and raids without number. The English, under William Marshal, De Burgo, or others, were mixed up in most of these contests, now siding with one of the parties, now with another; but always keeping an eye to their own interests. And thus the havoc and ruin went on unchecked. The Irish annalists who have recorded the history of those evil times, mention one pathetic incident which will give some idea of the miseries suffered by the people—who were here, it should be observed, all Irish. During one terrible raid by Marshal and one of the O'Conors, a frightened crowd of peasants—men, women, and children—fleeing from the pursuing army, perished by scores on the way. In their headlong flight they attempted to cross a wide and deep river, midway between Ballina and Foxford, in Mayo, where great numbers were drowned; and next day the baskets set at the weirs to catch fish were found full of the bodies of little children that had been swept down by the stream. This state of horror lasted in Connaught for many years. Meantime the wretched hunted people were unable to attend to their tillage: famine and pestilence followed; and the inhabitants of whole towns and districts were swept away.

At length one of the O'Conors—Felim, nephew of the old Ard-ri Roderick—established himself in 1249, by sheer force of energy and bravery, on the throne of Connaught, in spite of all enemies, both English and Irish, and reigned without interruption till his death in 1265.

The condition of Leinster and Connaught has been sketched: the state of things in Ulster and Munster was almost as bad.

Maurice Fitzgerald, who had been twice lord justice—he who had conspired with the others against Richard Marshal—marched with his army northwards through Connaught, resolved to bring Ulster completely under English rule. But he was intercepted by Godfrey O'Donnell, chief of Tirconnell, at Credran, beside Rosses, near Sligo, where a furious battle was fought. The two leaders, Fitzgerald and O'Donnell, met in single combat and wounded each other severely; the English were routed; and Fitzgerald retired to the Franciscan monastery of Youghal, in which he died the same year, probably of his wounds.

As for O'Donnell, he had himself conveyed to an island in Lough Beagh in Donegal, where he lay in bed for a whole year sinking daily under his wounds; and all this time the Tirconnellians had no chief to lead them. There had been, for some time before, much dissension between this O'Donnell and Brian O'Neill, prince of Tyrone; and now O'Neill, taking advantage of his rival's misfortune, invaded Tirconnell. O'Donnell, still lying ill, ordered a muster of his army, and as he was quite helpless

Tomb of Felim O'Conor, King of Connaught, in Roscommon Abbey.
From Kilkenny Archaeological Journal.
A full page engraving of the whole tomb, with the eight galloglasses full length
(the rubbish having recently been cleared away), may be seen in The O'Conors
of Connaught, *by the Right Hon.* The O'Conor Don. *Two of these fine figures are*
given at the end of this chapter.

and unable to lead them, expecting death daily, he had himself borne on
a bier at their head to meet the enemy. And while the bier was held aloft
in full view of the Kinel Connell, the armies attacked each other near the
river Swilly, and the Tyrone men were routed. Immediately afterwards the
heroic chief died: and the same bier from which he had witnessed his last
victory, was made use of to bear him to his grave.

Some of the Irish chiefs now attempted to unite against the common
enemy, choosing Brien O'Neill for leader (A.D. 1260): but they were
defeated by the English in a bloody battle at Downpatrick; and O'Neill
and a large number of chiefs were slain.

In the south, the Mac Carthys of Desmond, seeing their ancient
principality continually encroached upon by the Geraldines, became
exasperated, and attacked and defeated them in 1261 at Callan, near
Kenmare; after which they demolished numbers of the English castles.
But they soon quarrelled among themselves, and the Geraldines gradually
recovered all they had lost.

While this universal strife was raging in Ireland, Henry III died, and
was succeeded by Edward I in 1272. During Edward's reign, as will be
related further on, the Irish chiefs petitioned to be placed under English
law; but though this great king was himself willing to grant the petition,
the Anglo-Irish lords persuaded him to reject it.

Two of the eight Galloglasses on King Felim O'Conor's Tomb in Roscommon Abbey. From *Kilkenny Archaeological Journal,* 1870–1, p. 252.

Chapter XXII
Edward Bruce
A.D. 1315–1318.—Edward II

ATTERS were, as we have seen, in a very disturbed state during the preceding century; but we might almost say that it was peace itself compared with the three and a half years of Bruce's expedition to Ireland.

The Irish people, especially those of the north, viewed with great interest and sympathy the struggles of their kindred in Scotland for independence; and Robert Bruce's glorious victory over Edward II at Bannockburn (in 1314) filled them with joy and hope. Soon after the battle the native chiefs of Ulster, headed by Donall O'Neill, prince of Tyrone, with the Anglo-Irish De Lacys and Bissetts, who then owned Glenarm and Rathlin, despatched messengers praying Bruce to send his brother Edward to be king over them.

He eagerly accepted the proposal; and on the 25th of May, Edward Bruce, accompanied by many of the Scottish nobles, landed at Larne with an army of 6,000 of the best soldiers of Scotland. He was immediately joined by Donall O'Neill, and by numbers of the northern Irish; and the combined forces overran a great part of Ulster, destroying everything belonging to the English that came in their way, and defeating their armies in several battles. Moving southwards, they stormed and burned Dundalk and Ardee; and at this latter place they set fire to the church of the Carmelite friary, in which a number of people had taken refuge, and burned them all to death. From first to last the campaign was carried on with great cruelty, and with reckless waste of life and property. All food except what was needed for the use of the army was destroyed, though there was a famine, and the people were starving all over the country.

The two leading Anglo-Irish noblemen at this time were Richard De Burgo the Red Earl of Ulster, and Sir Edmund Butler the lord justice. The Red Earl, who was lord of the greatest part of the two provinces of Ulster and Connaught, and was by far the most powerful nobleman in Ireland— much more high and mighty than even the lord justice—raised a large army, chiefly in Connaught, and set out in quest of the invaders. His march north through the Irish districts was perhaps more savagely destructive than that of Bruce, if indeed that were possible; and his reason for thus destroying the property of the Irish people as he marched along, was that he believed they were all in favour of Bruce, which was not the case.

Felim O'Conor the young king of Connaught had joined De Burgo and accompanied the English army. But he was recalled to Connaught to suppress a rebellion of some of his subjects. This weakened De Burgo, who was now attacked by Bruce at Connor near Ballymena and wholly defeated; and he fled back to Connaught crestfallen, with the broken remnants of his forces. A body of the defeated English fled eastwards to Carrickfergus and took possession of the castle, which they gallantly defended for months against the Scots. Soon after the battle at Connor, Bruce had himself proclaimed king of Ireland and formally crowned. Marching next into Meath—still in 1315—he routed an army of 15,000 men under Roger Mortimer at Kells; and at the opening of the new year (1316) he defeated the lord justice, Sir Edmund Butler, at Ardscull near Athy.

The preceding harvest had been a bad one, and scarcity and want prevailed all over the country. Nevertheless the Scottish army, wherever they went, continued to ravage and destroy all they could not consume or bring away, multiplying tenfold the miseries of the people, both English and Irish.

Carrickfergus Castle.

Felim O'Conor, having crushed in blood the revolt in Connaught, now changed sides and declared for Bruce. Intending to expel all the English from the province, he marched to Athenry with a large army; but was there defeated and slain, in 1316, in a great battle by William De Burgo and Richard Bermingham. This was by far the most decisive and fatal defeat ever inflicted on the Irish since the invaders first set foot on Irish soil. Eleven thousand of O'Conor's army fell, and among them nearly all the native nobility of Connaught; so that of all the O'Conor family there survived only one chief, Felim's brother, able to bear arms.

The band of English who had taken possession of Carrickfergus castle held out most heroically, and now Bruce himself came to conduct the siege in person. Reduced to starvation, the brave garrison at last surrendered on condition that their lives should be spared.

King Robert had come over to aid his brother; and early in the spring of 1317 they both set out for Dublin with an army of 20,000, destroying everything in their march. They encamped at Castleknock; but the citizens of Dublin took most determined measures for defence, burning all outside the walls, both houses and churches, to deprive the Scots of shelter; so that the Bruces did not think it prudent to enter on a siege; and they resumed their destructive march till they reached Limerick. But as they found this city also well prepared for defence, and as there was still great scarcity of provisions, they returned northwards after a short stay. They had to traverse the very districts they had wasted a short time before; and in this most miserable march, vast numbers of them perished of cold, hunger, and disease—scourged by the famine they had themselves created.

After this, King Robert, believing it hopeless to attempt the complete conquest of the country, returned to Scotland; but Edward remained, determined to fight it out to the end. The two armies rested inactive, and there was a lull for a time, probably on account of the terrible dearth of food. But now came an abundant harvest, and both sides prepared for action. Bruce turned south for another conquering progress, but was met at Faughart two miles north of Dundalk by an army much more numerous than his own, under Sir John Bermingham. He was strongly advised not to fight till more men, who were on their way from Scotland, should arrive; but he was rash and headstrong, and despised his opponents, declaring he would fight if they were four times more numerous. The battle fought here on the 14th October terminated the war. The issue was decided chiefly by Sir John Maupas, an Anglo-Irish knight, who made a dash at Bruce and slew him in the midst of the Scots. Maupas was instantly cut down; and after the battle his body was found pierced all over, lying on that of Bruce. The invading army was defeated with great slaughter; and the main body of the survivors, including the De Lacys, escaped to Scotland. Bermingham had the body of Bruce cut in pieces to be hung up in the chief towns in the colony, and brought the head salted in a box to king Edward II, who immediately created him earl of Louth and gave him the manor of Ardee.

And so ended the celebrated expedition of Edward Bruce. Though it was a failure, it shook the Anglo-Irish government to its foundation and weakened it for centuries. Ulster was almost cleared of colonists; the native chiefs and clans resumed possession; and there were similar movements in other parts of Ireland, though not to the same extent. There had been such general, needless, and almost insane destruction of property, that vast numbers of the people of all classes, settlers and natives, chiefs and peasants, lost everything and sank into hopeless poverty. The whole country was thrown into a state of utter disorder from which it did not recover till many generations had passed away. And to add to the misery, there were visitations of famine and pestilence—plagues of various strange kinds—which continued at intervals during the whole of this century. The native Irish historians of the time regarded the expedition of Bruce with great disfavour; for they looked upon it as answerable for a large part of the evils and miseries that afflicted their unfortunate country.

Sculpture on a Capital: Priest's House, Glendalough: Beranger, 1779. From Petrie's *Round Towers.*

CHAPTER XXIII

THE STATUTE OF KILKENNY
A.D. 1318–1377. Edward II (to 1327).
Edward III (1327).

T the end of the last chapter it was stated that the Anglo-Irish government was greatly shaken by the Bruce invasion: it now grew weaker year by year; and the English, far from invading new territories, had more than they could do to defend those they had already acquired. For the Irish, taking advantage of their dissensions and helplessness, attacked them everywhere and recovered a great part of their lands.

Moreover, about this time, the English all over the country were fast becoming absorbed into the native population. The Irish, like the Celtic tribes everywhere, have always had a sort of fascinating power over people of other races settling among them, a power to make them in all respects like themselves: and in fact all the settlers before the Ulster Plantation, and most of those after it, have fallen under this spell. But about the time we are now dealing with, there were two powerful artificial influences to help this natural process. First: the colonists, seeing the Irish prevailing everywhere, joined them for mere protection, intermarrying with them and adopting their language, dress, and customs. Second: the government had all along made a most mischievous distinction between New English and Old English—English by birth and English by blood. They favoured Englishmen who came over to better their fortunes—men who never did anything for Ireland—and gave them most of the situations of trust, putting them over the heads of the Old English, those who had borne the brunt of the struggle. This so incensed the old colonists that a large proportion of them—Geraldines, Butlers, De Burgos, and others—turned against the government and joined the Irish. These "degenerate English," as they were called, were regarded by the loyal English with as much aversion as the

110

Irish, and returned hate for hate quite as cordially; and later on, as we shall see, some of the most dangerous leaders of rebellion were Anglo-Irish noblemen. So completely did they become fused with the native population, that an English writer complained that they had become "more Irish than the Irish themselves."

The whole country was now feeling the consequences of the Bruce invasion; and there were murderous broils everywhere among the English themselves, with little or no check. At Bragganstown near Ardee, Sir John Bermingham, the victor of Faughart, who had brought on himself the jealousy and hate of his neighbours by that victory, was led into a trap, in 1329, and treacherously slain, together with his brothers, nephews, and retainers, to the number of 160, by the Gernons and Savages. About the same time a similar outrage was perpetrated in Munster; when Lord Philip Hodnet and 140 of the Anglo-Irish were massacred by their brethren, the Barrys, the Roches, and others. A little later on (in 1333) De Burgo the Brown Earl of Ulster, then only twenty-one years of age, was murdered on his way to Carrickfergus church on a Sunday morning, by Richard de Mandeville, his own uncle by marriage, a crime that caused great and widespread indignation. The Anglo-Irish people of the place, by whom the young lord was much liked, rose up in a passionate burst of vengeance, and seizing on all whom they suspected of having a hand in the deed, killed 300 of them.

The murder of this young earl lost a great part of Ireland to the government, and helped to hasten the incorporation of the English with the Irish. He left one child, a daughter, who according to English law was heir to her father's vast possessions in Ulster and Connaught, about one-fourth of the whole Anglo-Irish territory. The two most powerful of the Connaught De Burgos, knowing that whoever this girl might marry, when she grew up, would come over their heads, seized the estates, declared themselves independent of England, and adopted the Irish dress, language, and law. They took also Irish names, one of them calling himself Mac William Oughter (Upper) as being lord upper, or south, Connaught; who was ancestor of the earls of Clanrickard: the other, Mac William Eighter, *i.e.* of Lower or North Connaught, from whom descend the earls of Mayo. And their example was followed by many other Anglo-Irish families, especially in the west and south. Almost the only part of the settlement that remained English, and loyal to England, was the district round Dublin, which was afterwards called the Pale. The poor settlers of this district were all this time in a most miserable condition. They were scourged by the Black Death and other terrible plagues, and oppressed and robbed by their own rulers. And as the government was not able to afford them protection, they had to pay "black rents" to some of the Irish chiefs round the borders, to protect them from the fierce attacks of the natives. These black rents too were often paid by the Irish government as well as by private individuals.

The uprising of the Irish became so general and alarming that the viceroy called in the aid of the most powerful nobleman in the country, Maurice Fitzgerald, who was at the same time created first Earl of Desmond. This only made matters worse; for Fitzgerald, after some successful expeditions, quartered his army, to the number of 10,000, on the colonists, that they might pay themselves by exacting coyne and livery: the first time the English adopted this odious impost, which afterwards became so frequent among them. The unfortunate colonists, exposed to all sorts of exactions and hardships, depressed by poverty and scourged by pestilence, quitted the doomed country in crowds—everyone fled who had the means—and the settlement seemed threatened with speedy extinction. The native Irish were not less wretched than the English; for the Black Death visited them too, and the continual wars brought quite as much misery on them as on the people of the Pale.

While the Pale was daily becoming more and more enfeebled, the great barons, in their strong castles all over the country, caring nothing for the English interest, but very much for their own authority and grandeur, became more dangerously powerful year by year; so that King Edward III feared them, and came to the determination to break down their power. He made three attempts to do so, by sending over three governors, at different times from 1331 to 1344, with instructions to carry out his design; but all three failed, and in the end the nobles remained in much the same position as before, till the time of Henry VIII.

Wherever a colony of English were settled, the two people—English and Irish—after some time, when they came to know each other, generally lived on good terms and often intermarried—Englishmen generally taking Irish wives—and the English learned to speak the Irish language, instead of the Irish learning English. But there were some evil influences from the outside to prevent this kindly intercourse—tending to make the people hostile rather than friendly towards each other. One of these was the state of the law.

After the English settlement in 1172 there were two distinct codes of law in force in Ireland—the English and the Brehon. The English law was for the colonists; it did not apply to the Irish: and an Irishman that was in any way injured by an Englishman had no redress. He could not seek the protection of English law, which gave the judges and magistrates no power to try the case; and if he had recourse to the Brehon law, the Englishman need not submit to it. But on the other hand, an Irishman who injured an Englishman in any manner was at once tried by English law and punished, if the matter was proved against him. So that all those of the native race who lived among or near the colonists were in a position of great hardship, humiliation, and danger. This state of things was not indeed brought about with any intention to give the English license to injure their Irish neighbours. The colonists were simply placed under English law without any thought of the Irish one way or the other. But the fact that it was unintentional in no way lessened the danger; and many instances are on record of Englishmen inflicting great injury on Irishmen—sometimes even killing them—knowing well that there was no danger of punishment. Accordingly, about this time, the Irish several times petitioned to be placed under English law; but though both Edward I and Edward III were willing to grant this petition, the selfish Anglo-Irish barons persuaded them that it would do great injury to the country, and so prevented it; for it was their interest that the Irish should be regarded as enemies, and that the country should be in a perpetual state of disturbance.

But there were also direct attempts made to keep the English and Irish people asunder, especially by a law known as the "Statute of Kilkenny," which was brought about in this way. King Edward III, when he was made aware of the critical state of the colony, resolved to send over his third son Lionel, afterwards duke of Clarence, as lord lieutenant. This young prince had married Elizabeth, the only child of the Brown Earl of Ulster, who had been murdered, and in her right had become earl of Ulster and lord of Connaught. But he was a most unsuitable person to have the government of the country in his hands, for he had an insane hatred of the Irish, whether of native or English blood. With a force of 1,500 trained soldiers he came to Ireland in 1361, but in his expeditions against the natives he was very unsuccessful: and twice afterwards he came as lord lieutenant, in 1364 and 1367. After this experience he became convinced that it was impossible ever to subdue the Irish and bring them under English rule; and he seemed to think that all the evils of the country arose from the intercourse of the colonists with them. This state of things he attempted to remedy by an act which he caused to be passed by a parliament held in Kilkenny, and which he imagined would be the means of saving the colony from destruction.

"The Statute of Kilkenny" was intended to apply only to the English, and was framed entirely in their interests. Its chief aim was to withdraw them from all contact with the "Irish enemies," as the natives are designated all through the act; to separate the two races for evermore.

According to this law, intermarriage, fosterage, gossipred, traffic, and close relations of any kind with the Irish were forbidden as high treason:— punishment, death.

If any man took a name after the Irish fashion, used the Irish language or dress, rode a horse without a saddle, or adopted any other Irish custom, all his lands and houses were forfeited, and he himself was put into jail till he could find security that he would comply with the law. The Irish living among the English were forbidden to use the Irish language under the same penalty: that is, they were commanded to speak English, a language they did not know. To use the Brehon law—as many of the English, both high and low, were now doing—or to exact coyne and livery was treason.

No Englishman was to make war on the Irish without the special permission of the government, who would carry on all such wars, "so that," as the Act expresses it, "the Irish enemies shall not be admitted to peace until they be finally destroyed or shall make restitution fully of the costs and charges of that war."

No native Irish clergyman was to be appointed to any position in the church within the English district, and no Irishman was to be received into any English religious house in Ireland.

It was forbidden to receive or entertain Irish bards, pipers, story-tellers, or mowers, because, as the Act said, these and such like often came as spies on the English.

But this new law, designed to effect so much, was found to be impracticable, and became after a little while a dead letter. It would require a great army to enable the governor to carry it out: and he had no such army. Coyne and livery continued to be exacted from the colonists by the three great earls, Kildare, Desmond, and Ormond; and the Irish and English went on intermarrying, gossiping, fostering, dressing, speaking Irish, riding horse without saddle, and quarrelling on their own account, just the same as before.

The reign of Edward III was a glorious one for England abroad, but was disastrous to the English dominion in Ireland. Great battles were fought and won for the French possessions: while Ireland, which was more important than all the French possessions put together, was neglected. At the very time of the battle of Cressy, the Irish settlement had been almost wiped out of existence: the English power did not extend beyond the Pale, which now included only four counties round Dublin; for the three great earls of Kildare, Desmond, and Ormond acted as independent princes, and made no acknowledgment of the authority of the English king. If one-half of the care and energy expended uselessly in France had been directed to Ireland, the country could have been easily pacified and compacted into one great empire with England.

Sculpture on Window Cathedral Church, Glendalough: Beranger, 1779.
From Petrie's *Round Towers*.

CHAPTER XXIV
ART MAC MURROGH KAVANAGH
Richard II (1377 to 1399).
A.D. 1377–1417. Henry IV (1399 to 1413).
Henry V (1413).

HE man that gave most trouble to the English during the reigns of Richard II and Henry IV was Art Mac Murrogh Kavanagh, the renowned king of Leinster. He was elected king in 1375, when he was only eighteen years of age. Soon afterwards he married the daughter of Maurice Fitzgerald fourth earl of Kildare; whereupon the English authorities seized the lady's vast estates, inasmuch as she had violated the Statute of Kilkenny by marrying a mere Irishman. In addition to this, his black rent—eighty marks a year—was for some reason stopped a little time after the accession of Richard II. Exasperated by these proceedings, be devastated and burned many districts in Leinster, till the Dublin council were at last forced to pay him his black rent. This rent continued to be paid to his descendants by the Irish government till the time of Henry VIII.

Meantime Ireland had been going from bad to worse; and at last King Richard II resolved to come hither himself with an overwhelming force, hoping thereby to overawe the whole country into submission and quietness. He made great preparations for this expedition; and on the 2nd October, attended by many of the English nobles, he landed at Waterford with an army of 34,000 men, the largest force ever yet brought to the shores of Ireland.

As soon as Mac Murrogh heard of this, far from showing any signs of fear, he swept down on New Ross, then a flourishing English settlement strongly walled, burned the town, and brought away a vast quantity of booty. And when the king and his army marched north from Waterford to Dublin, he harassed them on the way after his usual skilful fashion, attacking them from the woods and bogs and cutting off great numbers.

But the Irish chiefs saw that they could not resist the king's great army; and accordingly most of them—about 75 altogether—including Mac Murrogh the most dreaded of all—came forward and made submission. They were afterwards invited to Dublin, where they were feasted in great state for several days by the king, who knighted the four provincial kings, O'Neill of Ulster, O'Conor of Connaught, Mac Murrogh of Leinster, and O'Brien of Thomond.

King Richard, though shallow and weak-minded, had sense enough to perceive the chief causes of the evils that afflicted Ireland. In a letter to the duke of York, the English regent, he describes the Irish people as of three classes:—Irish *savages* or enemies, who were outside the law; Irish rebels, *i.e.* colonists who had once obeyed the law but were now in rebellion; and English subjects: and he says the rebels were driven to revolt by injustice and ill-usage.

Richard II knighting young Henry of Lancaster. Histoire rimée de Richard II, *Jean Creton.*

But this magnificent expedition, which cost an immense sum of money, produced no useful result whatever. It did not increase the king's revenue or the number of loyal subjects; and it did not enlarge the English territory by a single acre. As for the submission and reconciliation of the Irish chiefs, it was all pure sham. They did not look upon King Richard as their lawful sovereign; and as the promises they had made had been extorted by force, they did not consider themselves bound to keep them. After a stay of nine months the king was obliged to return to England, leaving as his deputy his cousin young Roger Mortimer, earl of March, who, as Richard had no children, was heir to the throne of England. Scarcely had he left sight of land when the chiefs one and all renounced their allegiance, and the fighting went on again; till at last, in a battle fought at Kells in Kilkenny in 1397, against the Leinster clans, amongst them a large contingent of Mac Murrogh's kern, the English suffered a great overthrow, and Mortimer was slain.

Ships relieving army. Histoire rimée de Richard II, *Jean Creton.*

When news of this calamity reached the king, he was greatly enraged, and foolishly resolved on a second expedition to Ireland, in order as he said, to avenge the death of his cousin, and especially to chastise Mac Murrogh. Another army was got together quite as numerous as the former one. In the middle of May the king landed with his army at Waterford, and after a short stay there he marched to Kilkenny on his way to Dublin. But instead of continuing his march on the open level country, he turned to the

117

right towards the Wicklow highlands to attack Mac Murrogh: and here his troubles began.

Making their way slowly and toilsomely through the hills, the English at length descried the Leinster army under Mac Murrogh, about 3,000 in number, high up on a mountain side, coolly looking down on them, with impassable woods between. Having waited for some time, vainly hoping to be attacked, the king had the adjacent villages and houses burned down: and while they were blazing he knighted Henry of Lancaster, then a lad of thirteen, afterwards the great King Henry V of England. Getting together 2,500 of the inhabitants, whose houses he had destroyed, he caused them to cut a way for his army through the woods, and then pushed on, determined to overwhelm the little body of mountaineers. But he was soon beset with difficulties of all kinds, bogs, fallen trees, hidden gullies, and quagmires in which the soldiers sank up to their middle. And all this time flying parties of the Irish continually darted out from the woods on every side, flinging their lances with terrible force and precision which no armour could withstand, and cutting off foraging parties and stragglers. All this is described in verse by a French gentleman, Jean Creton, who accompanied the expedition; and he goes on to say that after each attack the Irish disappeared into the woods, "so nimble and swift of foot that like unto stags they run over mountains and valleys, whereby we received great annoyance and damage."

In this dire strait the army made their way across hill, moor, and valley, never able to overtake the main body of Mac Murrogh's mountaineers, who continually retired before them. The weather was bad: no provisions could be procured, for there was nothing but bog and moor all round; and besides those that fell by the Irish, great numbers of the men—and of the horses too—were perishing from hunger, rain, and storm. At the end of eleven days of toil and suffering, they came in sight of the sea, somewhere on the south part of the Wicklow coast. Here they found three ships which had been sent from Dublin laden with provisions, and the starving multitude rushed down to the shore and into the water, struggling and fighting for every morsel of food. The timely arrival of these ships saved the army from destruction. Next day they resumed march, moving now along the coast towards Dublin; while flying parties of the Irish hung on their rear and harassed their retreat, never giving them an hour's rest.

But now Mac Murrogh sent word that he wished to come to terms. "This news," says Creton, "brought much joy unto the English camp, every man being weary of toil and desirous of rest": and the young earl of Gloucester was despatched by the king to confer with him.

When the party of English had come to the place of conference, Mac Murrogh was seen descending a mountainside between two woods, accompanied by a multitude of followers. He rode, without saddle, a noble horse that had cost him four hundred cows, and he galloped like the wind down the face of the hill: "I never in all my life"—Creton goes on to say—"saw hare, or deer, or any other animal go with such speed as his horse." He brandished a long spear, which, when he had arrived near the meeting place, he flung from him with great dexterity. Then his followers fell back, and he met the earl alone near a small brook; and those that saw him remarked that he was tall of stature, well knit, strong, and active, with a fierce and stern countenance.

Meeting of Mac Murrogh Kavanagh and Gloucester. Histoire rimée de Richard II, *Jean Creton.*

But the parley ended in nothing, for Gloucester and Mac Murrogh could not agree to terms; at which King Richard was greatly disappointed and incensed; and he vowed he would never leave Ireland till he had taken Mac Murrogh alive or dead. Accordingly on his arrival in Dublin he made arrangements to have Mac Murrogh hunted down. But before they could be carried out he was recalled to England by alarming news; and when he arrived there he was made prisoner, and a new king, Henry IV, was placed on the throne. By these two Irish expeditions Richard II lost his crown.

After the king's departure, Mac Murrogh's raids became so intolerable that the government agreed to compensate him for his wife's lands.

There was now a short period of quietness; but he renewed the war in 1405, plundered and burned Carlow and Castledermot—two English settlements—and again overran the county Wexford. But now came a turn of ill fortune. The deputy, Sir Stephen Scroope, utterly defeated him near Callan in Kilkenny, and immediately afterwards surprised O'Carroll lord of Ely, and killed O'Carroll himself and 800 of his followers. Altogether 3,000 of the Irish fell in these two conflicts—the greatest reverse ever sustained by Mac Murrogh. This disaster kept him quiet for a time. But in 1413 he inflicted a severe defeat on the men of the English colony of Wexford. Three years afterwards these same Wexford men combined, with the determination to avenge all the injuries he had inflicted on them. But he met them on their own plains, defeated them with a loss of three or four hundred in killed and prisoners, and so thoroughly frightened them, that they were glad to escape further consequences by making peace and giving hostages for future good behaviour.

This was the old hero's last exploit. He died in New Ross a week after the Christmas of 1417, in the sixtieth year of his age, after a reign of forty-two years over Leinster. O'Doran his chief brehon, who had been spending the Christmas with him, died on the same day; and there are good grounds for suspecting that both were poisoned by a woman who had been instigated by some of Mac Murrogh Kavanagh's enemies. He was the most heroic and persevering defender of his country, from Brian Boru to Hugh O'Neill; and he maintained his independence for nearly half a century just beside the Pale, in spite of every effort to reduce him to submission.

<hr>

CHAPTER XXV
HOW IRELAND FARED DURING THE WARS OF THE ROSES
Henry V (1413 to 1422).
A.D. 1413–1485. Henry VI (1422 to 1461).
Edward IV (1461).

ITTLE or no change in Irish affairs marked the short reign of Henry V, who ascended the throne in 1413, and who was so engrossed with France that he gave hardly any attention to Ireland. There was strife everywhere, and the native chiefs continued their fierce inroads on the Pale. Matters at last looked so serious that the king sent over an able and active military man as lord lieutenant, Sir John Talbot Lord Furnival, subsequently earl of Shrewsbury, who became greatly distinguished in the French wars. He made a vigorous circuit round the Pale, and reduced O'Moore, Mac Mahon, O'Hanlon, and O'Neill. But this brought the Palesmen more evil than good; for the relief was only temporary; and when the brilliant exploit was all over, he subjected them, in violation of the Statute of Kilkenny, to coyne and livery, having no other way of paying his soldiers, exactly as the earl of Desmond had done eighty-five years before. No sooner had he left than the Irish resumed their attacks, and for years incessantly harried and worried the miserable Palesmen, except indeed when kept quiet in some small degree by the payment of black rent.

The accession of Henry VI (in A.D. 1422) made no improvement in the country, which continued to be everywhere torn by strife: and the people of the Pale fared neither better nor worse than those of the rest of the country. But what greatly added to their misfortunes at this time was a long and bitter feud between two of the leading Anglo-Irish families, the Butlers and the Talbots, which was carried on with such violence that it put a stop to almost all government business in the Pale, and brought ruin on thousands of the poor people. For more than twenty years this fierce dissension continued; while within the Pale all was confusion and corruption. The leading English officials forced shopkeepers and others to supply goods, but hardly ever paid their debts; while at the same time they robbed the king of his lawful revenues and enriched themselves. During this time the soldiers were under little or no restraint and did just as they pleased. In harvest time they were in the habit of going, *with their wives, children, servants, and friends,* sometimes to the number of a hundred, to the farmers' houses in the country round Dublin—all inhabited by the people of the English colony—eating and drinking, and paying for nothing. They robbed and sometimes killed the tenants and husbandmen; and their horses were turned out to graze in the meadows and in the ripe corn, ruining all the harvest. Some little relief came when Richard Plantagenet, duke of York, a distinguished man, a prince of the royal blood and heir to the throne of England, was appointed lord lieutenant. He won the affections of the Irish both of native and English descent, by treating them with fairness and consideration; a thing they had been little accustomed to. The native chiefs sent him, unasked, as many beeves as he needed for his great household: a record creditable to both sides, for it showed that he was a kind and just man, and that they could be grateful and generous when they were fairly treated. He was appointed for ten years; but he had not been in Ireland for more than one year when Jack Cade's rebellion broke out; on which he went to England in 1451 to look after his own interests, and during his absence Ireland was governed by deputies appointed by himself.

During this heartless and miserable tumult it is pleasant to be able to record that the native people still retained all their kindly hospitality and their ancient love of learning. This is shown by what we read of Margaret, the wife of O'Conor of Offaly, a lady celebrated for her benevolence. Twice in one year (about 1450) she invited to a great banquet the learned men of Ireland and Scotland: poets, musicians, brehons, historians, &c. The first meeting was held at Killeigh, near Tullamore, when 2,700 guests were present; and the second at Rathangan in Kildare, to which were invited all who had been absent from the first. Lady Margaret herself was present, and she sat like a queen high up in the gallery of the church in view of the assembly, clad in robes of gold, surrounded by her friends and by the clergy and brehons. All were feasted in royal style, seated according to rank: after which each learned man was presented with a valuable gift: and the names of all present were entered on a roll by Mac Egan chief brehon to the lady's husband.

"The Colledge," Youghal, as drawn by Dinely, time of Charles II. From Kilkenny Archaeological Journal, *1862–3, p. 323.*

For the past century and a half the English kings had been so taken up with wars in France, Scotland, and Wales, that they had little leisure to attend to Ireland. Accordingly we have seen the Irish encroaching, the Pale growing smaller, and the people of the settlement more oppressed and more miserable year by year. But now began in England the tremendous struggle between the houses of York and Lancaster, commonly known as the Wars of the Roses, which lasted for about thirty years, and during which the colony fared still worse. The Geraldines sided with the house of York, and the Butlers with the house of Lancaster; and they went to England, with many others of the Anglo-Irish, to take part in the battles; going and returning as occasion required, and generally leaving the settlements in Ireland almost wholly unprotected during their absence. Then the Irish rose up everywhere, overran the lands of the settlers, and took back whole districts. The Pale became smaller than ever, till it included only the county Louth and about half of Dublin, Meath, and Kildare. At one time not more than 200 men could be got together to defend it.

Carbury Castle, Co. Kildare. From a photograph.

When the Yorkists prevailed, and Edward IV was proclaimed king (1461), the Geraldines, both of Desmond and Kildare, were in high favour, while the Butlers were in disgrace. These two factions enacted a sort of miniature of the Wars of the Roses in Ireland. Among many other encounters, they fought a battle at Pilltown in Kilkenny in 1462, where the Butlers were defeated, and 400 or 500 of their men killed. As showing how completely these Anglo-Irish families had adopted the Irish language and customs, it is worthy of mention that the ransom of Mac Richard Butler, who had been taken prisoner in the battle, was two Irish manuscripts, the Psalter of Cashel and the Book of Carrick. A fragment of the Psalter of Cashel is still preserved in the Bodleian Library in Oxford, and in one of its pages is written a record of this transaction.

Thomas the eighth earl of Desmond—the Great Earl as he was called—was appointed lord deputy, in 1463, under his godson the young duke of Clarence, the king's brother, who though appointed lord lieutenant, never came to Ireland. Desmond was well received by the Irish of both races. He loved learning as well as any of the native princes, and he showed it by founding a college in Youghal, which was richly endowed by him and by the succeeding earls, and which long continued to flourish. Some of the events that took place about this period give us curious glimpses of those wild and lawless times. In 1466 Earl Desmond was defeated in open fight by his own brother-in-law, O'Conor of Offaly, who took him prisoner and confined him in Carbury Castle in Kildare. But when the people of Dublin, with whom he was a great favourite, heard of his imprisonment, a number of active young fellows banded together, and marching all the way to Carbury, about thirty miles off, they rescued the earl and brought him back in triumph to Dublin. This is a bright part of the picture; but there is a sad and dark side also, where we see how the ruin of the great earl was brought about. It seems he had imprudently let fall some words disrespectful to the queen, who, when the matter was reported to her, had John Tiptoft—"the butcher," as he was called, from his cruelty—sent to Ireland to replace him in the deputyship. Acting on the secret instructions of the queen, this new deputy caused the two earls of Kildare and Desmond to be arrested for exacting coyne and livery, and for making alliance with the Irish, contrary to the Statute of Kilkenny. Desmond was at once executed (1467), while Kildare was pardoned; and "the butcher" returned to England, where he was himself executed soon after.

To the people of the Pale, the Irish were a constant source of terror; and when they failed to crush them in open fight they sometimes attempted to do so by act of parliament. One of these acts, passed by the Irish parliament in 1465, ordained that every Irishman dwelling in the Pale was to dress and shave like the English, and to take an English surname:—from some town as Trim, Sutton, Cork; or of a colour as Black, Brown; or of some calling, as Smith, Carpenter, etc., on pain of forfeiture of his goods. Then began the custom of changing Irish surnames to English forms, which afterwards became very general. Another and more mischievous measure forbade ships from fishing in the seas of Irish countries (that is, those parts of Ireland still belonging to the native chiefs) *because the dues went to make the Irish people prosperous and strong.* But the worst enactment of all was one providing that it was lawful to decapitate thieves found robbing "or going or coming anywhere" unless they had an Englishman in their company; and whoever did so, on bringing the head to the mayor of the nearest town, was licensed to levy a good sum off the barony. This put it in the power of any evil-minded person to kill the first Irishman he met, pretending he was a thief, and to raise money on his head. The legislators indeed had no such evil intention: for the act was merely a desperate attempt to keep down marauders who swarmed at this time everywhere through the Pale: but all the same it was a very wrong and dangerous law.

CHAPTER XXVI
POYNINGS' LAW
A.D. 1485–1494.—Henry VII.

Y the accession, in 1485, of Henry VII, who belonged to the Lancastrians, that great party finally triumphed. The Tudors, of whom he was the first, were a strong-minded and astute race of sovereigns. They paid more attention to Irish affairs than their predecessors had done; and they ultimately succeeded in recovering all that had been lost by neglect and mismanagement, and in restoring the English power in Ireland. At this time all the chief state offices in Ireland were held by the Geraldines; but as the new king felt that he could not govern the country without their aid, he made no changes, though he knew well they were all devoted Yorkists. He had a very insecure hold on his own throne, and he thought that the less he disturbed matters in Ireland the better. Accordingly the great earl of Kildare, who had been lord deputy for several years, with a short break, was still kept on.

But the Irish retained their affection for the house of York; and when the young impostor Lambert Simnel came to Ireland and gave out that he was the Yorkist prince Edward earl of Warwick, he was received with open arms, not only by the deputy, but by almost all the Anglo-Irish:—nobles, clergy, and people. But the city of Waterford rejected him and remained steadfast in its loyalty; whence it got the name of *Urbs Intacta,* the "untarnished city." After a little time an army of 2,000 Germans came to Ireland to support the impostor; and in 1487 he was actually crowned as Edward VI, by the bishop of Meath, in Christchurch Cathedral, Dublin, in presence of the deputy Kildare, who was the chief instigator and manager of the whole affair, the archbishop of Dublin, and a great concourse of

Anglo-Irish nobles, ecclesiastics, and officers, all of whom renounced their allegiance to Henry VII. In order that he might be seen well by the people, he was borne through the streets on the shoulders of a gigantic Anglo-Irishman named Darcy, amidst the loud huzzas of the Dublin mob: an incident that gives us a view of the rough and ready methods of those times.

But this foolish business came to a sudden termination when Simnel was defeated and taken prisoner in England. Then Kildare and the others humbly sent to ask pardon of the king; who, dreading their power if they were driven to rebellion, took no severer steps than to send over Sir Richard Edgecomb to exact new oaths of allegiance; retaining Kildare as deputy. In the following year the king invited them to a banquet at Greenwich; and they must have felt greatly crestfallen and humiliated when they saw that one of the waiters who attended them at table was none other than their idolised prince Lambert Simnel. How heartily the king must have enjoyed it: for he loved a good joke.

A little later on, reports of new plots in Ireland reached the king's ears; whereupon in 1492 he removed Kildare from the office of deputy. These reports were not without foundation, for now a second claimant for the crown, a young Fleming named Perkin Warbeck, landed in Cork in 1492 and announced that he was Richard, duke of York, one of the two princes that had been kept in prison by Richard III. After the ridiculous termination of the Simnel imposture one would think it hard for another to gain a footing in Ireland; yet Warbeck was at once accepted by the citizens of Cork; but his career, which belongs to English rather than to Irish history, need not be followed up here. It is enough to say that after causing considerable disturbance in Ireland, he was at length taken and hanged at Tyburn, along with John Walter mayor of Cork, his chief supporter in that city. It was mainly the English colonists who were concerned in the episodes of Simnel and Warbeck; the native Irish took little or no interest in either claimant.

The Irish parliament was always under the control of a few great lords, who could have any acts they pleased passed in it, so that it gave them great power, and its laws were often hasty, harsh, and oppressive, and sometimes dangerous to the king's sovereignty. Henry knew all this; and the experience of Simnel and Warbeck taught him that his Anglo-Irish subjects might, at any favourable opportunity, again rise in rebellion for the house of York. He came to the resolution to lessen the power of the nobles by destroying the independence of their parliament; and having given Sir Edward Poynings instructions to this effect, he sent him over as deputy. Poynings' first proceeding was to lead an expedition to the north against

O'Hanlon and Magennis, who had given shelter to some of Warbeck's supporters. But he heard a rumour that the earl of Kildare was conspiring with these two chiefs to intercept and destroy himself and his army; and news came also that Kildare's brother had risen in open rebellion and had seized the castle of Carlow. On this, Poynings, patching up a peace with O'Hanlon and Magennis, returned south and recovered the castle.

Carlow Castle in 1845. From Mrs. Hall's Ireland.

In order to carry out the king's commands, he convened a parliament at Drogheda in November, the memorable parliament in which the act since known as "Poynings' Law" was passed. The following are the most important provisions of this law:

1. No parliament was in future to be held in Ireland until the heads of all the acts intended to be passed in it had been sent to the king, with a full statement of the reasons why they were required, and until these acts had been approved and permission to pass them granted by the king and privy council of England. This single provision is what is popularly known as "Poynings' Law." It was the most important of all, and was indeed the only one that turned out permanent.

2. All the laws lately made in England, affecting the public weal, should hold good in Ireland. This referred only to English laws then existing; but we must carefully bear in mind that it gave no power to the English parliament to make laws for Ireland in the future.

3. The Statute of Kilkenny, which had become quite disregarded, was revived and confirmed, except the part forbidding the use of the Irish tongue, which could not be carried out, as the language was now used everywhere, even throughout the English settlements. But this attempt at revival failed as completely as the original act: for no one minded it.

4. For the purpose of protecting the settlement, it was made felony to permit enemies or rebels to pass through the marches; and the owners of march lands were obliged to reside on them or send proper deputies, on pain of losing their estates.

5. The exaction of coyne and livery was forbidden any shape or form.

6. Many of the Anglo-Irish families had adopted the Irish war-cries: the use of these was now strictly forbidden.[1]

In this parliament the earl of Kildare was attainted for high treason, mainly on account of his supposed conspiracy with O'Hanlon to destroy the deputy; in consequence of which he was soon afterwards arrested and sent a prisoner to England. The next chapter will tell all about his subsequent career.

The general purpose of Poynings' legislation was to increase the power of the king and diminish that of the nobles, who were the chief source of danger to the crown. Up to this the Irish parliament had been independent; it was convened by the chief governor whenever and wherever he pleased; and it made its laws without any interference from the parliament of England. Now Poynings' Law took away all these great privileges; and the Irish parliament could no longer make laws of any kind whatever without the knowledge and consent of the English king and council. This indeed was of small consequence at the time; for the parliament was only for the Pale, or rather for the few lords who summoned and controlled it, and no native Irishman could sit in it. But when at a later period English law was made to extend over the whole country, and the Irish parliament made laws for all the people of Ireland, then Poynings' Law, which still remained in

---

[1]The war-cry of the O'Neills was *Lamh-derg aboo, i.e.,* the Red-hand to victory (*lamh,* pron. lauv, a hand). That of the O'Briens and Mac Carthys, *Lamh-laidir aboo,* the Strong-hand to victory (*laidir,* pron. lauder, strong). The Kildare Fitzgeralds took as their cry *Crom aboo,* from the great Geraldine castle of Crom or Croom in Limerick; the earl of Desmond, *Shanit aboo,* from the castle of Shanid in Limerick. The Butlers' cry was *Butler aboo.* Most of the other chiefs, both native and Anglo-Irish, had their several cries.

force, was felt by the people to be one of their greatest grievances. In chapter LX we shall see that the Irish parliamentary leaders succeeded after a long struggle in having it repealed.

The English rule in Ireland, which had been steadily declining since the time of John, reached its lowest ebb about the time of Poynings' Law. In obedience to one provision of this law, a double ditch or rampart was built at the time all along on the boundary of the Leinster settlement from sea to sea to keep out the Irish; of which some remains can still be traced. This little territory was called the Pale; and it remained so circumscribed for many years, but afterwards became enlarged from time to time.

Group showing arms and costumes of the period. Irish soldiers and peasants, from a drawing by Albert Durer in 1521, preserved at Vienna.

Over the two soldiers is an inscription in German: "Here go the war-men of Ireland beyond England." Over the three peasants: "Here go the poor men of Ireland beyond England." Between the two is the date A.D. 1521.

Sculpture on Chancel Arch, Monastery Church, Glendalough. From Petrie's *Round Towers,* 1845.

CHAPTER XXVII
THE GERALDINES
A.D. 1495–1534. Henry VII (to 1509).
Henry VIII (1509).

N all their branches the Geraldines had become thoroughly Irish. They spoke and wrote the Irish language in their daily life, read and loved Irish books and Irish lore of every kind, kept bards, physicians, brehons, historians, and story-tellers, as part of their household, and intermarried, fostered, and gossiped with the leading Irish families. They were nearly always at war; and although they directed their hostilities oftenest against the native chiefs, the Irish people thought no worse of them on that score, for it was only what the native chiefs themselves were continually doing. In short, they were as much attached to all the native customs as the natives themselves; and when the Reformation came, they were champions of the Catholic religion. When we add to all this, that they were known to be of an ancient and noble family, which told for much in Ireland, we have a sufficient explanation of the well-known fact, that the old Irish were rather more devoted to those Geraldines than to their own chiefs of pure Celtic blood.

The man of most consequence of the Leinster Geraldines, at the beginning of the reign of Henry VII, was Garrett or Gerald Fitzgerald, the eighth earl of Kildare—"The Great Earl"—who stood in near relations by intermarriage with the O'Neills, the Butlers, and others, and was a man of great ability, though somewhat odd and eccentric. We have seen in the last chapter how he had headed the Simnel conspiracy and was pardoned, and how he had been subsequently arrested, and sent to London on suspicion of conspiring against deputy Poynings. He was now in the Tower awaiting trial.

As Ireland had meantime become almost unmanageable, it struck King Henry VII that perhaps the best course to follow was to govern the country through him; but it was necessary that he should first answer the charges

130

brought against him by Poynings and others. He had many enemies in Ireland, of whom a great number now came forward clamouring for his condemnation. One of the worst accusations was that he had impiously burned the cathedral church of Cashel; to which he replied, with a rough sort of simplicity, that he would not have done so only he thought the archbishop was in it. The archbishop himself (David Creagh) was present listening; and this reply was so unexpectedly plain and blunt, the excuse only making the crime all the worse, that the king burst out laughing. The king advised him to have the aid of counsel, saying that he might have anyone he pleased; to which the earl answered that he would have the best counsel in England, namely, the king himself: at which his majesty laughed as heartily as before. At last when one of his accusers exclaimed with great vehemence: "All Ireland cannot rule this man!" the king ended the matter by replying: "Then if all Ireland cannot rule him, he shall rule all Ireland!" Thus the earl triumphed; and he was restored and made lord lieutenant.

The king was not mistaken in his choice: the great earl was loyal to his trust, and turned out a faithful and successful governor. The most important event he was ever engaged in was the battle of Knockdoe, which came about in this way. O'Kelly chief of Hy Many, having a quarrel with William Burke of Clanrickard, and finding himself unable to stand against him, applied for help to the earl of Kildare. The earl was only too glad to take part in the feud; for his daughter had been married to Burke, who used her so ill that she had to leave him. Kildare and O'Kelly enlisted on their side the chiefs of almost all the north of Ireland except O'Neill. On the other side Burke, knowing what was coming, collected a considerable army, being joined by many of the native chiefs of the south, among others O'Brien of Thomond, Macnamara, and O'Carroll; and he awaited the approach of his adversary on a low hill called Knockdoe—the hill of the battle-axes—about eight miles from Galway. The battle that followed was the most obstinate, bloody, and destructive fought in Ireland since the Invasion, with the single exception of the battle of Athenry. The southern men, who were far outnumbered by the earl's forces, held the field for several hours; but in the end they suffered a total overthrow, with a loss of upwards of 2,000; and the other side also suffered severely. Though the battle of Knockdoe resulted from a private quarrel, it was really a battle of Irish against Irish; one of those senseless conflicts in which they merely slaughtered each other without any counterbalancing advantage. It was considered to have done so great a service to the English cause, by weakening the Irish, that the king rewarded Kildare by making him a knight of the garter.

The great earl was retained as deputy by Henry VIII in 1509; and in the very next year he set out on an expedition, which did not end so well for him as the battle of Knockdoe. Having overrun a good part of south Munster, he invaded Thomond, but was utterly routed at the bog of Monabraher near Limerick, by O'Brien and Burke of Clanrickard, two of his old adversaries at Knockdoe, and barely saved himself and the remnant of his army by flight. In no degree checked by this defeat, the warlike earl continued his fierce raids, west, north, south, and east in succession; but in an attempt to take O'Carroll's Castle of Leap in King's County, halfway between Kinnitty and Roscrea, he received a wound of which he died in a few days.

He was succeeded as deputy, in 1513, by his son Garrett Oge Fitzgerald, the ninth earl, who was quite as fond of fighting as his father had been, and was very successful in his expeditions against the Irish chiefs. His unbroken career of victory excited the jealousy of some of the other Anglo-Irish lords, especially the Butlers, the hereditary foes of his house, who employed every means in their power to turn the king against him. But Kildare counteracted all these schemes so skilfully, that for a long time his enemies were unsuccessful; till at last Pierce Roe earl of Ormond managed to gain the ear of Cardinal Wolsey, who disliked the Geraldines. Through the cardinal's influence Kildare was now summoned to England to answer charges of enriching himself from the crown revenues and of holding traitorous correspondence with the Irish enemies. Soon afterwards King Henry VIII, at Wolsey's suggestion, sent over Thomas Howard earl of Surrey as lord lieutenant.

From the very day of Surrey's arrival he applied himself to collect evidence against the earl of Kildare; taking down reports and stories of every kind, aided all through by Pierce Roe of Ormond. But all this came to nothing; for meantime Kildare married Lady Elizabeth Grey, a near relative of the king, which stopped for the time any further proceedings against him.

Surrey at last became heartily tired of his never-ending wars with the Irish chiefs, which had no effect in quieting the country; for no sooner was one ended than another broke out. He grew sick in mind and sick in body, and besought the king for leave to retire, which was at last granted; and he returned to England in 1521, after a stay of nearly two years, appointing as lord deputy Pierce Roe, Kildare's mortal enemy. The chief use this new deputy made of his power was to do all the injury he could to Kildare, several of whose castles he took and destroyed. But while he was still lord deputy, Kildare was permitted to return to Ireland. He was enraged beyond measure on finding all the damage done in his absence; and as might have been expected, the feud now blazed up with tenfold fury; so that the king had to send over commissioners to investigate the dispute. Their decision was for Kildare, whom they appointed deputy in 1524 in place of Ormond.

But now Kildare was exposed to danger from another quarter. He was directed by the king to arrest the earl of Desmond, who had been foolishly holding correspondence with the king of France about an invasion of Ireland. He led an army southwards on this unpleasant mission; but Desmond eluded pursuit, and the deputy returned without him to Dublin. It was afterwards alleged against him that he had intentionally allowed Desmond, who was his kinsman, to escape arrest, which was probably true. Meantime his enemies, especially the two most powerful, Pierce Roe in Ireland, and Wolsey in England, kept wide awake, watching his proceedings and continually sending damaging reports about him. They succeeded at last so far as to have him again summoned to England in 1526, to answer several charges. But his great influence and good fortune again prevailed, and he was released and restored to favour. Sir William Skeffington was appointed lord deputy, and Kildare was sent with him to Ireland to advise and aid him. It was easy to foresee that this arrangement would not last long; for Kildare, earl as he was, and like a king in his own land, was too high and proud to act as a mere adviser and subordinate to any English knight. There were disagreements and bickerings and open quarrelling, till at last the earl managed his business so well with the king, that Skeffington was recalled, and he himself was appointed deputy once more.

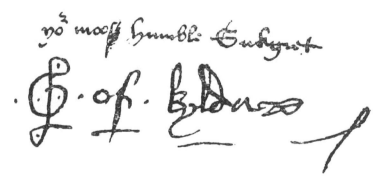

Signature of Gerald, 9th earl of Kildare. "Your moost humble subjiet, G. of Kyldare." From Gilbert's "Fac-Sim. Nat. MSS."

There was now no single enemy that he feared, and he used his great power unsparingly. He removed Archbishop Allen from the post of lord chancellor, and put George Cromer, archbishop of Armagh, in his place.

He drew around him the most powerful of the Irish chiefs, and gave one of his daughters in marriage to O'Conor of Offaly, and another to O'Carroll of Ely. He ravaged the territory of the Butlers in Kilkenny; and at his instigation his brother James Fitzgerald and his cousin Conn O'Neill entered Louth—a part of the Pale—burned the English villages, and drove away the cattle. All these proceedings were eagerly watched and reported to the king with exaggeration by Kildare's enemies; the result of which was that for the third time he was summoned to England to give an account of his government. There is some reason to suspect that he contemplated open rebellion and resistance; for now he furnished his castles with great guns, pikes, powder, etc., from the government stores in the castle of Dublin. At any rate he delayed obeying the order as long as he could. But at last there came a peremptory mandate from the king; and the earl, with a heavy heart, set about preparing for his journey: for he seems to have had some forebodings of coming evil.

CHAPTER XXVIII
THE REBELLION OF SILKEN THOMAS
A.D. 1534–1535.—Henry VIII.

ARRETT OGE FITZGERALD, the lord deputy, when setting out for England in obedience to the king's mandate, left his son, the young Lord Thomas, as deputy in his place. Before bidding the young man farewell, he spoke in this manner to him in presence of the council:—"Son Thomas, you know that my sovereign lord the king hath sent for me into England and what shall betide me God knoweth, for I know not. But however it falleth, I am now well stept in years, and so I must soon decease, because I am old. Wherefore insomuch as my winter is well nigh ended, and the spring of your age is now budding, my will is that you behave so wisely in these your green years, as that with honour you may grow to the catching of that hoary winter in which you see your father fast faring. And whereas it pleaseth the king his majesty that upon my departure here hence I should substitute in my room such a one as I could answer for: albeit I know your years are tender and your judgment not fully rectified: and therefore I might with good cause be excused from putting a naked sword in a young man's hand; yet forasmuch as I am your father I am well contented to bear that oar-stroke with you in steering your ship, because as your father I may commend you [for steering well], and correct you as my son for the wrong handling of your helm. And now I am resolved day by day to learn rather how to die in the fear of God, than to live in the pomp of the world. Wherefore my son in all your affairs be ruled by this Board, that for wisdom is able to lesson you with sound and sage advice. For albeit in authority you rule them, yet in counsel they must rule you. My son, although my fatherly affection would make my discourse longer, yet I trust your good inclination permits it to be shorter. And upon that assurance, here in the presence of this honourable assembly, I deliver you this sword of office." Thus in tears the earl spoke his last farewell; and committing his son and the members of the council to God, he set sail for England. On his arrival in London he was sent prisoner to the Tower on various charges. He might possibly have got through his present difficulties, as he had through many others, but for what befell in Ireland, which will now be related.

Lord Thomas Fitzgerald, who was afterwards known as "Silken Thomas," from the gorgeous trappings of himself and his retinue, was then in his twenty-first year, brave, open, and generous. But the earl his father could not have made a more unfortunate choice as deputy; for there were in Dublin plotting enemies who hated all his race, and they led the young man to ruin by a base trap. They spread a report that his father had been beheaded in England, and that all his relations were going to be treated in the same way. Whereupon, with his brilliant retinue of seven score horsemen, the impetuous young lord rode through the streets to St. Mary's Abbey; and entering the chamber where the council sat, he openly renounced his allegiance, and proceeded to deliver up the sword of office and the robes of state. His friend Archbishop Cromer, lord chancellor, besought him with tears in his eyes to forego his purpose; but at that moment the voice of an Irish bard was heard from among the young nobleman's followers, praising the Silken Lord, and calling on him to avenge his father's death. Casting the sword from his hand, he rushed forth with his men to enter on that wild and hopeless struggle which ended in the ruin of himself and his family. The earl, his father, on hearing of his son's rebellion, took to his bed, and being already sick of palsy, died in a few days broken-hearted. By his death, his son Lord Thomas became the tenth earl of Kildare.

Collecting a large force of the Irish septs in and around the Pale, Lord Thomas led them to Dublin, and laid siege to the castle, to which several of the leading citizens, including Archbishop Allen, had retired on the first appearance of danger. The archbishop, having good reason to dread the Geraldines, for he had always shown himself bitterly hostile to them, attempted during the siege to make his escape by night in a vessel that lay in the Liffey; but he was taken and brought before Lord Thomas at Artaine. He threw himself on his knees to beg for mercy, and the young lord, pitying him, ordered his attendants to take him away in custody and then turned aside; but they, wilfully taking a wrong meaning from his words, murdered the archbishop on the spot. This fearful crime brought a sentence of excommunication against Lord Thomas and his followers. Nevertheless the rebellion went on, and several powerful Irish chiefs joined his standard. But his men were not able to take Dublin Castle; and at last the citizens, tired of their disorderly conduct, turned on them and chased them outside the walls of the city.

Sir William Skeffington had been appointed deputy by the king to put down the rebellion: but he was ill, and could do nothing during the whole winter; so that the havoc and ruin went on unchecked. In March, 1535, he began his measures by laying siege to the castle of Maynooth, the strongest of Fitzgerald's fortresses, which was defended by 100 men. After a siege of nine days, during which the castle was battered by artillery, then for the first time used on any important occasion in Ireland, he took it by storm, except the great keep; and the garrison who defended this, now reduced to thirty-seven men, seeing the case hopeless, surrendered, doubtless expecting mercy. But they were all executed. The fall of Maynooth damped the spirits of Lord Thomas's adherents; and one of his best friends, O'Moore of Leix, was induced by the earl of Ossory, one of the Butlers, to withdraw from him.

The rebellion had already brought the English Pale to a frightful state, three-fourths of Kildare and a great part of Meath burned and depopulated; while to add to the ruin and misery of the people, the plague was raging all over the country. Lord Leonard Grey, marshal or military commander of Ireland, was at last directed to place himself at the head of the army and to take more active measures. He made short work of the rebellion. Lord Thomas's remaining allies rapidly fell off; and he and his faithful friend O'Conor sent offers of submission. O'Conor was received and pardoned; and Lord Thomas delivered himself up to Lord Grey, on condition that his life should be spared.

He was conveyed to England in 1535 and imprisoned in the Tower. Here he was left for about eighteen months, neglected and in great misery. There is extant a pitiful letter written by him while in the Tower in 1536 to an old servant in Ireland, asking that his friend O'Brien should send him £20 to buy food and clothes:—"I never had any money since I came into prison but a noble, nor I have had neither hosen, doublet, nor shoes, nor shirt but one; nor any other garment but a single frieze gown, instead of a velvet furred with lambskin [as formerly], and so I have gone shirtless and barefoot and barelegged divers times (when it hath not been very warm); and so I should have done still, but that poor prisoners, of their gentleness, hath sometimes given me old hosen and shoes and shirts."

Maynooth Castle: Photograph. From Journal of the Kildare Archaeological Society.

At the time of his arrest his five uncles were treacherously taken by Grey, who invited them to a banquet, and had them seized and manacled on their arrival. Though it was well known that three of them had openly discountenanced the rebellion, and notwithstanding the promise made by Grey to the young lord, he and his uncles were all executed at Tyburn in 1537. Thus fell, at one cruel blow, the great and illustrious house of Kildare: for though the earldom and an heir to it remained, and the lands were ultimately restored, the family never attained its former power and magnificence. During the rebellion, though it lasted little more than a year, the county Kildare was wasted and depopulated, and the whole Pale, as well as the country round it, suffered unspeakable desolation and misery. It was a reckless enterprise, for there never was the remotest chance of success: the only excuse was the extreme youth and inexperience of Lord Thomas Fitzgerald.

Notwithstanding the efforts of King Henry VIII to extirpate the house of Kildare, there remained the two sons of the ninth earl by Lady

Elizabeth Grey. Gerald (or Garrett) the elder, then about twelve years of age, was at Donore near Naas in Kildare, sick of smallpox, at the time of the apprehension of his five uncles. His faithful tutor Thomas Leverous, afterwards bishop of Kildare, fearing for his safety, wrapped him up warm in flannels, and had him secretly conveyed in a *cleeve* or basket to Thomond, where he remained under the protection of O'Brien. The other son, then an infant, was in England with his mother. It must be remembered that Leonard Grey, now lord justice, was uncle to these two children, for their mother Lady Elizabeth was his sister; but notwithstanding this he was quite earnest in his endeavours to capture the boy.

Great efforts were now made to discover the place of young Gerald's retreat; and certain death awaited him if he should be captured. But he had friends in every part of Ireland, for the Irish, both native and of English descent, had an extraordinary love for the house of Kildare. By sending him from place to place disguised, his guardians managed to baffle the spies that were everywhere on the watch for him. Sometimes the Irish chiefs that were suspected of protecting him were threatened, or their territories were wasted by his uncle the lord justice; and large bribes were offered to give him up; but all to no purpose.

Signature of Silken Thomas to letter of 1536. "By me Thomas fytz Gerald." From Gilbert's "Fac-Sim. Nat. MSS.," in which is a facsimile of the whole letter.

When Thomond became an unsafe asylum, he was sent by night to Kilbrittain in Cork, to his aunt Lady Eleanor Mac Carthy, widow of Mac Carthy Reagh and sister of the boy's father, who watched over him with unshaken fidelity. While he was under her charge, Manus O'Donnell chief of Tirconnell made her an offer of marriage, which she accepted, mainly for the sake of seeming a powerful friend for her outlawed nephew. In the middle of June, 1537, the lady travelled with young Gerald all the way from Cork to Donegal, through Thomond and Connaught, escorted and protected everywhere by the chiefs through whose territories they passed. The illustrious wayfarers must have been well known as they moved slowly along, yet none of the people attempted to betray them. The journey was performed without the least accident; and she and O'Donnell were immediately married.

The earls of Kildare were connected, either by blood or marriage, with most of the leading Irish families, both native and Anglo-Irish, who were all incensed at the execution of the six Geraldines; and the chiefs, headed by Conn O'Neill prince of Tyrone, a near cousin of the Kildare family, now (1537) formed a league—the First Geraldine League—which included the O'Donnells, the Desmonds, the O'Conors, the O'Briens, the M'Carthys, and many others, with the object of restoring the young nobleman to his rightful place, appointing a guard of twenty-four horsemen to wait on him continually. This greatly alarmed the authorities, and extraordinary efforts were made to capture him, but all in vain.

At the end of two years Lady Eleanor, having reason to believe that her husband was about to betray the boy, had him placed, disguised as a peasant, on board a vessel which conveyed him to St. Malo. On the Continent he was received with great distinction. He was however dogged everywhere by spies, greedy to earn the golden reward for his capture; but he succeeded in eluding them till. And he was pursued from kingdom to kingdom by the English ambassador, who in vain demanded from the several sovereigns that he should be given up. He found his way at last to Rome to his kinsman Cardinal Pole, who gave him safe asylum, and educated him as became a prince.

After a career full of adventure and many narrow escapes, he was reinstated in all his possessions by Edward VI in 1552; and in 1554 Queen Mary restored his title, and he succeeded as the eleventh earl of Kildare.

Chapter XXIX
Submission of the Chiefs
A.D. 1535–1541.—Henry VIII.

ATTERS had now (1535) come to such a pass in Ireland that the English government had to choose one or the other of two courses: either to give up the country altogether, or to put forth the strength they had hitherto held back and regain their authority. Henry VIII, with his strong will, determined to attempt the restoration of the English power, and, as we shall see, he succeeded.

A few years before the time we have now arrived at, King Henry had begun his quarrel with Rome, the upshot of which was that he threw off all spiritual allegiance to the Pope, and made himself supreme head of the church in his own kingdom of England. He made little or no change in religion: on the contrary he did his best to maintain the chief doctrines of the Catholic church, and to resist the progress of the Reformation. All he wanted was that he, and not the Pope, should be head.

He was now determined to be head of the church in Ireland also; and to carry out his measures, he employed the deputy Skeffington, the earl of Ormond, and George Brown, formerly a London friar, whom the king appointed archbishop of Dublin in place of the murdered Archbishop Allen. Brown now—1535—went to work with great energy; but he was vehemently opposed by Cromer, archbishop of Armagh; and he made no impression on the Anglo-Irish of the Pale, who showed not the least disposition to go with him. Finding all his efforts fail, a parliament was convened by his advice in Dublin, which passed an act making the king supreme spiritual head of the church. An oath of supremacy was to be taken by all government officers, *i.e.* an oath that the king was spiritual head of the church; and anyone who was bound to take it and refused was adjudged guilty of treason. Appeals to the Pope in matters connected with the church were forbidden: the king would henceforward settle all these. The monasteries all through Ireland, except a few in some remote districts, were suppressed; and their property was either kept for the king or given to laymen: about four hundred altogether were broken up, and the great body of the inmates were turned out on the world without any provision.

The deputy, Lord Grey, now entered vigorously on the task of restoring quietness; for the Geraldine League was still kept up, and the disturbances caused by the rebellion continued. After a great deal of fighting he reduced most of the chiefs; and though he failed to bring Desmond and O'Brien to submission, he so weakened the League that it never came to anything.

Hitherto the English kings, from the time of John, had borne the title of "Lord of Ireland": it was now resolved to confer on Henry the title of "King of Ireland." With this object a parliament was assembled in Dublin on June 12th; and in order to lend greater importance to its decisions, a number of the leading Irish chiefs were induced to attend. This parliament accordingly is remarkable as being the first ever attended by native chiefs. Among them were also many Anglo-Irish chiefs who had seldom or never before been in parliament. For the king had instructed his deputy, Sir Anthony Sentleger, to treat with them all in a kindly and generous spirit; and as they were by this time heartily weary of strife, they showed a general disposition to meet the king's offers of reconciliation and peace. The act conferring the title of King of Ireland on Henry and his successors was passed through both houses rapidly, and without opposition. The Irish, and many of the Anglo-Irish lords, did not understand one word of English; and they were much pleased when the earl of Ormond translated into Irish for them the speeches of the lord chancellor and the speaker. There was general rejoicing, and titles were conferred on many of the chiefs. Conn O'Neill was made earl of Tyrone, and his (reputed) son Matthew was made baron of Dungannon, with the right to succeed as earl of Tyrone. O'Brien was made earl of Thomond; Mac William Burke was created earl of Clanrickard; and many other chiefs all over the country had minor titles.

With the career of Henry VIII in England we have no concern here; for this book is an Irish, not an English history. Putting out of sight the question of supremacy and the suppression of the Irish monasteries, Henry's treatment of Ireland was on the whole considerate and conciliatory, though with an occasional outburst of cruelty. He persistently refused to expel or exterminate the native Irish people to make room for new colonies, though often urged to do so by his mischievous Irish officials. The result was that the end of his reign found the chiefs submissive and contented, the country at peace, and the English power in Ireland stronger than ever it had been before. Well would it have been, both for England and Ireland, if a similar line of conduct had been followed in the succeeding reigns. Then our history would have been very different, and the tragic story that follows would never have to be told.

Chapter XXX
New Causes of Strife

F there had been no influences from the outside to stir up discord after the time of Henry VIII, it is pretty certain that the Irish people of all classes, with their own parliament, would have settled down in peace, prosperity, and contentment under the rule of the kings of England; and there now appeared every prospect that this state of things would come to pass. But there were causes of strife in store for Ireland that no one at the time ever dreamed of; so that the condition of the country, instead of improving, became gradually much worse than ever it had been, even during the evil times we have been treating of. Before resuming our regular narrative, it will be better to state the circumstances that brought about this state of things.

After the death of Henry VIII, the government in course of time entered on the task of forcing the Irish people to become Protestant; and they also began to plant the country with colonies from England and Scotland, for whom the native inhabitants were to be expelled. These two projects were either directly or indirectly the causes of nearly all the dreadful wars that desolated this unhappy country during the next century and a half: for the Irish people resisted both. One project—the Plantations—partially succeeded: the other—the religious one—failed.

But there were other circumstances that tended to bring on disturbance, though of less importance than the two above-mentioned. It will be recollected that an Irish chief had a tract of land for life, which, after his death went, by the Law of Tanistry, to his successor. But now when a chief who had got an English title from the king died, his eldest son or his next heir succeeded to title and land, according to English law; but according to the Irish custom, he whom the tribe elected succeeded to the chiefship and to the mensal land. Thus when this titled chief died, English and Irish law were, in a double sense, opposed to each other, and there was generally a contest, both for the headship and for the land, in which the government supported the heir, and the tribe the new chief elected by them. This was the origin of many very serious disturbances.

Another fruitful source of bitter heartburnings was the continual and most unwise harshness of the government, by which they turned both natives and colonists against them. To such an extent was this carried—so odious did the authorities make themselves—without the least necessity, that any invader, no matter from what quarter, would have been welcomed and aided, by both native Irish and Anglo-Irish.

A disquieting agency less serious than any of the preceding, but still a decided cause of disturbance, was the settled policy of the Tudors to anglicise the Irish people; to make them, as it were, English in everything. To accomplish this the government employed all the means at their disposal, and employed them in vain. Acts of parliament were passed commanding the natives to drop their Irish language and learn English—a thing impossible for a whole people—to take English names instead of their own, and to ride (with saddle), dress, and live after the English fashion. The legislators undertook to regulate how the hair was to be worn and how the beard was to be clipped; and for women, the colour of their dresses, the number of yards of material they were to use, the sort of hats they were to wear, and many other such like silly provisions. These laws, as might be expected, were hardly ever obeyed, so that they generally came to nothing: for the people went on speaking Irish, shaving, riding without saddle, and dressing just the same as before. But like all such laws, they were very exasperating, for they put it in the power of any ill-conditioned person to insult and harass his Irish neighbours; and they were among the causes that rendered the Irish government of that time so universally hated in Ireland.

The death of Henry VIII removed all check to the Reformation, which was now pushed forward vigorously in England. In 1551, the fifth year of Edward's reign, the chief Protestant doctrines and forms of worship were proclaimed in Ireland by Sir Anthony Sentleger, while George Brown archbishop of Dublin exerted himself to spread the Reformation: but they could only reach the few people in the service of the government, and the Reformation made no progress. The work was carried on, however, without violence; and there was on the whole little disturbance in Ireland on the score of religion during Edward's short reign.

Queen Mary, who succeeded Edward VI in 1553, restored the Catholic religion in England and Ireland; but Ireland, during her reign, was quite free from religious persecution. The Catholics were now the masters; but they showed no disposition whatever to molest the few Protestants that lived among them, allowing them full liberty to worship in their own way. Ireland indeed was regarded as such a haven of safety, that many Protestant families fled hither during the troubles of Mary's reign in England.

On the death of Mary in 1558, Elizabeth became queen. Henry VII had transferred the headship of the church from the Pope to himself; Edward VI had changed the state religion from Catholic to Protestant; Mary from Protestant to Catholic; and now there was to be a fourth change, followed by results far more serious and lasting than any previously experienced. A parliament was assembled in Dublin in 1560, to restore the Protestant religion; and in a few weeks the whole system introduced by Mary was reversed. The Act of Supremacy was revived, and all officials and clergymen were to take the oath or be dismissed. The Act of Uniformity was also reintroduced. This was an act commanding all people to use the Book of Common Prayer (the Protestant Prayer Book), and to attend the Protestant service on Sunday under pain of censure and a fine of twelve pence for each absence—about twelve shillings of our money.

Wherever these new regulations were enforced, the Catholic clergy had of course to abandon their churches, for they could not hold them without taking the oath. But they went among the people and took good care of religion just the same as before. In some places the new Act of Uniformity was now brought sharply into play, and fines were inflicted on those who absented themselves from church; but this compulsion prevailed only in the Pale and in some few other places. In far the greatest part of Ireland the government had no influence, and the Catholics were not interfered with. Even within the Pale the great body of the people took no notice of proclamations, the law could not be enforced, the Act of Uniformity was very much a dead letter, and the greater number of the parishes remained in the hands of the priests. From the time of Elizabeth till the disestablishment of the church in 1869, Protestantism remained the religion of the state in Ireland.

During the century following the death of King Henry VIII there were four great rebellions which almost depopulated the country: the Rebellion of Shane O'Neill, the Geraldine Rebellion, the Rebellion of Hugh O'Neill, and the Rebellion of 1641: after which came the War of the Revolution. In the following chapters these will be all related in the proper order.

CHAPTER XXXI
THE REBELLION OF SHANE O'NEILL
Edward VI (to 1553).
A.D. 1551–1567. Mary (1553 to 1558).
Elizabeth (1558).

T will be remembered that when Conn O'Neill was created earl of Tyrone, the young man Matthew, his reputed son, was made baron of Dungannon with the right to succeed to the earldom. Conn had adopted this Matthew, believing him to be his son, though there was then, as there has been to this day, a doubt about it. The earl's eldest legitimate son Shane, afterwards well known by the name of John the Proud, was a mere boy when Matthew was made baron. But now that he was come of age and understood his position, he claimed the right to be his father's heir and to succeed to the earldom, alleging that Matthew was not an O'Neill at all. The father, repenting his preference for Matthew, now took Shane's part; whereupon the authorities, who were of course on the side of Matthew, allured Earl Conn to Dublin, on some pretence or another, in 1551, and kept him there a captive. Shane was instantly up in arms to avenge his father's capture, and to maintain what he believed was his right against Matthew and the government: and so commenced a quarrel that cost England more men and money than any single struggle they had yet entered upon in Ireland.

The deputy, Sir James Croft, made three several attempts during 1551 and 1552 to reduce him to submission, and failed in all. The first was an expedition by sea against the Mac Donnells of Rathlin, Shane's allies: but they unexpectedly fell on his army, of whom, we are told, only one man escaped alive. The next year Croft marched north, and was joined by

Matthew: but both were routed by the young rebel chief and his adherents. He made the third attempt in the autumn of the same year, but the only injury he was able to inflict was to destroy the poor people's crops over a large stretch of country. These hostilities went on till a great part of Ulster was wasted: but still O'Neill showed not the least disposition to yield. On the contrary, the authorities complain that when they went to "parle" with him (in 1553) they "found nothing in Shane but pride and stubbornness." At last they thought it as well to let him alone, and for the next five or six years no serious attempt was made to reduce him.

In the year of Queen Elizabeth's accession, some of his people killed his rival, Matthew the baron of Dungannon, in a night attack, so unfairly that it almost deserved the name of assassination; but Shane himself was not present. In the following year the earl his father died in Dublin, and Shane was elected "The O'Neill" in accordance with the ancient Irish custom; but this was in open defiance of English law, according to which Matthew's eldest son should succeed to title and lands. These movements of the great chief gave the government much uneasiness; and in 1560 they raised up rivals all around him, who were directed to attack him simultaneously at various points: but he quickly defeated them separately, before they had time to combine. In 1561 the lord deputy—the earl of Sussex—marched north against him; but Shane defeated him; and soon afterwards he made himself master of all Ulster, including Tirconnell, the territory of the old rivals of his family, the O'Donnells. At last Sussex—as he tells us himself in one of his letters—tried to have him assassinated, but failed, because the fellow he employed got afraid and backed out of the business.

Signature of Shane O'Neill in 1561. "Misi O'Neill." Misi, pronounced Mish'ĕ two syllables. "Mise O'Neill" means Myself O'Neill. This form of signature was often used by Irish chiefs. From Gilbert's "Fac-Sim, Nat. MSS."

But now the queen adopted a pacific method: she invited him to London. He went there in December 1561, much against the wishes of Sussex, who suggested that he should be treated coldly. But this spiteful recommendation was disregarded, and the queen received him very graciously. The redoubtable chief and his retainers, all in their strange native attire, were viewed with curiosity and wonder. He strode through the court to the royal presence, as Camden tells us, between two lines of wondering courtiers; and behind him marched his galloglasses, their heads bare, their long hair curling down on their shoulders and clipped short in front just above the eyes. They wore a loose wide-sleeved saffron-dyed tunic, and over this a short shaggy mantle flung across the shoulders. On the 6th of January 1562, he made formal submission to the queen, in presence of the court and the foreign ambassadors.

If the London authorities had acted straight, O'Neill would probably have returned loyally disposed, and all might have been well: but they adopted a different course, and the natural result followed. They laid a cunning trap for him, and took an unfair advantage of his presence, while he was in their power, to make him sign certain severe conditions; but though he signed them, it was against his will, and it would seem he had no intention to carry them out. It was craft against craft; and the crooked officials in London met their match. Shane managed his business so adroitly with the queen, that in May 1562, he was permitted to return to Ulster, with the queen's pardon in his pocket, all his expenses having been paid by the government.

But he was very indignant at being forced to sign conditions: and he now quite disregarded them and renewed the war. At last the queen, heartily sick of the quarrel, instructed Sussex to end it by reasonable concessions; and peace was signed in November 1563, in O'Neill's house at Benburb, on terms much to his advantage. Among other things, it was agreed to confirm him in the old Irish name of "The O'Neill," "until the queen should decorate him by another honourable name": meaning no doubt to make him an earl. After this, things were quiet for some time.

There were at this time in Antrim great numbers of Scottish settlers from the western coasts and islands of Scotland, of whom the most distinguished were the Mac Donnells—the "Lords of the Isles." They were greatly feared and disliked by the government, who made many unsuccessful attempts to expel them. One of the conditions that Shane had to sign in London bound him to make war on these Scots and reduce them to obedience. Whether it was that he wished to carry out this condition, or what is more likely, that he himself dreaded the Scots as neighbours, he attacked and defeated them at Glenshesk, near Ballycastle in Antrim, where 700 of them were killed. The news of this victory at first gave great joy to the English; but seeing how much it increased his power, their joy soon turned to jealousy and fear; and they sent two commissioners to have an interview with him; to whom he gave very little satisfaction. He said to them, among many other things:—"For the queen, I confess she is my sovereign: but I never made peace with her but at her own seeking. My ancestors were kings of Ulster, and Ulster is mine, and shall be mine.

O'Donnell shall never come into his country [Tirconnell], nor Bagenall into Newry, nor Kildare into Dundrum or Lecale. They are now mine. With the sword I won them; with this sword I will keep them."

But this career of triumph came at last to an end. The defeat that finally crushed the great chief was inflicted, not by the government, but by the O'Donnells. Hugh O'Donnell, chief of Tirconnell, made a plundering excursion into Tyrone, Shane's territory. Shane retaliated by crossing the Swilly into Tirconnell; but he was met by O'Donnell at the other side and utterly routed; and he barely escaped with his life by crossing a ford two miles higher up the river. This action, in which 1,300 of his men perished, utterly ruined him. He lost all heart, and now formed the insane resolution of placing himself at the mercy of the Scots, whose undying enmity he had earned by the defeat at Glenshesk two years before. He came to their camp at Cushendun with only fifty followers, trusting to their generosity. They received him with a show of cordiality; but in the midst of the festivities they raised a dispute, which obviously had been prearranged, and suddenly seizing their arms, they massacred the chief and all his followers.

O'Neill's rebellion cost the government a sum nearly equal to two millions of our present money, besides the cesses laid on the country and the damages sustained by the subjects. At the time of his death he was only about forty years of age. We are told by several English historians of the time that he governed his principality with great strictness and justice.

Chapter XXXII
The Geraldine Rebellion
A.D. 1565–1583.—Elizabeth.

ERHAPS at no time since the Invasion did the dissensions of the great Anglo-Irish lords bring more misery to the general body of the people than at the present period. The Fitzgeralds and the Butlers were perpetually at war, with no authority to quell them. The earl of Desmond, head of the southern Geraldines, was a Catholic, and took the Irish side; the earl of Ormond, leader of the Butlers, had conformed to the Protestant faith, and had taken the side of the English all along. By the tyranny and oppression of these two earls, as well as by their never-ending disputes, large districts in the south were devastated, and almost depopulated. At the same time Connaught was in a state almost as bad, by the broils of the earl of Clanrickard and his sons with each other, and with the chiefs all round.

At last the deputy, Sir Henry Sydney, set out on a journey through Connaught and Munster to make peace; and having witnessed the miseries of the country, he treated those he considered delinquents with excessive and merciless severity, hanging and imprisoning great numbers. He brought Desmond a prisoner to Dublin, leaving his brother John Fitzgerald, or John of Desmond as he is called, to govern South Munster in the earl's absence. Sydney describes what he saw, and the wonder is that things could have been permitted to come to such a pass in any civilised land. The farther south he went the worse he found the country. Speaking of the districts of Desmond and Thomond, he states that whole tracts, once cultivated, lay waste and uninhabited: the ruins of burned towns, villages, and churches everywhere: "And there heard I the lamentable cries and doleful complaints made by that remnant of poor people which are yet left, hardly escaping sword and fire, or the famine which their tyrannical lords have driven them unto, either by taking their goods from them or by spending the same by taking coyne and livery. Yea, the view of the bones and skulls of dead subjects, who partly by murder, partly by famine, have died in the fields, as in truth hardly any Christian with dry eyes could behold."

After the arrest of the earl of Desmond, his brother John continued to govern South Munster, and was well affected towards the government. But at Ormond's instigation he was seized without any cause, and he and the earl were sent to London and consigned to the Tower, where they were detained for six years. All this was done without the knowledge of Sydney, who afterwards quite disapproved of it; and it made great mischief, for it was one of the causes of the rebellion, and it changed John Fitzgerald from a loyal man to a bitter rebel.

Signature (in 1574) of Garrett Fitzgerald, earl of Desmond: "Gerot Desmond."
From Gilbert's "Fac-Sim. Nat. MSS."

About this time or a little previously, the English government had some intention to colonise a large part of Ireland: and although they tried to keep the matter secret, it leaked out, and alarming rumours went among the chiefs and people, both native and Anglo-Irish. Another disquieting circumstance was that the Irish government in Dublin had been taking active steps to force the Reformation among Catholics. At last matters were brought to a crisis by the arrest of the earl of Desmond and John Fitzgerald. James Fitzmaurice Fitzgerald, the earl's first cousin, now went among the southern chiefs, and induced them all, both native Irish and Anglo-Irish, to unite in defence of their religion and their lands: and thus was formed the Second Geraldine League. Thus also arose the Geraldine rebellion.

When Sydney heard of these alarming proceedings he made another journey south with his army, in 1569, during which he and his officers acted with great severity. This circuit of Sydney's went a good way to break up the confederacy; many of the leaders were terrified into submission; and at length, after a hopeless struggle, Fitzmaurice was forced to submit. On this, as the rebellion was considered at an end, the earl and his brother were released, and returned home.

Fitzmaurice fled to France after his submission, and for about six years there was quietness; but at the end of that time he returned with three ships, which he had procured in Spain, accompanied by about eighty Spaniards, and landed in Kerry, where he was joined by Desmond's brothers, John and James Fitzgerald. Immediately the lord justice sent Sir Henry Davells and Arthur Carter to the earl of Desmond, directing him to attack the Spaniards; but as they were returning, John Fitzgerald forced his way at night into their inn in Tralee and murdered them both in their beds, a crime calculated to bring discredit and ruin on any cause. The little invading force was soon scattered, and Fitzmaurice was killed in a skirmish; on which John Fitzgerald took command of the Munster insurgents. The earl of Desmond had hitherto held aloof; but the studied ill-grained harshness of the lord justice, Sir William Pelham, at last forced him to join the rebellion; at which the queen was much displeased.

The frightful civil war broke out now more ruthlessly than before, and brought the country to such a state as had never yet been witnessed. Several hostile bands belonging to both sides traversed the country for months, destroying everything and wreaking vengeance on the weak and defenceless, but never meeting, or trying to meet, in battle. At Christmas, 1579, Desmond utterly ruined the rich and prosperous town of Youghal, which belonged to the party of his opponents, leaving not even one house fit to live in; but in his marches through those parts of the country belonging to the English he did not kill the inhabitants. Not so with the government commanders, Pelham and Ormond: they carried fire and sword through the country; and Pelham himself tells us that every day, in their marches, they hunted the peasantry fleeing with their families through the woods, and killed them by hundreds. For the rebels it was a losing game all through. James Fitzgerald was captured and executed: and a little later on, his brother John was intercepted and killed.

While Pelham and Ormond still continued to traverse Munster, burning, destroying, and slaying, from Limerick to the remote extremities of the Kerry peninsulas, the insurrection suddenly blazed up in Leinster. About two years before this, Sir Henry Sydney, the lord deputy, had excited great discontent and violent commotion among the loyalist people of the Pale, by imposing on them an oppressive tax without consulting the Irish parliament, a proceeding which was quite illegal; and partly for this reason, and partly on account of the measures taken by government to force the Reformation, one of the principal men among them, James Eustace, Viscount Baltinglass, and his people, rose up in open rebellion. Just at this time, Lord Grey of Wilton was appointed lord justice; and no sooner had he landed in Dublin than he marched into Wicklow to put down this new rebellion. But he was a bad general, and incautiously led his army in pursuit of the rebel forces into the wooded and dangerous defile of Glenmalure, where he was suddenly attacked by viscount Baltinglass and by the great Wicklow chief, Fiach Mac Hugh O'Byrne; and his army was almost annihilated.

The insurgents had long expected aid from the Continent, and a small force at length arrived: 700 Spaniards and Italians landed about the 1st October 1580, from four vessels at Smerwick in Kerry. They took possession of an old fort beside the sea, called Dunanore, and proceeded to fortify it. After about six weeks spent in collecting forces, Lord Grey, burning with rage after his defeat at Glenmalure, laid siege to the fort, and battered it with cannon till the garrison was forced to surrender. The Irish authorities assert that they had promise of their lives: the English say they surrendered at discretion. At any rate, as soon as they had delivered up their arms, Grey had the whole garrison massacred. This deed of horror caused great indignation all over England as well as on the Continent, and brought upon Grey the displeasure of the queen. During the next year, he and his officers carried on the war with relentless barbarity; till at length it began to be felt that instead of quieting the country he was rather fanning rebellion. The queen was assured that his proceedings had left in Ireland little more for her majesty to reign over but carcases and ashes: and she recalled him in 1582.

Things had come to a hopeless pass with the rebels. And now the great earl of Desmond, the master of almost an entire province, the inheritor of vast estates, and the owner of numerous castles, was become a homeless outlaw with a price on his head, dogged by spies everywhere, and hunted from one hiding place to another. Through all his weary wanderings he was accompanied by his faithful wife, who never left him, except a few times when she went to intercede for him. On one of these occasions she sought an interview with Pelham himself, and on her knees implored mercy for her husband; but her tears and entreaties were all in vain. Once in the depth of winter a plan was laid to capture him. The soldiers led by the spy had actually arrived by night at the hut where he was hiding, when he heard the noise of footsteps, and he and the countess rushed out in the darkness, and plunging into the river that flowed close by, concealed themselves under a bank, with only their heads over the water, till the party had left. Another time, he and his company of sixty galloglasses were surprised in the glen of Aherlow while cooking part of a horse for their dinner. Many of the galloglasses were killed while defending their master: twenty were captured and executed on the spot, and the others, with the earl and countess, escaped. He was at length taken and killed by some soldiers and peasants in Kerry, which ended the great Geraldine rebellion.

The war had made Munster a desert. In the words of the Four Masters:—"The lowing of a cow or the voice of a ploughman could scarcely be heard from Dunqueen in the west of Kerry to Cashel." To what a frightful pass the wretched people had been brought may be gathered from Edmund Spenser's description of what he witnessed with his own eyes:—"Notwithstanding that the same [province of Munster] was a most rich and plentiful countrey, full of corne and cattle, yet ere one yeare and a halfe the people were brought to such wretchedness as that any stony hart would have rued the same. Out of every corner of the woods and glynnes they came creeping forth upon their hands, for their legges could not beare them, and if they found a plot of watercresses or shamrocks there they flocked as to a feast for the time: that in short space of time there were almost no people left, and a most populous and plentifull country suddainely left voide of man and beast."

From Miss Stokes's *Early Christian Architecture,* 76.

Chapter XXXIII
The Plantations

EFORE proceeding further with our regular narrative, it is necessary that we here turn back a little in point of time, in order to trace the history of the plantations, and to describe what they were and how they were carried out. In the time of Queen Mary, an entire change was made in the mode of dealing with Irish territories whose chiefs had been subdued. Hitherto whenever the government deposed or banished a troublesome Irish chief, they contented themselves with putting in his place another, commonly English or Anglo-Irish, more likely to be submissive, while the general body of occupiers remained undisturbed. But now when a rebellious chief was reduced, the lands, not merely those in his own possession, but also those belonging to the whole of the people over whom he ruled, were confiscated, that is, seized by the crown, and given to English adventurers— undertakers as they were commonly called. These men got the lands on condition that they should bring over, and plant on them, a number of English or Scotch settlers; for whom it was of course necessary to clear off the native population. What became of the doomed people no one cared. Some went away quietly and faced hardship and want. But others refused to give up their homes, and then there was fighting and bloodshed, as will be seen as we go along.

Our first example of this kind of colonisation occurred in Leix and Offaly, from which their two chiefs O'Moore and O'Conor had been banished in 1547, immediately after the death of King Henry. These two districts were, in the first instance, not exactly taken possession of by the crown, but given directly to an Englishman named Francis Bryan and to some others, who proceeded straightway to expel the native people and parcel out the lands to new tenants, chiefly English. But the poor people clung to their homes and struggled hard to retain them. The fighting went on during the whole of the reign of Edward VI with great loss of life to

152

both sides; and the settlement, exposed to the constant vengeful attacks of those who had been dispossessed, decayed year by year.

As this attempt at plantation did not succeed, the whole district was taken possession of by the crown in the reign of Queen Mary, and replanted. The natives still resisted; but they had now the full strength of the government forces to contend with; and a pitiless war of extermination went on for many years, till the original owners and peasantry were as a body almost completely banished or extirpated. But this settlement never succeeded: and the natives gradually crept back till in course of time they in great measure absorbed the settlers, as happened in older times.

After the death of Shane O'Neill, more than half of Ulster was confiscated; and the attempt to clear off the old natives and plant new settlers was commenced without delay. In 1570 the peninsula of Ardes in Down was granted to the queen's secretary Sir Thomas Smith, who sent his son with a colony to take possession. But this attempt at plantation was a failure too; for the owners, the O'Neills of Clannaboy, not feeling inclined to part with their homes without a struggle, attacked and killed the young undertaker in 1573. The next undertaker was a more important man, Walter Devereux, earl of Essex. In 1573 he undertook to plant the district now occupied by the county Antrim, together with the island of Rathlin. He waged savage war on the natives, killing them wherever he could find them, burning their corn and depopulating the country to the best of his ability by sword and starvation. He treacherously seized young O'Donnell of Tirconnell and Brian O'Neill chief of Clannaboy, and sent them prisoners to Dublin, having first caused two hundred of O'Neill's people to be killed at a banquet to which he had invited them. And he hunted down and massacred many hundreds of the Scots of Clannaboy and of Rathlin Island, all without distinction, men, women, and children, to gain possession of their lands. Yet after all this fearful work, he failed in the end and returned to Dublin, where he died.

On the suppression of the Geraldine rebellion, the vast estates of the earl of Desmond, and those of 140 of the leading gentlemen of Munster, his adherents, were confiscated by a parliament held in Dublin. In the following year proclamation was made all through England, inviting gentlemen to "undertake" the plantation of this great and rich territory. Estates were offered at two pence or three pence an acre, and no rent at all was to be paid for the first five years. Every undertaker who took 12,000 acres was to settle eighty-six English families as tenants on his property, but no Irish; and so in proportion for smaller estates down to 4,000 acres.

Many of the great undertakers were absentees: English noblemen who never saw Ireland. Of those who came over to settle down on their

Raleigh's House. From Kilkenny Archaeological Journal, *1856–7.*

estates, two are well known. Sir Walter Raleigh got 42,000 acres in Cork and Waterford, and resided in Youghal, where his house is still to be seen. Edmund Spenser the poet received 12,000 acres in Cork, and took up his residence in one of Desmond's strongholds, Kilcolman Castle, the ruin of which, near Buttevant, is still an object of interest to visitors.

Kilcolman Castle. From Cork Historical and Archaeological Society's Journal.

In the most important particulars, however, this great scheme turned out a failure. The English farmers and artisans did not come over in sufficient numbers; and the undertakers received the native Irish everywhere as tenants, in violation of the conditions. Some English came over indeed; but they were so harassed and frightened by the continual onslaughts of the dispossessed proprietors and tenants, that many of them returned to England. And lastly, more than half the confiscated estates remained in possession of the original owners, as no others could be found to take them. So the only result of this plantation was to root out a large proportion of the old gentry, and to enrich a few undertakers.

There were many other plantations during these times and subsequently, some of which will be described farther on; but all of them resembled, in their main features, those sketched here. From beginning to end they were the cause of frightful bloodshed and misery to both natives and settlers; and they left to posterity a disastrous legacy of hatred and strife.

Chapter XXXIV
Hugh Roe O'Donnell
A.D. 1584–1592.—Elizabeth.

Sir JOHN PERROT, a brave bluff old soldier, was lord deputy from 1584 to 1588. He treated the Irish with some consideration, much against the wishes of his Dublin council, many of whom were his bitter enemies. Yet his action was not always straight, as the following narrative will show. Fearing hostilities with Spain, where the Armada was at this time in preparation, he had already secured hostages from many of the Irish chiefs, but none from the O'Donnells whom he feared most of all. In this strait he bethought him of a treacherous plan to seize either Sir Hugh O'Donnell or his son and heir.

Sir Hugh O'Donnell chief of Tirconnell had a son Hugh, commonly known as Hugh Roe (the Red), who was born in 1572, and who was now—1587—in his fifteenth year. Even already at that early age, he was remarked for his great abilities and for his aspiring and ambitious disposition. "The fame and renown of the above-named youth, Hugh Roe," say the Four Masters, "had spread throughout the five provinces of Ireland even before he had come to the age of manhood, for his wisdom, sagacity, goodly growth, and noble deeds; and the English feared that if he should be permitted to arrive at the age of manhood, he and the earl of Tyrone [Hugh O'Neill his brother-in-law] might combine and conquer the whole island."

Perrott's plan for entrapping young Red Hugh was skilfully concocted and well carried out. In the autumn of 1587 he sent a merchant vessel laden with Spanish wines to the coast of Donegal on pretence of traffic. The captain entered Lough Swilly and anchored opposite the castle of Rathmullan, where the boy lived with his foster-father Mac Sweeny. When Mac Sweeny heard of the arrival of the ship, he sent to purchase some wine. The messengers were told that no more was left to sell; but that if any gentlemen wished to come on board they were quite welcome to drink as much as they pleased. The bait took. A party of the Mac Sweenys, accompanied by Hugh, unsuspectingly went on board. The captain had previously called in all his men; and while the company were enjoying themselves, their arms were quietly removed, the hatchway door was closed down, and the ship weighed anchor. When the people on shore observed this, they were filled with consternation, and flocked to the beach; but they were quite helpless, for they had no boats ready. Neither was it of any avail when Mac Sweeny rushed to the point of shore nearest the ship, and cried out in the anguish of his heart, offering any amount of ransom and hostages. Young Hugh O'Donnell was brought to Dublin, and safely lodged in the Castle.

This dishonourable and unwise transaction, however, so far from tending to peace, as Perrott no doubt intended, did the very reverse. It made bitter enemies of the O'Donnells, who had been hitherto for generations on the side of the government. In young O'Donnell himself more especially, it engendered lifelong feelings of exasperation and hatred; and it was one of the causes of the O'Neill rebellion, which brought unmeasured woe and disaster to both English and Irish.

Three years and three months passed away: Perott had been recalled, and Sir William Fitzwilliam was now lord deputy; when O'Donnell, in concert with some of his fellow-prisoners, made an attempt to escape. Round the castle there was a deep ditch filled with water, across which was a wooden footbridge opposite the door of the fortress. Early one dark winter's evening, before the guard had been set, they let themselves down on the bridge by a long rope, and immediately fastened the door on the outside. They were met on the bridge by a young man of Hugh's people with two swords, one of which Hugh took, the other was given to Art Kavanagh, a brave young Leinster chief who had been O'Donnell's companion in bondage. They made their way noiselessly through the people along the dimly lighted streets, guided by the young man, while Kavanagh brought up the rear with sword grasped ready in case of interruption. Passing out through one of the city gates which had not yet been closed for the night, they crossed the country towards the hills, avoiding the public road, and made their way over that slope of the Three Rock Mountain overlooking Stillorgan and the sea. They pushed on till far in the night; when being at last quite worn out, they took shelter in a thick wood, somewhere near the present village of Roundwood, in Wicklow, where they remained hidden during the remainder of the night. Next morning O'Donnell was so fatigued that he was not able to keep up with his companions; for the thin shoes he wore had fallen in pieces with wet, and his feet were torn and bleeding from sharp stones and thorns. So, very unwillingly, his companions left him in a wood and pursued their journey, all but one servant who went for aid to Castlekevin, a little way off, near the mouth of Glendalough, where lived Felim O'Toole, one of Hugh's friends, who at once took steps for his relief.

Now to return to Dublin Castle. Not long after the captives had left, the guards, going to lock them up in their cells for the night, missed them, and instantly raising an alarm, rushed to the door; but finding themselves shut in, they shouted to the people in the houses at the other side of the street, who removed the fastening of the door and released them. They were not able to overtake the fugitives, who had too much of a start, but they traced them all the way to the hiding place. O'Toole now saw that his friend could no longer be concealed, for the soldiers had actually surrounded the wood; and making a virtue of necessity, he and his people arrested him and brought him back to Dublin. The council were delighted at his capture; and for the better security in the future they shackled him and his companions in the prison with heavy iron fetters.

Another weary year passed away. On Christmas night, before suppertime, Hugh and his two companions, Henry and Art O'Neill, the sons of the great rebel Shane O'Neill, who were also in the prison, cut through their iron fetters with a file which had somehow been conveyed to them, and let themselves down on the bridge by a long silken rope which had been sent in with the file.[1] They crept through the common sewer of the castle, and, making their way across the ditch, were met at the other side by a guide sent by Fiach Mac Hugh O'Byrne of Glenmalure.

They glided through the dim streets, as in their former attempt at escape, the people taking no notice of them; and passing out at one of the city gates

[1]There is good reason to believe that the deputy Fitzwilliam, who was a very avaricious man, was bribed by Hugh O'Neill earl of Tyrone, to secretly permit O'Donnell to escape.

which had not been closed, they made their way across the country; but in this part of their course they lost Henry O'Neill in the darkness. Greatly distressed at this, they still pressed on; but they found it hard to travel and suffered keenly from cold; for rain and sleet fell thick, and they had thrown aside their soiled outer mantles after leaving the castle. They crossed the hills, shaping their way this time, it would appear, more to the west, up by Killakee and along the course of the present military road.

But Art O'Neill, who had grown corpulent in his prison for want of exercise, was unable to keep pace with the others: and Hugh and the attendant had to help him on at intervals by walking one on each side, while he rested his arms on their shoulders. In this manner they toiled on wearily across the snowy waste through the whole of that Christmas night and the whole of next day, without food, hoping to be able to reach Glenmalure, O'Byrne's home, without a halt. But they became at last so worn out with fatigue and hunger, that they had to give up and take shelter under a high rock, while the servant ran on to O'Byrne's Castle for help. Fiach instantly despatched a small party with a supply of food, but found the two young men lying under the rock to all appearance dead:— "Unhappy and miserable," write the Four Masters, "was the condition [of the young chiefs] on their arrival. Their bodies were covered over with white-bordered shrouds of hailstones freezing around them, and their light clothes and fine-threaded shirts adhered to their skin, and their large shoes and leather thongs to their legs and feet: so that it did not appear to the men who had arrived that they were human beings at all, but like masses of earth covered with snow; and when they lifted them up, they found scarce any life in them."

They tried to make the unhappy sufferers take food and drink, but neither food nor drink could they swallow; and while the men were tenderly nursing them, Art O'Neill died in their arms. And there they buried him under the shadow of the rock. Hugh, being hardier, however, fared better: after some time he was able to swallow a little ale, and his strength began to return. But his feet still remained frozen and dead, so that he could not stand: and when he had sufficiently recovered, the men carried him on their shoulders to Glenmalure. Here he was placed in a secluded cottage, where he remained for a time under cure, till a young chief named Turlogh O'Hagan, a trusty messenger from Hugh O'Neill earl of Tyrone, came for him.

Meantime, the council hearing that O'Donnell was in Glenmalure with O'Byrne, placed guards on the fords of the Liffey to prevent him from passing northwards to Ulster. Nevertheless, as O'Neill's message was urgent, O'Donnell, though weak and suffering, set out with the messenger, accompanied by a troop of horse sent by O'Byrne as a guard: but his feet were still so helpless that he had to be lifted on and off his horse. They crossed the Liffey at a deep and dangerous ford just beside Dublin, which had been left unguarded. Here O'Byrne's escort left them; and from Dublin they made their way northwards, attended by Felim O'Toole and his brother, who had accompanied the party from Glenmalure. Having escorted them to a safe distance beyond Dublin, the O'Tooles bade Hugh farewell, and having given him their blessing, departed from him."

There were now only two, O'Donnell himself and O'Hagan, and they rode on till they reached the Boyne a little above Drogheda: here they crossed in a boat, while the ferryman brought the horses round by the town. They next reached Mellifont, where resided a friend, Sir Garrett Moore, a young Englishman, with whom they remained for the night; and in the evening of the following day set off with a fresh pair of horses.

They arrived at Dundalk by morning. Having been made aware that all the ordinary roads and passes were guarded, for news of Hugh's flight had reached Dundalk from Dublin, they took the bold course of riding into the town, passing through in open day without attracting any notice or exciting suspicion: and they next reached the residence of Hugh O'Neill's half brother, chief of the Fews in Armagh. Next day they came to the city of Armagh, where they remained in concealment for one night. The following day they reached the house of Earl Hugh O'Neill at Dungannon, where O'Donnell rested for four days; but secretly, for O'Neill was still in the queen's service.

The earl sent him with a troop of horse as an escort to Enniskillen Castle, the residence of O'Donnell's cousin Maguire of Fermanagh, who rowed him down Lough Erne, at the far shore of which he was met by a party of his own people. With these he arrived at his father's castle at Ballyshannon, where he was welcomed with unbounded joy. Here he remained under cure for two months. The physicians had at last to amputate his two great toes; and a whole year passed away before he had fully recovered from the effects of that one terrible winter night in the mountains.

In May this year, 1592, a general meeting of the Kinel Connell was convened; and Sir Hugh O'Donnell, who was old and feeble, having resigned the chieftainship, young Hugh Roe—now in his twentieth year—was elected The O'Donnell, chief of his race.

Sculpture on a Capital of the Church of the Monastery, Glendalough. Beranger, 1779. From Petrie's *Round Towers,* 258.

CHAPTER XXXV
THE REBELLION OF HUGH O'NEILL
A.D. 1585–1597.—Elizabeth.

ATTHEW, baron of Dungannon, had two sons, of whom the younger, Hugh O'Neill, succeeded to the title when very young, after the death of his father and brother. He was born about 1545 and was educated among the English, his father having been always on the side of the government; and he began his military life in the queen's service as commander of a troop of horse. He is described by the contemporary English historian Moryson as "Of a medium stature but a strong body, able to endure labours, watching, and hard fare, being withal industrious and active, valiant, affable, and fit to manage great affairs, and of a high, dissembling, subtile, and profound wit." The Irish parliament of 1585 made him earl of Tyrone in succession to his (reputed) grandfather, Earl Conn O'Neill, but they had no power to give him the land inheritance, the former patrimony of the O'Neills; as it had been confiscated after the death of Shane the Proud. This, however, was granted to him by the queen, on the condition that he should give up 240 acres on the Blackwater as a site for a fort. This fort was built soon afterwards and called Portmore; and it was kept garrisoned with English troops; for it was considered very important, as it commanded a ford on the river, which was the usual pass from Armagh into Tyrone, O'Neill's territory. The site of the fort is now marked by the village of Blackwatertown.

Not long after this, the earl and Mabel Bagenal, sister of Sir Henry Bagenal, marshal or military commander of Ireland, wished to be married; for O'Neill's first wife, Red Hugh O'Donnell's sister, was at this time dead. But Bagenal bitterly opposed the match, and sent the lady out of the

160

way, to the house of his sister in Dublin, whither O'Neill followed her; and they were married in the house of a friend at Drumcondra. The marshal from that day forth was O'Neill's deadly enemy; and he kept the lady's fortune, £1,000 (about £12,000 of our money), which her father had left her.

Enniskillen Castle in or about 1600. From Speed's Map of Ireland.

In 1593 the government made O'Neill master of all Tyrone. But his movements were now considered suspicious, and the queen and government were greatly puzzled how to deal with him; for he was continually drilling his men; and he brought home vast quantities of lead to roof his new house at Dungannon, which it was reported was not intended for roofs but for bullets. He secured the friendship of the most powerful of the Ulster chiefs; and we have seen how he aided young O'Donnell to escape from Dublin castle, a matter which was very well known to the authorities. Still he was in the queen's service, and in this same year, 1593, he fought with deputy Fitzwilliam against O'Ruarc, who had been goaded into rebellion by the sheriff of Fermanagh. In 1594 Fitzwilliam took Maguire's castle at Enniskillen. But Maguire and O'Donnell besieged it immediately after; and when the deputy sent forces to relieve the garrison, they were intercepted at a ford near Enniskillen by Maguire and O'Neill's brother Cormac, and defeated. In their flight they abandoned all the provisions intended for the garrison; so that the place got the name of Bellanabriska, the ford of the biscuits; after which the garrison at Enniskillen surrendered the castle to Maguire, who sent them away unharmed and under protection to a place of safety. But no one could tell whether or not it was with O'Neill's consent his brother had joined Maguire.

The friendly relations between the earl and the government may be said to have ended with the close of the year 1594. Up to this it does not appear that he had any intention of rebelling; for though maintaining his rights, he endeavoured to avoid displeasing the authorities. But he was continually harassed by the untiring enmity of Marshal Bagenal, who intercepted many of his letters of submission and explanation to the deputy: and this and his determination to regain all the ancestral power of his family in Ulster gradually drew him into rebellion.

There were now many alarming signs and rumours of coming disturbance; and at the request of the deputy a force of 3,000 troops was sent over from England early in 1595, under the command of Sir John Norris president of Munster, an officer of great ability and experience, on whom was conferred the title of "Lord General." O'Neill evidently regarded this movement as the first step towards the subjugation of the whole country, including his own province of Ulster; and he decided on immediate action. His young brother Art seized Portmore; and he himself plundered the English settlements of Cavan.

He next, in the same year, laid siege to Monaghan and reduced its English garrison to great distress. Norris and his brother Sir Thomas managed to reach the town with a store of provisions, without meeting with any opposition; but on their return march to Newry, they found O'Neill with his army drawn up on the far bank of a small stream at Clontibret, six miles from Monaghan. After a brave contest the English were defeated; the two Norrises were severely wounded: and O'Neill himself slew in single combat a gigantic officer named Segrave, who had attacked and attempted to crush him by main strength.

In midsummer of this year (1595) Lord General Norris marched north, determined to recover Portmore; but he was opposed and harassed by O'Neill and O'Donnell, so that he did not venture to attack the fort; and he returned without much result. There were next many negotiations and conferences, in which O'Neill always insisted, among other conditions, that the Catholics should have full liberty to practise their religion; but this was persistently refused, and the war still went on. Nevertheless the queen was anxious for peace; and she was greatly exasperated when she heard of the cruelties of Sir Richard Bingham president of Connaught, who had driven nearly all the chiefs of that province into rebellion. She removed him in January 1597, and sent in his place Sir Conyers Clifford, a just and humane man.

A few months afterwards, Thomas Lord Borough was appointed lord deputy, and made preparation for a combined attack on Ulster from three different points:—he himself to march from Dublin towards Portmore against O'Neill; Sir Conyers Clifford to move from Galway to Ballyshannon against O'Donnell; and young Barnewell, son of Lord Trimblestone, to proceed from Mullingar: all three to form a junction near Ballyshannon. O'Neill and O'Donnell made preparations to intercept them. In July the deputy marched with his Leinster forces towards Portmore, and after much destructive skirmishing, O'Neill attacked and defeated him at Drumflugh on the Blackwater, near Benburb. Borough himself and the earl of Kildare were wounded, and both died soon after. But the deputy accomplished one important object:—he regained Portmore, and left in it a garrison of 300 men in charge of a brave and capable officer, Captain Williams. Sir Conyers Clifford forced his way across the Erne and laid siege to O'Donnell's castle at Ballyshannon. But the garrison, commanded by a Scotchman named Crawford, after desperate fighting, forced the attacking party to retire with considerable loss. Clifford was harassed daily by O'Donnell and reduced to great distress; till at last he was forced to recross the river in great haste just above the waterfall of Assaroe, and retreat back to Connaught, abandoning all his cannons, carriages, and stores to O'Donnell, and losing many men in the deep and dangerous ford. As to young Barnewell: he marched towards the north with 1,000 men; but he was intercepted in a well-planned ambuscade by Captain Tyrrell at Tyrrell's Pass, where his army was exterminated, and he himself was taken and sent prisoner to the earl of Tyrone.

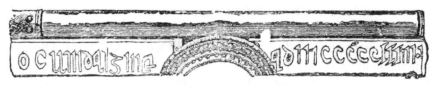

Ornament, with Inscription, on the cover of the "Misach," an ancient reliquary belonging to Inishowen. From Miss Stokes's *Christian Inscriptions,* ii. 102.

CHAPTER XXXVI
THE BATTLE OF THE YELLOW FORD
A.D. 1597–1598.—Elizabeth.

ORTMORE was now occupied by Captain Williams and his garrison of three hundred. No sooner had lord deputy Borough turned southward after his defeat at Drumflugh than O'Neill laid siege to it; and watching it night and day, tried every stratagem; but the vigilance and determination of Williams completely baffled him. At last he attempted a storm by means of scaling ladders (A.D. 1597); but the ladders turned out too short, and the storming party were met by such a fierce onslaught that they had to retire, leaving thirty-four of their men dead in the fosse. After this, O'Neill, having had sufficient experience of the captain's mettle, tried no more active operations, but sat down, determined to starve the garrison into surrender. When this had continued for some time, Williams and his men began to suffer sorely; and they would have been driven to surrender by mere starvation, but for the good fortune of having seized and brought into the fort a number of O'Neill's horses, on which they now chiefly subsisted. Even with this supply they were so pressed by hunger that they ate every weed and every blade of grass they could pick up in the enclosure: but still the brave captain resolutely held out.

When tidings of these events reached Dublin, the council sat in long and anxious deliberation, and at first decided to order Williams to surrender; but Marshal Bagenal arriving at this moment, persuaded them to entrust him with the perilous task of relieving the fort. Marching north, he arrived at Armagh with an army of 4,000 foot and 350 horse. The five miles highway between this city and Portmore was a narrow strip of uneven ground, with bogs and woods at both sides; and right in the way, near Bellanaboy or the Yellow Ford, on the little river Callan, two miles north of Armagh, O'Neill had marshalled his forces, and determined to dispute the passage. His army was perhaps a little more numerous than that of his adversary, well trained and disciplined, armed and equipped after the English fashion, though not so well as Bagenal's army—they had no armour, for instance, while many of the English had; and he had the advantage of an excellent position selected by himself. He had with him Hugh Roe O'Donnell, Maguire, and Mac Donnell of the Glens of Antrim, all leaders of ability and experience. At intervals along the way he had dug deep holes and trenches, and had otherwise encumbered the line of march with felled trees and brushwood; and right in front of his main body extended a trench a mile long, five feet deep, and four feet across, with a thick hedge of thorns on top. Over these tremendous obstacles, in face of the whole strength of the Irish army, Bagenal must force his way, if he is ever to reach the starving little band cooped up in Portmore.

But Bagenal was not a man easily daunted: and on the morning of the 14th August he began his march with music and drum. The army advanced in six regiments, forming three divisions. The first division—two regiments—was commanded by Colonel Percy: the marshal himself, as commander-in-chief, riding in the second regiment—the general's regiment, as it was called; the second division, consisting of the third and fourth regiments, was commanded by Colonel Cosby and Sir Thomas Wingfield; and the third division by captains Coneys and Billings: and these six infantry regiments marched one behind another at intervals of 600 or 700 paces. The horse formed two separate divisions, one on each wing, right and left, under Sir Calisthenes Brooke, with captains Montague and Fleming.

On the night before, O'Neill had sent forward 500 light-armed kern, who concealed themselves till morning in the woods and thickets along the way; and the English had not advanced far when these opened fire from both sides, which they kept up during the whole march past. Through all obstacles—fire, bog, and pitfalls—the army struggled and fought resolutely, till the first regiment reached the great trench. A determined rush across, a brief and fierce hand-to-hand struggle, and in spite of all opposition they got to the other side. Instantly reforming, they pushed on, but had got only a little way when they were charged by a solid body of Irish and utterly overwhelmed. It now appeared that a fatal mistake in tactics had been made by Bagenal. The several regiments were too far asunder, and the men of the vanguard were almost all killed before the second regiment could come up. When at last this second line appeared, O'Neill with a body of horse, knowing that Bagenal was at their head, spurred forward to seek him out and settle wrong and quarrel hand to hand. But they were not fated to meet. The brave marshal, fatigued with fighting, lifted his visor for a moment to look about him and take breath; and hardly had he done so when a musket ball pierced his brain and he fell lifeless.

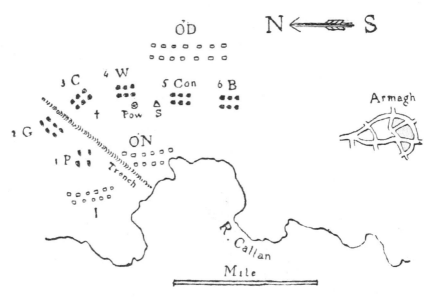

Plan of the Battle of the Yellow Ford, after the two first English regiments had crossed the trench. English regiments numbered and made dark for distinction.

> O'D. O'Donnell, Maguire, and Mac Donnell of the Glens: horse and foot, about to attack last two regiments.
> O'N. O'Neill's horse and foot.
> S. The "Saker" or cannon bogged.
> Pow. Where the powder blew up.
> † Spot where Marshal Bagenal fell.
> I. Irish regiment that overwhelmed the first two English regiments, G and P.

Constructed from a Contemp. Plan of Battle in Gilbert's "Fac-Sim. Nat. MSS."

Even after this catastrophe the second regiment passed the trench, and were augmented by those of the first who survived. These soon found themselves hard pressed; which Cosby becoming aware of, pushed on with his third regiment to their relief; but they were cut to pieces before he had come up. A cannon had got bogged in Cosby's rear, straight in the line of march; and the oxen that drew it having been killed, the men of the fourth regiment made frantic efforts to free it, fighting for their lives all the time, for the Irish were swarming all round them. Meantime, during this delay, Cosby's regiment was attacked and destroyed, and he himself was taken prisoner. While all this was taking place in the English front, there was hard fighting in the rear. For O'Neill, who with a small party of horse had kept his place near the trench, fighting and issuing orders, had, at the beginning of the battle, sent towards the enemy's rear O'Donnell, Maguire, and Mac Donnell of the Glens, who passing by the flank of the second division, hotly engaged as they were, fell on the last two regiments, which after a prolonged struggle to get forward, "being hard sett to, retyred foully [in disorder] to Armagh."

The fourth regiment, at last leaving their cannon in the bog, made a dash for the trench; but scarcely had they started when a waggon of gunpowder exploded in their midst, by which they were "disrancked and rowted" and great numbers were killed, "wherewith," as the English account says, "the traitors were encouraged and our men dismayed." O'Neill, observing the confusion, seized the moment for a furious charge. The main body of the English had been already wavering after the explosion, and now there was a general rout of both middle and rear. Fighting on the side of the English was an Irish chief, Mailmora or Myles O'Reilly, who was known as Mailmora the Handsome, and who called himself the Queen's O'Reilly. He made two or three desperate attempts to rally the flying squadrons, but all in vain; and at last he himself fell slain among the others.

The multitude fled back towards Armagh, protected by the cavalry under captain Montague, an able and intrepid officer, for Sir Calisthenes Brooke had been wounded; and the Irish pursued them—as the Four Masters express it—"by pairs, threes, scores, and thirties." Two thousand of the English were killed, together with their general and nearly all the officers; and the victors became masters of the artillery, ammunition, and stores of the royal army. On the Irish side the loss is variously estimated from 200 to 700. This was the greatest overthrow the English ever suffered since they had first set foot in Ireland.[1]

A large body of fugitives shut themselves up in Armagh, where they were closely invested by the Irish. But Montague, with a company of horse, most courageously forced his way out and brought the evil tidings to Dublin. In a few days the garrisons of Armagh and Portmore capitulated— the valiant Captain Williams yielding only after a most pressing message from Armagh—and were permitted to retire to Dundalk, leaving colours, drums, and ammunition behind.

When the southern chiefs heard of O'Neill's great victory, the Munster rebellion broke out like lightning. The confederates, including the Geraldines, attacked the settlements to regain the lands that had been taken from them a dozen years before; they expelled the settlers; and before long they had recovered all Desmond's castles. The lord lieutenant and Sir Thomas Norris, president of Minister, were quite unable to cope with the rebellion, and left Munster to the rebels.

---

[1] The above account of the battle has been taken chiefly from English sources.

Ornament on top of Devenish Round Tower. From Petrie's *Round Towers.*

CHAPTER XXXVII
THE EARL OF ESSEX
A.D. 1599–1600.—Elizabeth.

HE queen was greatly exasperated when news reached her of the Battle of the Yellow Ford; and she wrote to the Dublin Council, censuring them bitterly, and expressing her belief that this catastrophe, and many others, were owing to their incapacity and mismanagement. At this grave juncture she appointed, as lord lieutenant, Robert Devereux, second earl of Essex, son of Essex of the Plantations. He brought an army of 20,000 men, and the queen invested him with almost as much power as if she had made him king of Ireland; giving him at the same time distinct instructions to direct all his strength against the earl of Tyrone and the other rebels of Ulster, and to plant garrisons at Lough Foyle and Ballyshannon. Though he was a brave and distinguished soldier, he did not understand how to carry on war in Ireland; and, as we shall see, he mismanaged the whole campaign. He delayed proceeding against Tyrone, and he neglected altogether the order for planting garrisons. Soon after his arrival in Dublin, he foolishly scattered a good part of his army, by sending detachments to various minor stations through the country. Then, probably deeming it not yet quite safe to attempt the reduction of O'Neill, he deliberately disobeyed the queen's instructions by setting out for the South in May, with 7,000 men, chiefly with the object of chastising the Geraldines.

Through the whole of this disastrous journey, which occupied about six weeks, the insurgents constantly hung round his army and never gave him an hour's rest, so that he had to fight every inch of his way. The O'Moores killed 500 of his men at the "Pass of the Plumes," near Maryborough, which was so called from the number of English helmet-plumes that remained strewn about after the fight. Having extricated himself from this pass, Essex pushed on for Caher in Tipperary, where he took the castle from Thomas Butler, one of O'Neill's confederates, after a siege of ten days—the only successful exploit of the whole expedition. Passing round by Limerick, Fermoy, Bismore, and Waterford, he returned to Dublin in June, "the soldiers," as the historian Moryson says, "being weary, sick, and incredibly diminished in numbers."

Caher Castle in 1845. From Mrs. Hall's Ireland.

Matters were going on no better in the West of Ireland. In Collooney in Sligo, was a strong castle held by O'Conor of Sligo, one of the Government supporters, which was now closely besieged by O'Donnell; whereupon Sir Conyers Clifford, by orders of Essex, marched from Galway to relieve it. Having arrived at Boyle, he started to cross the Curlieu Hills into Sligo; but he was intercepted by O'Donnell in a difficult part of the mountain road, called Ballaghboy or the Yellow Pass. After a very sharp fight the English were defeated, and fled; and Sir Conyers, endeavouring to rally his men, was killed in the pass. He was greatly regretted by the Irish, who buried him with much respect.

Essex's fine army had melted away in a few months; and at his own request he now got 2,000 more from the queen; who, however, was very indignant against him, and wrote him a bitter letter commanding him to proceed at once against O'Neill. In August 1599, he set out at last for the north, with only 2,500 men: but he found the insurgent earl so strongly entrenched in his camp on a high bank over the little river Lagan, about halfway between Carrickmacross and Ardee, that he did not dare to attack him. O'Neill now requested a conference, which was granted. Early on a morning in September, the two leaders rode down unattended, from the heights on either side of the river. O'Neill saluted the earl with great respect; and spurring his horse into the stream, to be near enough to hold converse, he remained there up to his saddle-girths during the whole conference, while he laid down the conditions he demanded. A truce was agreed on: but nothing ever came of this conference; for, immediately afterwards, Essex suddenly sailed for England. The remainder of his short career, ending on the block, belongs to the history of England.

For some time after the departure of Essex there were negotiations for peace; but they were all rendered fruitless by the refusal of the queen and government on the one vital point of freedom of religious worship, which O'Neill always insisted on. He visited Munster in January, 1600, and encamped with his army at Inishcarra on the Lee, six miles above Cork; where most of the southern chiefs visited him and acknowledged him as their leader.

For the last two years victory and success had attended the Irish almost without interruption; and Hugh O'Neill, earl of Tyrone, had now attained the very summit of his power. But after this the tide began to turn; and soon came the day of defeat and disaster. In the next four chapters will be related the waning fortunes of the earl of Tyrone, and the waning fortunes of his cause.

CHAPTER XXXVIII
THE TURN OF THE TIDE: BATTLE OF KINSALE
A.D. 1600–1602.—Elizabeth.

HARLES BLOUNT Lord Mountjoy, a man of great ability, and a more formidable adversary than any yet encountered by O'Neill, was the person chosen by the queen to succeed Essex as governor. He came to Ireland in February, and as soon as O'Neill heard of his arrival he broke up his camp at Inishcarra, where he had tarried for six weeks, and returned to Ulster. Along with Mountjoy came Sir George Carew as president of Munster, a man quite as able and courageous, but crafty and avaricious. He had an intense hatred for the Irish, mainly because his brother had been killed by them in the battle of Glenmalure.

170

Carew directed all his energies against the Munster rebels, capturing their castles one after another; and he caused his soldiers to destroy the crops wherever he went in order to produce a famine. The famine ultimately came, and the people—men, women, and children —perished by thousands of starvation.

While these events were taking place in the south, O'Neill and O'Donnell were kept busy in the north. It had long been the intention of the government to plant garrisons on the shores of Lough Foyle; and we have seen how Essex had neglected the queen's command to do so. Now a powerful armament of 4,000 foot and 200 horse, under the command of Sir Henry Docwra, with abundance of stores and building materials, sailed for Lough Foyle in May; at the same time, in order to divert O'Neill's attention and draw off opposition, Mountjoy marched north from Dublin as if to invade Tyrone. While O'Neill and O'Donnell were opposing Mountjoy, Docwra succeeded in building a fort at Culmore, just at the mouth of the river Foyle; and soon after, in spite of the opposition of the two chiefs, he erected two others, one at Derry, then almost uninhabited; and the other at Dunnalong five miles farther up the river, at the Tyrone side.

Leinster had shared in the O'Neill rebellion: and Owney O'Moore, the chief of Leix, had succeeded in winning back most of his principality. The country had quite recovered from the wars of the Plantations, nearly half a century before: the land was well cultivated, and the people were prosperous and contented. Moryson, the historian, Mountjoy's secretary, tells us that the ground was well tilled, the fields fenced in an orderly manner, the towns well inhabited, the highways in good repair: "The reason whereof," he says, "was that the queen's forces during these wars never till then came among them." But now all this was to be changed. To punish them for their part in the rebellion, Mountjoy set out in August 1600, from Dublin, with a large force, and a supply of sickles, scythes, and harrows to tear up the corn; and he soon destroyed the crops of the whole district; after which he returned to Dublin, leaving the people to despair and hunger, their smiling district turned to a black ruin. Soon after this he marched north and employed himself in the same manner, till he had destroyed the people's means of subsistence over a large part of Ulster. By the middle of 1601 the rebellion may be said to have been crushed in the three southern provinces. In Ulster, though O'Neill and O'Donnell were still actively engaged in defensive warfare, they had become greatly circumscribed. But the war was now fated to be renewed in another quarter of the island.

The aid which the Irish chiefs had long expected from Spain came at last. On the 23rd of September, a Spanish fleet entered the harbour of

Kinsale with 3,400 troops under the command of Don Juan del Aguila. They immediately took possession of the town: and Del Aguila despatched a message to Ulster to O'Neill and O'Donnell to come south without delay. An express messenger from Cork brought the news to Mountjoy and Carew, who at once began to muster their forces; and at the end of three weeks they encamped on the north side of Kinsale with an army of 12,000 men.

Signature of Hugh O'Neill earl of Tyrone in 1601, to a Proclamation in Irish written in his own hand: "O'Neill." From Gilbert's "Fac-Sim. Nat. MSS."

On the receipt of Del Aguila's message, the northern chiefs, though urgently needed in their own province, made a hasty preparation to march south. O'Donnell was first. Setting out from Ballymote, and crossing the Shannon into Tipperary, he encamped near Holycross. But here his further progress was barred; for Carew, whom Mountjoy had sent to intercept him,

Kinsale Harbour. From Mrs. Hall's Ireland.

lay right in his path near Cashel; the Slieve Felim mountains on his right— to the west—were impassable for an army with baggage on account of recent heavy rains; and he dared not go towards the left through Kilkenny, as he might encounter the army of the Pale. At the same time, wishing to reserve his strength, he was determined to reach Kinsale without fighting. Luckily there came a sudden and intense frost on the night of the 22nd of November, which hardened up bog and morass and made them passable. The Irish general, instantly taking advantage of this, set out that night westwards, crossed the Slieve Felim mountains with his hardy Tirconnell men, and reached Croom the next night after a march of forty English miles—"the greatest march with [incumbrance of] carriage," says Carew, "that hath been heard of."

During the month of November, the English had carried on the siege vigorously; but after O'Donnell's arrival things began to go against them; for they were hemmed in by the town on one side, and by the Irish army on the other, so that they were now themselves besieged. They were threatened with famine, for hardly any food could be procured for either men or horses; and the weather was so inclement that they lost numbers of their men every day by cold and sickness.

Red Hugh O'Donnell's signature: it is in Irish, and contracted:—Aodh Odomn: that is Aodh Odomhnaill, *Hugh O'Donnell. From* Ulster Journal of Archaeology, *II, Pl. I., No. 9.*

O'Neill arrived on the 21st December with an army of about 4,000. He saw at once how matters stood, and his counsel was, not to attack the English, but to let their army melt away; for already 6,000 of them had perished; but he was overruled in a council of war, and a combined attack of Irish and Spaniards was arranged for the night of the 3rd of January 1602. Meantime an Irish traitor, Brian Mac Mahon, sent secret information of the intended attack to the English.

The night was unusually dark, wet, and stormy; the guides lost their way, and the army wandered aimlessly and wearily, till at length at the dawn of day, O'Neill unexpectedly found himself near the English lines, which he saw were quite prepared to receive him. His own men were wearied and his lines in some disorder, so he ordered the army to retire a little, either to place them in better order of battle or to postpone the attack. But Mountjoy's quick eye caught the situation at once, and he hurled his cavalry on the retreating ranks. For a whole hour O'Neill defended himself, still retiring, till his retreat became little better than a rout. All efforts to rally his ranks were vain; by some mistake Del Aguila's attack did not come off; and the Irish lost the battle of Kinsale. A short time after the battle Del Aguila surrendered the town; quite needlessly, for he could have held it till further help came, both from O'Neill and from the king of Spain; and having agreed also to give up the castles of Baltimore, Castlehaven, and Dunboy, which were garrisoned by Spaniards, he returned to Spain. He was justly blamed by King Philip III of Spain, and on his arrival he was placed under arrest, which so affected him that he died of grief.

On the night after the fatal day of Kinsale, the Irish chiefs retired with their broken army to Innishannon. Here they held a sad council, in which it was resolved to send O'Donnell to Spain for further help. Leaving his Tirconnellian forces in command of his brother Rory, O'Donnell set out and arrived in Spain in due course. He was treated everywhere with the greatest respect and honour; and King Philip received him most cordially, assuring him that he would send with him to Ireland an armament much more powerful than that of Del Aguila. But Red Hugh O'Donnell never saw his native Ulster more. He took suddenly ill at Simancas; and his bodily ailment was intensified by sickness of heart, for he had heard of the surrender of Kinsale and of the fall of Dunboy (next chapter); and he died on the 10th of September 1602, in the twenty-ninth year of his age.

CHAPTER XXXIX
THE SIEGE OF DUNBOY
A.D. 1602.—Elizabeth.

 HE Irish chiefs were very indignant with Del Aguila for surrendering Kinsale; and they were incensed beyond measure when they heard that he had agreed to hand over to the deputy the castles of Baltimore, Castlehaven, and Dunboy. The castles had not yet been given up however, and Donall O'Sullivan, chief of Beare and Bantry, the owner of Dunboy, hoping that O'Donnell would soon return with help from Spain, resolved to regain possession of it and defend it. It was situated on a point of the mainland jutting into the channel west of Beare Island, and had the reputation of being impregnable. In February he threw in a body of native troops under the command of Richard Mac Geoghegan and Thomas Taylor, an Englishman. The Spaniards who held

it were sent away; and now Mac Geoghegan's whole garrison amounted to 143 men, who straightway began to make preparations for a siege.

Carew set out on his march from Cork with 3,000 men to lay siege to the castle, sending round his ships with ordnance and stores. At Bantry Sir Charles Wilmot joined him with 1,000 more. The whole army was conveyed to Great Beare Island by sea, in the first few days of June; and encamped near the ill-starred castle. The devoted little garrison never flinched at sight of the powerful armament of 4,000 men, and only exerted themselves all the more resolutely to strengthen their position.

Bearhaven and Dunboy Castle in 1845. Castle in the foreground to the right. From Mrs. Hall's Ireland.

And now the siege was begun and carried on with great vigour; and day after day the ordnance thundered against the walls. On the 17th of June the castle was so shattered that Mac Geoghegan sent to Carew offering to surrender, on condition of being allowed to march out with arms: but Carew's only answer was to hang the messenger and to give orders for a final assault. The storming party were resisted with desperation, and many were killed on both sides; but the defenders were driven from turret to turret by sheer force of numbers; till at last they had to take refuge in the eastern wing which had not yet been injured. The only way to reach this was by a narrow passage where firearms could not be used; and a furious hand-to-hand combat was kept up for an hour and a half, while from various standpoints the defenders poured down bullets, stones, and every available missile on the assailants, killing and wounding great numbers.

While this was going on, some of the besiegers, by clearing away a heap of rubbish, made their way in by a back passage, so that the garrison found themselves assailed on all sides; whereupon forty of them sallying out, made a desperate rush for the sea, intending to swim to the island. But before they had reached the water they were intercepted and cut down, all but eight who plunged into the sea; and for these the president had provided by stationing a party with boats outside, "who," in Carew's words, "had the killing of them all."

This furious struggle had lasted during the whole long summer day, and it was now sunset; the castle was a mass of ruins, and the number of the garrison was greatly reduced. Late as it was the assault was maintained vigorously; and after another hour's fighting the assailants gained all the upper part of the castle; and the Irish, now only seventy-seven, took refuge in the cellars. Then Carew, leaving a strong guard at the entrance, withdrew his men for the night; while those in the castle enjoyed their brief rest as best they could, knowing what was to come with the light of day.

On the next morning—the 18th of June—Taylor was in command; for Mac Geoghegan was mortally wounded; and the men resolved to defend themselves to the last, except twenty-three who laid down their arms and surrendered. Carew now directed his cannons on the cellars till he battered them into ruins on the heads of the devoted band; and at length Taylor's men forced him to surrender. When a party of English entered to take the captives, Mac Geoghegan, who was lying on the floor, his life ebbing away, snatched a lighted candle from Taylor's hand, and exerting all his remaining strength, staggered towards some barrels of powder which stood in a corner of the cellar. But one of Carew's officers caught him and held him in his arms, while the others killed him with their swords. On that same day Carew executed fifty-eight of those who had surrendered. He reserved Taylor and fourteen others to tempt them to give information; but as they firmly refused to purchase their lives on such terms, he had them all hanged.

It is chiefly from Carew himself that this account of the siege is taken: and he concludes by saying that of the 143 defenders of Dunboy "no one man escaped but were either slain, executed, or buried in the ruins; and so obstinate and resolved a defence had not been seene within this kingdom." The powder that was in the vaults was heaped together and ignited; and all that remained of Dunboy was blown into fragments, except two parallel side walls which are still standing.

*Portion of a Bell-shrine found in the River Bann. From Miss Stokes's
Christian Inscriptions, ii. 106.*

CHAPTER XL
THE RETREAT OF SULLIVAN BEARE
A.D. 1603.—Elizabeth.

 FTER the capture of Dunboy, Donall O'Sullivan, the lord of Beare and Bantry, had no home; for his other castles, including those of Dursey Island and Carriganass, had also been taken. He was still however at the head of a formidable band among the glens of South Munster: and he kept up the struggle resolutely in Glengarriff and thereabout against Sir Charles Wilmot and his more numerous forces. But towards the end of the year (1602) ill news came from Spain: that O'Donnell was dead, and that King Philip, on hearing of the fall of Dunboy, had countermanded the intended expedition. Finding that he could no longer maintain himself and his followers where he was, he resolved to bid farewell to the land of his inheritance and seek a refuge in Ulster. On the last day of the year 1602 he set out from Glengarriff on his memorable retreat, with 400 fighting men, and 600 women, children, and servants. The march was one unbroken scene of conflict and hardship. They were everywhere confronted or pursued by enemies, who attacked them when they dared; and they suffered continually from fatigue, cold, and hunger. "O'Sullivan was not a day or night during this period," say the Four Masters, "without a battle, or being vehemently or vindictively pursued, all which he sustained and responded to with manliness and vigour."

They fled in such haste that they were able to bring with them only one day's provisions, trusting to be able to obtain food as they fared along; for O'Sullivan had plenty of money, which had been sent to him from Spain. But they found the people generally too much terrified by Carew's threats to give them help or shelter, or to sell them provisions. As they could not buy, they had either to take by force or starve, which explains much of the hostility they encountered; for no man will permit his substance to

177

be taken without resistance. Scarce a day passed without loss: some fell behind or left the ranks overcome with weariness; some sank and died under accumulated hardships; and others were killed in fight.

Carriganass Castle on the river Owvane, six miles N.E. from Bantry.

The first day, they made their way to Ballyvourney, after a journey of about twenty-four miles over the mountains. Here they rested for the night. On next through Duhallow, till they reached Liscarroll, where John Barry of Buttevant attacked their rear as they crossed the ford, and after an hour's fighting killed four of their men, but lost more than four himself. Skirting the north base of the Ballahoura Mountains, they encamped one night beside the old hill of Ardpatrick. Their next resting place was the Glen of Aherlow, where among the vast solitudes of the Galtys, they could procure no better food than herbs and water: and the night sentries found it hard to perform their duty, oppressed as they were with fatigue and hunger. For the first part of their journey they made tents each evening to sleep in; but they were not able to continue this, so that they had to lie under the open sky, and they suffered bitterly from the extreme cold of the nights. Next northwards from the Galtys across the Golden Vale, over the great plain of Tipperary, fighting their way through enemies almost every hour. While one detachment of the fighting men collected provisions, the others remained with the main body to protect the women and children; and the whole party were preserved from utter destruction only by the strict discipline maintained by the chief.

O'Sullivan's wife, who accompanied the party, carried and nursed so far, through all her hardships, her little boy, a baby two years old; but now she had to part with him. She entrusted him to the care of one of her faithful dependents, who preserved and reared him up tenderly, and afterwards sent him to Spain to the parents. We are not told how it fared with this lady and some others; but as they did not arrive with the rest at the end of the journey, they must, like many others, have fallen behind during the terrible march, and been cared for, as they are heard of afterwards.

The ninth day of their weary journey found them beside the Shannon near Portland in the north of Tipperary; and here they rested for two nights. But their enemies began to close in on them from the Tipperary side; and as there was no time to be lost, they prepared to cross the broad river opposite the castle of Kiltaroe or Redwood. Among them was a man, Dermot O'Hoolahan by name, skilled in making *currachs* or hide-boats. Under his direction they constructed boat frames of boughs, interwoven with osier twigs in the usual way. They then killed twelve of their horses, and carefully husbanding the flesh for food, they finished their currachs by covering the skeleton boats with the skins. In these they crossed the river; though at the last moment their rearguard had a sharp conflict with the sheriff of Tipperary, Donogh Mac Egan the owner of Redwood Castle, who with his party came up, and in spite of O'Sullivan's earnest expostulations, attacked them, and attempted to throw some of the women and children into the river. But O'Sullivan turned on him, and killed him and many of his men.

Nothing better awaited them on the other side of the Shannon. Pushing on northwards through O'Kelly's country, they had to defend themselves in skirmish after skirmish. As most of the horses had by this time quite broken down, O'Sullivan had to abandon the wounded to their certain fate; and their despairing cries rang painfully in the ears of the flying multitude. Sometimes when they came near a village, a party were despatched for provisions, who entered the houses and seized everything in the shape of food they could lay hands on, satisfying their own hunger while they searched, and bringing all they could gather to their starving companions. At Aughrim they were confronted by Captain Henry Malbie with a force much more numerous than their own. O'Sullivan, addressing his famished and desperate little band of fighting men in a few encouraging words, placed them so that they were protected on all sides except the front, where the assailants had to advance on foot through a soft boggy pass. Malbie, despising the fugitives, sprang forward at the head of his followers, but fell dead at the first onset. On rushed O'Sullivan and his men: it must be either victory or destruction; and after a determined and bitter fight,

O'Sullivan Beare. From portrait in Irish College, Salamanca.

they scattered their assailants, and freed themselves from that great and pressing danger.

Onwards over Slieve Mary near Castlekelly, and through the territory of Mac David Burke, where the people, headed by Mac David himself, harassed them all day long to prevent them from obtaining provisions. Near Ballinlough in the west of Roscommon they concealed themselves in a thick wood, intending to pass the night there. But they got no rest: for a friendly messenger came to warn them that Mac David and his people were preparing to surround them in the morning and slay them all. So they resumed their march and toiled on wearily through the night in a tempest of sleet, splashing their way through melting snow, and in the morning found themselves pursued by Mac David, who however was cowed by their determined look, and did not dare to come to close quarters.

Arriving at another solitary wood they found the people friendly; and they lighted fires and refreshed themselves. They next crossed the Curlieu Hills southwards to Knockvicar, beside the river Boyle where it enters Lough Key, and here they took some rest. For days past they had undergone unspeakable sufferings. Avoiding the open roads, they had to cross the country by rugged, rocky, and unfrequented ways, walking all the time, for horses could not be used. The weather was inclement, snow falling heavily, so that they had sometimes to make their way through deep drifts; and many of those who continued able to walk had to carry some of their companions who were overcome by fatigue and sickness.

Their hope all through had been to reach the territory of O'Ruarc prince of Brefney; and next morning when the sun rose over Knockvicar, their guide pointed out to them, only five miles off, the towers of one of O'Ruarc's residences, Leitrim or Brefney Castle. At eleven o'clock that same day they entered the hospitable mansion, where a kind welcome awaited them. They had set out from Glengarriff a fortnight before, one thousand in number; and that morning only thirty-five entered O'Ruarc's castle: eighteen armed men, sixteen servants, and one woman, the wife of the chief's uncle, Dermot O'Sullivan. A few others afterwards arrived in twos and threes; all the rest had either perished or dropped behind from fatigue, sickness, or wounds. There is still a village at Leitrim; but of the castle only a few fragments of the walls remain.

Signature of O'Sullivan Beare in 1601: "Yours most faythfull and bounden Don. OSulyvan Beare." From Gilbert's "Fac-Sim. Nat. MSS."

How it fared with South Munster after the capture of Dunboy may be told in a few words. Though the province was now quiet enough, yet several of the rebels were still at large, and there were rumours of other intended risings. Against these dangers Carew took precautions of a very decided character; he had the country turned into a desert:—"Hereupon"— says Carew—"Sir Charles Wilmot with the English regiments overran all Beare and Bantry, destroying all that they could find meet for the reliefe of men, so as that country was wholly wasted. . . . The president therefore [*i.e.* Carew himself], as well to debarre those straglers from releefe as to prevent all means of succours to Osulevan if hee should return with new forces, caused all the county of Kerry and Desmond, Beare, Bantry, and Carbery to be left absolutely wasted, constrayning all the Inhabitants thereof to withdraw their Cattle into the East and Northern parts of the County of Corke."

Composed from the Book of Kells.

Chapter XLI
The Flight of the Earls
A.D. 1602–1608. Elizabeth (to 1603).
James I (1603).

 URING the whole of the interval from the autumn of 1600 to the end of 1602, the work of destroying crops, cattle, and homesteads was busily carried on by Mountjoy and Carew, and by the governors of the garrisons, who wasted everything and made deserts for miles round the towns where they were stationed. We have already seen how thoroughly this was done in Munster and Leinster: it was now the turn of Ulster. In June, 1602, Mountjoy marched north to prosecute the war against the rebels, and remained in Ulster during the autumn and winter, traversing the country in all directions, and destroying the poor people's means of subsistence.

And now the famine, so deliberately planned, swept through the whole country; and Ulster was, if possible, in a worse condition than Munster. For the ghastly results of the deputy's cruel policy we have his own testimony, as well as that of his secretary, the historian Moryson. Mountjoy writes:—"We have seen no one man in all Tyrone of late but dead carcases merely hunger starved, of which we found divers as we passed. Between Tullaghoge and Toome [seventeen miles] there lay unburied 1,000 dead, and since our first drawing this year to Blackwater there were about 3,000 starved in Tyrone." But this did not satisfy him; for soon after he says:— "tomorrow (by the grace of God) I am going into the field, as near as I can utterly to waste the county Tyrone." Next hear Moryson. "Now because I have often made mention formerly of our destroying the rebels' corn, and using all means to famish them, let me by one or two examples show the miserable estate to which the rebels were thereby brought." He then gives some hideous details, which show, if indeed showing was needed, that the women and children and peaceable people were famished as well as the actual rebels. And he goes on to say: "And no spectacle was more frequent in the ditches of towns than to see multitudes of these poor people dead with their mouths all coloured green by eating nettles, docks, and all things they could rend up above ground."

O'Neill was not able to make any headway against Mountjoy and Docwra, both of whom continued to plant garrisons all through the province. With the few followers that remained to him, he retired into impenetrable bogs and forests; and far from taking active measures, he had quite enough to do to preserve himself and his party from utter destruction. But he refused to submit, still clinging fondly to the expectation of help from abroad.

The news of the death of Red Hugh O'Donnell crushed the last hopes of the chiefs, and Rory O'Donnell and others submitted, and were gladly and favourably received. O'Neill himself, even in his fallen state, was still greatly dreaded; for the government were now, as they had been for years, haunted by the apprehension of another and more powerful armament from Spain. At length Mountjoy, authorised by the queen, sent Sir Garrett Moore, O'Neill's old friend, to offer him life, liberty, and pardon, with title and territory; and at Mellifont near Drogheda, a few days after the death of the queen, the chief made submission to the deputy. Soon afterwards O'Neill and O'Donnell went to England with Mountjoy. The king received them kindly and graciously; confirmed O'Neill in the title of earl of Tyrone; made Rory O'Donnell earl of Tirconnell; and restored both to most of their possessions and privileges.

Notwithstanding that the earl of Tyrone had been received so graciously by the king, and was now settled down quietly as a loyal subject, yet he was regarded with suspicion and hatred by the officials and adventurers, who could not endure to see him restored to rank and favour. Those who had looked forward to the forfeiture of his estates and to the confiscation of Ulster were bitterly disappointed when they found themselves baulked of their expected prey, and they determined to bring about his ruin. He was now constantly subjected to annoyance and humiliation, and beset with spies, who reported the most trivial incidents of his everyday life. At the same time the earl of Tirconnell was persecuted much in the same manner.

At last matters reached a crisis. In 1607 a false report of a conspiracy for another rebellion was concocted and spread; and the two earls were assured by some friends that it was intended to arrest them. Tyrone was on a visit at Slane with the deputy, Sir Arthur Chichester, when he heard of the matter, and, keeping his mind to himself, he took leave of his host and went to Sir Garrett Moore of Mellifont, where he remained for a few days. On a Sunday morning, he and his attendants took horse for Dundalk. He knew that he was bidding his old friend farewell for the last time; and Sir Garrett, who suspected nothing, was surprised to observe that he was unusually moved, blessing each member of the household individually, and weeping bitterly at parting. He and his party rode on in haste till they reached Rathmullan on the western shore of Lough Swilly, where a ship awaited them. Here he was joined by the earl of Tirconnell and his family. The total number of exiles taking ship was about one hundred. At midnight on the 14th of September they embarked, and bidding farewell forever to their native country, they made for the open sea, and landed in France, where they were received with great distinction by all, from the king downwards. From France the earls and their families proceeded to Rome, where they took up their residence, being allowed ample pensions by the Pope and the king of Spain. O'Donnell died in the following year, 1608; and O'Neill, aged, blind, and worn by misfortune and disappointment, died in 1616.

Hugh O'Neill earl of Tyrone. In an old work in Italian, La Spada d'Orione stellata nel Cielo di Marte, *by Damaschino, published in Rome, 1680, is an engraving of Hugh O'Neil, with the inscription, "Ugo Conte di Tirone General Ibernese" ("Hugh Earl of Tyrone, General of the Irish"). This engraving has been photographed for me from a copy of the book in the British Museum: photograph reproduced here.*

The profound quiet that followed the rebellion was suddenly broken by the hasty and reckless rising of Sir Caher O'Doherty. This chief, then only twenty-one years of age, had hitherto been altogether on the side of the English; and his rebellion was a mere outburst of private revenge, having nothing noble or patriotic about it. On one occasion he had an altercation with Sir George Paulett, governor of Derry, who being a man of ill-temper, struck him in the face. O'Doherty, restraining himself for the time, retired and concerted his measures for vengeance. He invited his friend Captain Harte, the governor of Culmore Fort, to dinner. After dinner the governor was treacherously seized by O'Doherty's orders, and threatened with instant death if he did not surrender the fort. Harte firmly refused; but his wife, in her terror and despair, went to the fort and prevailed on the guards to open the gates; on which O'Doherty and his men rushed in and immediately took possession; and having supplied himself with artillery and ammunition from the fort, he marched on Derry that same night. He took it by surprise, slew Paulett, slaughtered the garrison, and sacked and burned the town. He was joined by several other chiefs, and held out from May to July, 1608, when he was shot dead near Kilmacrenan in a skirmish; on which the rising collapsed as suddenly as it had begun.

No. 1.   No. 2.

No. 3.   No. 4.   No. 5.   No. 6.

Groups showing, costumes A.D. 1600. From Map of Ireland (published 1611) by Speed, who thus designates the three pairs of figures:—1. "The Gentleman of Ireland"; 2. "The Gentle Woman of Ireland" (i.e. persons belonging to the high classes); 3. "The Civill Irish Woman"; 4. "The Civill Irish Man" (persons of the middle rank); 5. "The Wilde Irish Man"; 6. "The Wilde Irish Woman" (i.e. peasants, whom the English commonly designated "Wild Irish").

Composed from the Book of Kells.

CHAPTER XLII
THE PLANTATION OF ULSTER
A.D. 1603–1625.—James I.

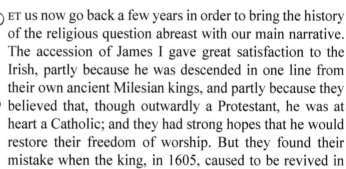

ET us now go back a few years in order to bring the history of the religious question abreast with our main narrative. The accession of James I gave great satisfaction to the Irish, partly because he was descended in one line from their own ancient Milesian kings, and partly because they believed that, though outwardly a Protestant, he was at heart a Catholic; and they had strong hopes that he would restore their freedom of worship. But they found their mistake when the king, in 1605, caused to be revived in Ireland two penal enactments, which during the late troubles had fallen very much into disuse:—those of Supremacy and Uniformity. By the Act of Supremacy, it will be remembered, no Catholic, without taking an oath that the king was spiritual head of the church, could hold any office under government, could practise as a lawyer, act as a magistrate, be appointed judge, or take possession of an estate to be held from the king; and as Catholics could not possibly take such an oath, they were excluded from all these offices wherever the act was enforced. By the Act of Uniformity any Catholic might be brought up and fined if he absented himself from Protestant worship on a Sunday; and in Dublin many of those who refused to attend—"Recusants" as they were called—were actually fined or imprisoned. But except in or near Dublin, it was impossible to carry out these laws, for the people were nearly all Catholics. And even in Dublin, the law, for the same reason, could not be enforced to any extent; and numbers of Catholic magistrates, lawyers, and government officers went on discharging their duties unmolested.

For a long time King James had intended, at the first opportunity, to colonise a large part of Ireland with Scotch and English settlers. He was not deterred by the terrible evils that all former attempts at plantation had brought on the country; and when it became known that the earls of Tyrone and Tirconnell had fled, he considered that the proper time had arrived for carrying out his favourite project. The earls had indeed committed no treasonable or unlawful act by leaving the country: nevertheless nearly all the fertile land of six counties—Donegal, Derry, Tyrone, Armagh, Fermanagh, and Cavan—amounting to more than half a million acres[1]— was confiscated to the crown and given to settlers. The person to whom the king entrusted the management of the whole plantation was the lord deputy, Sir Arthur Chichester.

A great part of the confiscated district was divided into lots of 2,000, 1,500, and 1,000 acres. The undertakers to whom the 2,000-acre lots were granted were all Scotch or English, who were required to people their land with Scotch and English tenants: but no Irish. Those who obtained the middle-sized lots were to be all Protestants who had been in the service of the crown in Ireland during the late wars—"servitors," as they were called; and they might take Scotch, English, or Irish tenants, but no Catholics. The 1,000-acre lots might be taken by English, Scotch, or Irish planters, who might be either Protestants or Catholics, and the Catholics were not required to take the oath of supremacy. Vast tracts were given to London companies of merchants or tradesmen, and to certain high officials; all of whom, both companies and individuals, were to plant their districts with English and Scotch Protestant settlers. Chichester had for his share the whole of Inishowen, Sir Cahir O'Doherty's territory. Large tracts were granted for religious and educational purposes, all Protestant: Trinity College, Dublin (which had been founded in 1592), getting 9,600 acres.

Of the whole body of old Irish proprietors, only 286 were provided for: these got 58,000 acres—about one-ninth of the escheated lands. All the rest of the natives were ordered "to depart with their goods and chattels at or before the first of May next [1609] into what other part of the realm they pleased." But, as Chichester well knew, there was really no other part of the realm for them to go to; for the people of other districts would naturally resist the encroachment of strangers. Moreover, it was found impossible to carry out the order for the removal of the whole body of the natives; and numbers remained among the new settlers as mere labourers or tenants of small plots of land. As for the rest, the greater number, instead of migrating to a distance, clung to their native place, and betook them to the hills, glens, and bogs, where they eked out a scanty subsistence, with bitter feelings in their hearts.

---

[1]About three quarters of a million English acres. There were bog and waste land besides: the total area of these six counties is about 3¾ millions of English acres; so that the waste land was then four times the extent of the arable land.

This turned out the most successful of all the plantations; and in a short time vast numbers of English Protestants and Scotch Presbyterians were settled on the rich lowland farms all over the confiscated counties. There was no resistance of any consequence this time: the native people, crushed and dispirited after the calamities of the late rebellion, seem to have submitted to their fate in sullen despair. But the fighting came later on, and in a very dreadful form; for this plantation was one of the main causes of the Great Rebellion of 1641.

Settlers' Houses on a Survey Map of London Company of Drapers made in 1622. From Gilbert's "Fac-Sim. Nat. MSS."

To help to pay the expenses of the plantation, the king created the order of "baronets"; who were to bear on their coat of arms the "bloody hand," the badge of the O'Neills, Each new baronet had his title on condition that he maintained thirty soldiers for three years, at 8*d.* a day each—about £1095 altogether, which represents something like £10,000 of our present money. As the title was to be hereditary, *i.e.* was to descend from father to son, it was eagerly sought after: but at that time there was little honour in it; for it was merely sold for money.

The lord deputy now resolved to summon a parliament, the first held for many years: and in order to enable him to pass measures pleasing to the king, he took steps to have a Protestant majority, by creating forty spurious "boroughs," nearly all among the settlers of Ulster; little hamlets with only a few inhabitants, which really did not deserve to be specially represented in parliament: each to return two members. There were many violent scenes in this parliament; for the Catholics, though in a minority, struggled hard, and not altogether unsuccessfully, for their rights. Large sums were voted for the king, who was always in want of money: and some old penal statutes against natives of Irish blood were repealed. English law was extended to the whole of Ireland, a concession the Irish had often previously asked for in vain, and for which James I should get full credit.

King James continued his plantations in other parts of the country; but instead of turning off the people openly as in Ulster, he adopted a more cunning plan: he sent persons to examine the titles of estates. These managed to find flaws, or pretended flaws, in almost all the titles they examined. If cases came to trial, witnesses and jurors were illegally forced to give evidence and verdicts in favour of the king; on which the owners were either turned out, or had to pay the king large sums to be let remain. And the country swarmed with persons called "Discoverers," who gave information of any titles that could be made out faulty; and who, in reward for their crooked proceedings, got, either the estates, or part of the money paid by the owners to buy themselves off. In consequence of these iniquitous law proceedings, there were several minor plantations in different parts of the country, especially in Leinster; and great numbers of industrious comfortable people were driven away from their homes and reduced to beggary. The whole country was in a miserable state of uncertainty; and no man was sure of his property for a day.

Chapter XLIII
Strafford
A.D. 1625–1640.—Charles I.

ARLY in the year 1625, in the midst of all the inquietude caused by the dishonest proceedings related at the end of the last chapter, King James died, and was succeeded by his son Charles I. This king was in perpetual straits for money; and the Irish Catholics hoped that by granting him subsidies he would have the penal laws relaxed. The Protestants also had their troubles, for many of them, like the Catholics, were threatened with the loss of their estates through the knaveries of the discoverers.

Accordingly in this same year (1625) the Irish gentry, Catholic and Protestant, encouraged by Falkland, the lord deputy, offered to pay £120,000 (nearly a million of our day) in instalments to the king, who agreed to grant certain concessions or "Graces" as they were called. There were altogether fifty-one Graces, of which the two most important were, that land owners should be reasonably secured in their estates (which affected Catholics and Protestants alike), and that the Catholics should not be molested on account of their religion. But the king, once he had the money, broke his promise, and dishonestly withheld the Graces: the land titles were not confirmed, and the laws were put in force against the Catholics, who suffered bitterly for a time.

In 1633 the king sent over as deputy, Lord Wentworth, afterwards the earl of Strafford, the most despotic ruler the Irish had yet experienced. He adopted a new course; for he did not follow up the attempt to suppress the Catholic religion: this he reserved for another opportunity. His two main objects were to make the king absolute master in Ireland, and to raise money for him; which he pursued through right and wrong, trampling on all that crossed him, Protestants and Catholics alike. The recusants were induced to give him £20,000 for the king, on promise that the penal statutes against them should not be enforced; and the landholders prevailed on him to summon a parliament with the object of having the Graces confirmed—for they could not be carried out without the sanction of parliament—paying at the same time another year's subsidy. Accordingly, parliament met and passed subsidies for the king, amounting to £240,000; but Wentworth, partly by bullying and partly by trickery, succeeded in evading the Graces.

The motive of all this soon appeared: for in the following year he proceeded to break the titles all over Connaught, on the pretence that they had not been completed according to law; so that he confiscated nearly the whole province. There was a regular trial for each case; and he obtained verdicts in all, for the good reason that he threatened, punished, and imprisoned sheriffs, juries, and lawyers who thwarted him—Catholics and Protestants without distinction. This caused a great outcry; but he persisted in his outrageous and reckless course, though admonished by his friends, who saw dark clouds ahead. There was no use in appealing against this intolerable tyranny; for his master the king, who was pursuing much the same course in England, supported him in everything. By similar iniquitous proceedings he confiscated the whole of Clare and a large part of Tipperary. One main object he accomplished all through; for out of every transaction he made money for the king. But though Connaught was confiscated it was not planted: Wentworth feared that any attempt to do so would raise a rebellion: and the king's position in England was now so precarious that it was thought better to postpone the plantation to some more favourable time: a time which never came for either Wentworth or the king.

At this period there was a flourishing Irish trade in wool and woollen cloths; but Wentworth adopted measures that almost destroyed it, lest it should interfere with the woollen trade of England. On the other hand he took means to create a linen trade, which could do no harm in England; and he thus laid the foundation of what has turned out a great and flourishing industry in Ulster.

Summoning a parliament in 1639, he managed to obtain another supply for King Charles, who was every day getting himself more deeply in conflict with his own parliament in England. But with all his tyranny and evil deeds Wentworth enforced order, and kept down petty tyrants; so that there was an increase of commerce and of general prosperity during his rule. He was now made earl of Strafford; and he raised an army of 9,000 men in Ireland, nearly all Catholics, who were well drilled and well armed, intending them to be employed in the service of the king. But his career was drawing to a close. He was recalled in 1640 to take command against the Scotch Covenanters. Soon afterwards he was impeached by the English house of commons, some of the most damaging charges against him coming from Ireland; and in May, 1641, he was beheaded on Tower Hill.

Chapter XLIV
The Rebellion of 1641
A.D. 1641.—Charles I.

HIS great and disastrous rebellion was brought about by the measures taken to extirpate the Catholic religion, and by the plantations, beginning with that of Ulster. The religious hardships of the Catholics were increasing year by year. The plantations went steadily on with hardly any intermission, and it was well known that Wentworth's tyrannical proceedings had the full approval of the king; so that it seemed plain to the Irish that it was the settled purpose of King Charles and his advisers to root out the whole native population in order to make room for new settlers. Besides all this, the country swarmed with persons wandering hopelessly about in abject poverty, who had been driven from their homes, all of whom longed for the first opportunity to fall on the settlers and regain their homesteads and farms. As to obtaining redress by peaceable means, no one now thought this possible after the experience of the Graces.

At last some of the old Irish chiefs and gentry held meetings and came to the determination to obtain their rights by insurrection. The leading spirit was Roger or Rory O'Moore of Leix, a man of great influence and unblemished character; and among many others were Sir Phelim O'Neill of the family of Tyrone, Lord Maguire of Fermanagh, Magennis of Iveagh, O'Reilly of Brefney, and the Mac Mahons of Oriell.

They hoped for help from abroad; for many of their exiled kindred had by this time risen to positions of great influence in France, Spain, and the Netherlands; and they sent to Owen Roe O'Neill, a soldier who had greatly distinguished himself in the service of Spain, nephew of the great Hugh O'Neill earl of Tyrone, inviting him home to lead the insurgent army. He replied urging an immediate rising and holding out expectations of help from France.

The 23rd of October was the day fixed on for a simultaneous rising. Dublin Castle with its large store of arms, and many of the fortresses and garrisons all over the country, were to be seized, and the arms taken. Instructions were given to make the gentry prisoners, but to kill or injure no one except in open conflict; and in general to have as little bloodshed as possible. The Ulster settlers from Scotland, being regarded as kinsmen, were not to be molested. On the evening of the 22nd of October, when the preparations had been completed in Dublin, a man named Owen O'Connolly, to whom Mac Mahon had confided the secret, went to Sir William Parsons, one of the lords justices, and told him of the plot. Parsons at first gave no heed to the story, for he perceived that O'Connolly was half drunk. But on consultation with his colleague Sir John Borlase, they arrested Maguire and Mac Mahon on the morning of the 23rd: these were subsequently tried in London and hanged. Rory O'Moore and some others then in Dublin escaped. Instant measures were taken to put the city in a state of defence.

But though Dublin was saved, the rising broke out on the 23rd all through the north. Sir Phelim O'Neill, by a treacherous stratagem, obtained possession of Charlemont fort; and the rebels took Newry, Dungannon, Castleblayney, and many smaller stations. Sir Phelim exhibited a forged commission giving him authority, which he alleged he had received from King Charles, to which was fraudulently attached the great seal he had found in one of the castles.

At the end of a week nearly all Ulster was in the hands of the rebels, and Sir Phelim had an army of 30,000 men, armed with knives, pitchforks, scythes, and every weapon they could procure. During this week the original orders of the leaders were carried out, and there was hardly any bloodshed. But Sir Phelim, who had none of the great qualities of his illustrious kinsmen, was a bad general, and soon lost all control over his irregular army. Many of those who had risen up were persons that had been deprived of their lands, who after a time broke loose from all discipline, and wreaked their vengeance without restraint and without mercy on the settlers. The country farmhouses all over the settlements were attacked by detached parties, under no orders and checked by no discipline. Multitudes were stripped and turned out half naked from house and home—old and young, men, women, and children; and hundreds, vainly trying to make their way to Dublin, or to other Government stations, perished by the wayside, of exposure, hardship, and hunger. But there was even worse: for numbers were murdered, often with great cruelty. Some of these excesses were carried out by the orders of O'Neill himself; but the greatest number were the acts of irresponsible persons taking vengeance for their own private wrongs. The outrages actually committed were bad enough; but the daily reports that reached England magnified them tenfold, and excited the utmost horror among the English people.

Charlemont Fort. From illustration in Kilkenny Archaeological Journal, *1883–4. p. 320: and this from a photograph.*

During this terrible outbreak of fury, many Protestants were protected by individual Catholics. The priests exerted themselves to save life, often at great personal risk, sometimes hiding the poor fugitives under the very altar cloths. The Protestant bishop of Kilmore, Dr. Bedell, who was very popular, was not molested; and many fugitive settlers had a safe asylum in his house. The people at last confined him in Cloghoughter Castle, merely to protect him; and on his death in February 1642, they attended his funeral in crowds, including a large military force sent by the Irish commanders, as a mark of respect and regret.

The numbers of victims have been by some writers enormously exaggerated: but Dr. Warner, an English writer, a Protestant clergyman, who made every effort to come at the truth, believes that in the first two years of the rebellion, 4,000 were murdered, and that 8,000 died of ill usage and exposure. Even this estimate is probably in excess.

The sanguinary Ulster episode of this memorable year reminds us of what took place on a much larger scale forty years before. One was an unpremeditated outburst of merciless popular rage, resulting in great suffering and loss of life: the other the slower and surer destruction of much larger numbers, by the cool and carefully planned arrangements of Mountjoy.

But we must not suppose that outrages were confined to the rebels. There were wholesale murders also on the other side; and the numbers of the Irish that were killed all over the country in places where there had been no rising, far exceeded those of the settlers that had fallen victims in Ulster. In November, the Scottish garrison of Carrickfergus sallied out and slaughtered a great number of harmless people in Island Magee, where there had been no disturbance of any kind. The two lords justices sent parties of military from Dublin through the country all round, who massacred all the people they met, whether engaged in rebellion or not. Their general, Sir Charles Coote, committed horrible cruelties, especially in Wicklow, surpassing the worst excesses of the rebels, killing and torturing women and infants, as well as men. In Munster, Sir William St. Leger slaughtered vast numbers of innocent persons, in order, as he said, to avenge the cruelties committed in Ulster, and forced the people of the province, the Anglo-Irish as well as the old Irish native race, to rise in rebellion, much against their will.

Towards the end of the year, the old Anglo-Irish nobility and gentry of the Pale, who were all Catholics and all thoroughly loyal, were treated by the two lords justices, Parsons and Borlase, with brutal harshness, merely because they were Catholics. He insulted them in every possible way, and Coote burned many of their houses: so that they were forced to combine for their own protection; and at last they were driven to join the ranks of the insurgents. There could not have been more unfit men at the head of affairs in this critical time than these lords justices; and their conduct is condemned by historians of all shades of opinion. In spite of the remonstrances of their best counsellors they acted in such a manner as to spread the trouble instead of allaying it; so that in a short time the rebellion had extended through all Ireland.

Composed from the Book of Kells.

CHAPTER XLV
THE CONFEDERATION OF KILKENNY:
THE BATTLE OF BENBURB
A.D. 1642–1649.—Charles I.

T the opening of 1642, there were in the distracted country four distinct parties, each with an army:—First: The Old Irish, whose leader was Rory O'Moore. These were oppressed by plantations and by religious hardships, and they aimed at total separation from England. Their army was chiefly confined to Ulster.

Second: The Old Anglo-Irish Catholics, nearly all of the middle and south of Ireland. These suffered on account of their religion as much as the old Irish; and also by the plantations, though not to the same extent; and they wanted religious and civil liberty, but not separation from England. These two parties represented all the Catholics of Ireland: but there was much jealousy and distrust between them; and this disunion ruined their cause in the end.

Third: The Puritans, including the Presbyterians and Scots of Ulster, under General Monro. At this time King Charles I was getting deeper and deeper into trouble with the parliament in England; and of all the Parliamentarians, his most determined and successful enemies were the Covenanters of Scotland. Monro and his army worked in harmony with the Covenanters: and as they were very hostile to Catholics and the Catholic religion, they were the special opponents of the old Irish party, with whom they constantly came into collision in Ulster.

Fourth: The Royalist party, who held Dublin. These were chiefly Protestants of the Established Church, who were opposed to the Parliamentarians. They were the party of the king; and they wished to make it appear that the Catholics were rebels against him.

The war went on during the early part of this year with varying fortunes; sometimes the rebels were victorious, sometimes the Government forces.

In Ulster the rebels were losing ground, and losing heart, chiefly through the incompetency of Sir Phelim O'Neill, who had no military knowledge or experience. The Scottish army there soon amounted to 20,000 men under Monro, who plundered and spoiled the province with little check.

Owen Roe O'Neill landed in Donegal in July 1642, with a single ship and a hundred officers, and taking command of the old Irish army in place of Sir Phelim, immediately set about organising the scattered Irish forces. He soon changed the whole aspect of affairs. He strongly denounced the past cruelties, severely punished the offenders, so far as he was able to reach them, and set free the Protestant prisoners, whom he caused to be escorted to a place of safety. Soon afterwards another important leader landed on the Wexford coast to join the Catholic party, Colonel Preston, brother of Lord Gormanstown, with 500 officers and some stores. He had distinguished himself in the wars on the Continent; and he now took command of the Anglo-Irish Catholic army.

Owen Roe O'Neill. From engraving in Ulster Journal of Archaeology, *iv., p. 25: and that from an original painting by Van Brugens.*

The two branches of the Catholics had hitherto acted independently of one another, each struggling for much the same cause, but without any unity of plan. But a great effort was now made by the Catholic bishops and other dignitaries to bring these two parties to act in concert: and in accordance with their arrangements a general assembly or parliament of the most distinguished men of both sections, consisting of eleven bishops, fourteen lay lords, and 226 commoners, met in Kilkenny on the 24th October. This is known as the "Confederation of Kilkenny." The Royalist party of Dublin represented them as in rebellion: but the Confederate leaders earnestly denied that they were rebels, and proclaimed themselves loyal subjects, standing up for the king, who, they said, would do them justice if the Puritans would only let him act freely. The assembly, having first proclaimed their loyalty to the king, took upon themselves for the time the government of the country, or of that part of it outside the influence of the lords justices, and appointed generals over the army: O'Neill for Ulster, Preston for Leinster, and two others for Munster and Connaught. To manage affairs with greater facility they elected from their number a "Supreme Council" of twenty-four, six from each province. And they issued a decree for raising and coining money, and for levying men, who were to be drilled by the officers that had come with O'Neill and Preston. For some time after this the two Catholic parties worked in union; and Owen Roe O'Neill with the Old Irish carried on the war in Ulster against Monro, and Preston with the Anglo-Irish Catholics in Leinster against the Royalists.

The king was most anxious to come to terms with the Confederates as a help against the English and Scotch Parliamentarians; and as his two lords justices, Borlase and Parsons, had by underhand practices prevented an agreement, he removed Borlase and appointed James Butler, marquis (afterwards duke) of Ormond, lord lieutenant, with full power to offer satisfactory terms to the Confederates. But Ormond was only half-hearted in the business; so the proceedings still dragged on: and besides this, the king was a double-dealer, ready to promise anything, but intending to perform as little as possible. When accused by the Parliamentarians of offering favourable terms to the Roman Catholics, he openly denied that he had done any such thing. He was in fact trying to deceive both parties, Catholics and Parliamentarians.

With the object of more closely uniting the Old Irish and Old English to defend the Catholic religion and to sustain the king against the Parliamentarians, the Pope sent to the Confederates, as nuncio, Archbishop Baptist Rinuccini, who brought them a supply of money and arms. But this encouragement was much more than counterbalanced by the ever-increasing fatal division in the Confederation. The bishops and those who represented the Old Irish party were for carrying on the war vigorously, and on their side were Rinuccini and O'Neill. On the other hand the Anglo-Irish party, chiefly consisting of the lay element, who had the majority in the assembly, were for treating with the Royalists; and following out this line of policy, they held back military operations and wasted time in fruitless negotiations. To make matters worse there was bitter rivalry between the two generals: Preston hated O'Neill, and O'Neill took no pains to conceal his contempt for Preston. The Anglo-Irish party, through mere jealousy of O'Neill, the only great soldier now in Ireland, refused to support him with the necessary supplies, so that for a long time he was unable to make head against Monro in the north. Though struggling against these great difficulties, he at last succeeded, partly by means of the money supplied by the nuncio, in collecting an army of 5,000 foot and 500 horse; which he kept stationed on the borders of Cavan. Meantime Monro, aware that Leinster was at this time almost unprotected—for Preston with his army was in Connaught—made preparations to march southwards to Kilkenny to annihilate the small Confederate force left there, and suppress the Confederation itself. When O'Neill received intelligence of this, he broke up camp and marched north in the beginning of June, determined to intercept him, and if possible, to draw him into battle. Monro had set out from Carrickfergus with 6,000 foot and 800 horse: and hearing, on arriving near Armagh, of O'Neill's movement, he turned aside from his course in order to crush the Irish army; and he sent word to Coleraine to his brother George Monro to meet him at Glasslough in Monaghan with a reinforcement of cavalry. For he had been warned to beware of O'Neill's consummate generalship; and he was unwilling to meet him except with very superior numbers. But O'Neill had been too quick for him. He arrived at Glasslough before the brothers had time to join; and crossing the Blackwater into Tyrone, he encamped at Benburb. Next morning, the 5th June, having first sent two regiments north under Bernard Mac Mahon and Patrick Mac Neny to intercept George Monro, he selected at his leisure an excellent position for battle on the Blackwater, between two small hills, with a wood in the rear. He made seven divisions of his army, placing four in front with wide spaces between, and three behind, so that they could at any time step into the spaces. The ranks faced south-east: and in this position he awaited the approach of the Scottish army.

Early on that same morning Monro marched from Armagh towards Benburb; but finding the ford, now crossed by Battleford Bridge, strongly guarded, he turned south-west, and crossing at Kinard (now Cale-don) without any opposition, he advanced along the river towards the Irish army. O'Neill sent forward a detachment under Colonel Richard O'Farrell to oppose the advancing columns in a narrow defile; but they had to retreat before the Scottish artillery. Having arrived on the ground, Monro arranged his army in nine divisions, five in front and four behind; but

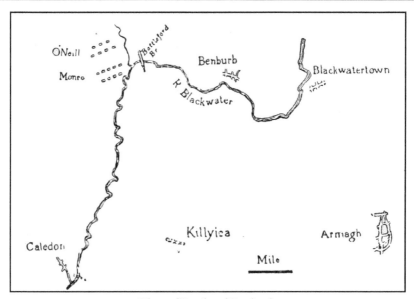

Plan of Battle of Benburb.

the spaces in front were too narrow to permit the rear divisions to come forward. The two armies now stood face to face; but O'Neill, knowing that his opponents were already wearied after their long morning's march, skilfully wasted the day in light skirmishes till late in the evening, when the sun had come round and shone full in the faces of the Scottish army. While the skirmishing was still going on, and growing every moment more hot, a large body of men were seen in the distance approaching from the north, whom Monro took to be his brother's reinforcements; but they were in reality Mac Mahon's and Mac Neny's regiments, returning after having scattered George Monro's party. When at last they were seen to join the Irish army, Monro became alarmed and prepared to retreat. But O'Neill seized the moment for a general assault. He first moved forward the three rear divisions, so as to form one continuous line. When all was ready, he was seen to pause for a moment and raise his hat, while his lips moved. Then issuing his orders, the whole army started forward and charged with sword and pike. Twice did Monro attempt to stop the advance by hurling against the ranks squadrons of cavalry, which in both cases were driven back among his footmen. He ordered forward his four rear detachments to support the front divisions; but there was not sufficient room for this movement, so that the ranks became closely packed; and this, with the commingling and furious prancing of the retreating cavalry, caused great disorder. In the midst of all this confusion, while the sun glared full in the faces of the Scots, down on them came O'Neill's well-arranged solid

199

battalions. At once they gave way before this terrible onset, and, turning round, rushed back in utter rout. But right in their way flowed the river, deep and rapid; and, besides those slain in fight, vast numbers were drowned in attempting to cross, so that the survivors were able to pass over the bodies lying in the water. Monro himself escaped and fled in panic, bareheaded, leaving on the field his cloak, helmet, and wig. Upwards of 2000 of his army fell, while the Irish lost only seventy.

This great victory of O'Neill, which was quite as brilliant as that of his uncle at the Yellow Ford, forty-eight years before, restored for a time the influence of the Old Irish party in the Confederation.

It became known to the Confederates that Ormond had been holding correspondence with the Parliamentarians; and fearing lest Dublin might be betrayed, they ordered O'Neill and Preston to combine their forces and attempt its capture—a thing that might have been easily accomplished; for, though Ormond had been making some hasty preparations, the defences were very weak. The two armies had arrived within a few miles of the city; but there was delay, owing mainly to the obstruction of Preston, who, following up the spirit of the Confederate majority, proposed to treat with Ormond instead of attacking the city at once. During this period of hesitation and suspicion, a trifling alarm occurred, on which both armies broke up camp and marched away. The end of the matter was that Ormond delivered up Dublin to the Parliamentarians and went to France. Soon afterwards—in August of this year—Preston was disastrously defeated by Colonel Jones, the Parliamentarian governor of Dublin, between "Lynch's Knock" and Dangan, near Summerhill in Meath, with a loss of more than 5,000 men; and in the same year (1647) Lord Inchiquin, formerly a Royalist but now on the side of the Parliament—who is known as Murrogh the Burner from his merciless ravages in Munster—inflicted quite as bad a defeat on the Confederate army at Knocknanuss near Mallow, owing to the incapacity of their commander Lord Taaffe.

After more than a year's absence Ormond returned and having resumed his place as head of the Protestant Royalists, he finally made peace with the Confederates, agreeing to their main condition that the laws against Catholics should be repealed; and it was also stipulated that both the Confederates and Ormond's forces should combine and act in support of the king. Thus came to a termination a seven years' war between the Confederates and the Royalists. But all this was too late. Dublin had been given up, and was now in the hands of the Parliamentarians; and about a fortnight after the peace had been signed, King Charles was beheaded. In the same year (1649) the Nuncio, finding his mission a failure, returned to Rome.

The death of the king caused a counter-movement in Ireland, and many abandoned the Parliamentary side. The Royalist cause was now favoured, as against the English Parliamentarians, by nearly all the Irish parties, including Ormond, the Confederates, and the Scots and Presbyterians of Ulster; and they proclaimed the Prince of Wales king as Charles II. On the side of the Parliament, Jones still held Dublin, and Sir Charles Coote, Derry. Inchiquin—now again turned royalist—took from them Drogheda, Dundalk, Newry, and Trim: and Ormond, with a view of following up Inchiquin's successes, besieged Dublin to recover what he had so easily given up two years before. He encamped at Rathmines, but took steps to move his encampment towards the mouth of the Liffey, in order to stop supplies coming by sea to the city. With this object he ordered Major-General Purcell to fortify the old castle of Bagot Rath, not far from the river mouth, standing on a site then in the open country, but now occupied by a part of Upper Baggot Street. But before the work had been even begun, Jones sallied forth in the night of the 2nd August, and surprised, not only Purcell but Ormond himself, and utterly routed the whole army. This great disaster, which was due to the dilatoriness of Purcell and the bad generalship of Ormond, almost ruined the Royalist cause in Ireland.

CHAPTER XLVI

OLIVER CROMWELL
A.D. 1649–1660.—The Commonwealth (1649 to 1660).

ENGLAND, the Parliamentarians, headed by Cromwell, were now triumphant, while the great majority of the Irish stood up for King Charles II. There was a small party of Parliamentarians in Ireland too, who held Dublin, Derry, and a few other important places; and in order to finally crush the Royalists it became necessary to reduce Ireland. With this object, Oliver Cromwell, as the best and most influential of the Parliamentarian generals, was appointed lord lieutenant and commander of the forces in Ireland, and landed at Dublin on the 14th August, with 9,000 foot, 4,000 horse, a supply of military stores, and £20,000 in money, accompanied by his son-in-law Ireton as second in command. Before commencing his military operations, he issued a proclamation against plunder and excesses of every kind, ordering that all supplies taken from the natives should be paid for. He first proceeded against Drogheda, which had been garrisoned by Ormond with 3,000 troops, chiefly English, under Sir Arthur Ashton. The walls were battered with cannon for two days till a sufficient breach was made, when the order was given to storm. Two desperate attempts to enter were repulsed; but the third succeeded; and immediately, on Cromwell's order, a general massacre was commenced, which lasted for several days; and Ashton and his garrison, with great numbers of the townspeople were killed. About thirty of the garrison who had escaped the massacre were shipped off to Barbados as slaves. After this, Trim, Dundalk, Carlingford, Newry, and several other places in the North, surrendered.

Cromwell returned to Dublin, and marching south, appeared before Wexford, which was well fortified and garrisoned with 3,000 men, under the command of David Sinnott. He began his cannonade on the 11th of October, and when some breaches had been made, Sinnott asked for a parley. But meantime Captain Stafford, the commander of the strong castle just outside the walls, treacherously delivered it up to Cromwell's troops; which enabled a party of the besiegers to get into the town and open the gates. The garrison, finding they were betrayed, retreated to the market-place, where they found the townspeople congregated. Here they defended themselves in desperation for an hour, but were overpowered by numbers; and Cromwell's soldiers, under his orders, killed garrison and townspeople without distinction, to the number of 2,000. The fate of Drogheda and Wexford struck the Irish with terror; Cork and many other southern towns now yielded on mere summons; and Cromwell rested his troops for a month in mid-winter at Youghal.

In the midst of all this havoc and clash of war, Owen Roe O'Neill, the only commander in Ireland that seemed a match for the great parliamentary general, was struck down by sickness on his way southward to join Ormond, and died at Cloghoughter Castle in Cavan on 6th November 1649; and with him passed away the chief hope of the Royalist party.

At the end of January Cromwell set out to traverse Munster. Most towns he came to were given up; and where there was serious resistance he usually put the garrison to the sword. At Clonmel, which was held by Hugh O'Neill, Owen Roe's nephew, he met with the most determined resistance he had yet experienced. For a long time all efforts to take the town wore foiled; and after a final assault in the month of May, he had to withdraw with a loss of 2,500 of his men. But O'Neill, having exhausted his ammunition, quietly withdrew in the night with his army to Waterford, and as Cromwell was not aware of this movement, the town was able to obtain favourable terms on surrender.

In the north his generals, Colonel Venables and Sir Charles Coote—son of Sir Charles Coote of Wicklow notoriety—were also very successful, capturing town after town; and by May the Parliamentarians had possession of the greater number of the fortresses of both North and South. On the surrender of Clonmel, Cromwell, seeing the country virtually subdued, sailed for England on the 29th May, after a stay of nine months, leaving Ireton to finish the war. At the very time that the Confederates were thus loyally fighting and suffering for Charles, this young king, who was then in Scotland, repudiated any agreement with the Irish, in order that he might gain the favour of the Scots, and declared himself against allowing them liberty to practise their religion.

Signet of Owen Roe O'Neill (from Kilkenny Archaeological Journal, *1858–9, p. 38); and signature, five days before his death (Gilbert's "Fac-Sim. Nat. MSS."). The signature plainly shows the hand of death.*

Ireton now turned his attention to Limerick, the most important place in possession of the Royalists, which was commanded by Hugh O'Neill, the defender of Clonmel. By forcing the passage of the Shannon at O'Brien's Bridge, he got at the Clare side of the city, which was now invested on both sides. O'Neill defended the place with great obstinacy; but there was disunion, and he was not supported by the magistrates; and besides, the plague was raging among the citizens. At length Colonel Fennell, encouraged by some of the officers of the corporation, betrayed his trust by opening St. John's Gate to Ireton, who took possession of the city on the 27th of October. The garrison of 2,500 laid down their arms and were allowed to march away unmolested. Ireton caused several of the prominent defenders to be executed, among them Dr. O'Brien, Catholic bishop of Emly; but he himself died of the plague within a month. The traitor Fennell was hanged with the others, though for a different reason. After Ireton's death, Lieutenant-General Edmund Ludlow taking command, marched to the aid of Coote at Galway, which surrendered on the 12th May, after a siege of nine months; and the capture of a few detached castles completed the conquest of Ireland by the Parliamentarians.

St. John's Gate: copied from a photograph.

Charles Fleetwood, who was Cromwell's son-in-law—having married Ireton's widow—took command of the army, and was afterwards appointed lord deputy. Under his direction a High Court of Justice was instituted in October, to punish those who had been concerned in the rising of 1641; about 200 were sentenced and hanged, and among them Sir Phelim O'Neill. On the very scaffold he was offered pardon if he only asserted that the forged commission he exhibited eleven years before had been really given him by King Charles, which would be a sort of justification for the king's execution; but he resolutely refused, and died with fortitude and Christian penitence.

The war was now—1652—ended: but for a long time there had been a terrible pestilence raging all over the country, which still continued. Famine came to help the work of destruction; and for two or three years these two scourges spread death and desolation and misery everywhere. But worse than even all this was to come. Cromwell's soldiers were to be paid by grants of confiscated estates when the country should be conquered. The English parliament now professed to consider the whole of Ireland forfeited; and that therefore they might do as they pleased with land and people. In August 1652, the Parliament passed an act to dispose of the Irish. The poorer sort of people of the three provinces of Ulster,

Leinster, and Munster—ploughmen, tradesmen, labourers, &c.—were not to be disturbed; for the settlers would need them as mere working men. All above these, the gentry of every class, whether Anglo-Irish or of old native blood, were ordered to transplant themselves and their families across the Shannon into Connaught and Clare, where they were to be given small allotments of lands that had been left waste. The same edict, though mainly directed against Catholics, was not exclusively confined to them. Many Protestants who had fought against the parliament were included in the proscription. The Presbyterians of Down and Antrim did not escape scathless, for they had shown some loyalty to the king. They were to transplant themselves, not to Connaught, but to the hilly parts of Leinster, where poor little plots of land were assigned to them.

The Catholic Irish were to move to the West by the 1st May 1654; and any of those ordered away—young or old—men or women—found in any of the three provinces after that date, might be killed by whoever met them. Moreover, they were not permitted to live within four miles of the sea or of any town, or within two miles of the Shannon.

Those who were forced to undertake this terrible migration were mostly families accustomed to a life of easy comfort. It so happened that the move had to be made chiefly in winter, and the season was unusually wet and severe. The roads were so bad as to be almost impassable, for people had something else to do in those times besides attending to roads; and as the miserable crowds trudged along, hundreds of women, children, and feeble persons perished of want and hardship.

But great numbers of the younger men, instead of migrating, formed themselves into bands to be avenged on the new settlers, like the expelled natives of Queen Mary's time. These "Tories" and "Rapparees," as they were called, gave great trouble, plundering and killing at every opportunity: they were hunted down by the settlers, and neither gave nor received quarter. This terrible war went on for many years till the Tories were in great measure exterminated.

The Irish soldiers who had fought against the Parliament were allowed to enlist in foreign countries; and 34,000 of them emigrated and entered the service of France, Spain, Austria, and Venice. There were widows and orphans everywhere, and a terrible fate awaited these: they were hunted down and brought forth from their hiding places, and large numbers of them, and many men also, were sent to the West Indian Islands to be sold as slaves.

A new survey of the country was made, and the lands were distributed to Cromwell's solders and to those who had advanced money to carry on the war. This vast exodus of the native population went on from 1652 to

1654. But it was found impossible to clear the gentry completely out of the land. Many settled in wild places; many were taken as under-tenants on their own lands; and in course of time many intermarried with the new settlers. The laws against the Catholic religion and against Catholic priests were now put in force with unsparing severity. But the priests remained among their flocks, hiding in wild places and under various disguises; and the Catholic religion was practised as earnestly and as generally as ever.

This dreadful Cromwellian episode must be taken as proceeding, not from the English government or the English people, but from the will of one man, who then ruled as despotically in England as in Ireland, though not with such cruelty.

CHAPTER XLVII
IRELAND AFTER THE RESTORATION
A.D. 1660–1688. Charles II (to 1685).
James II (1685–1688).

HARLES THE SECOND'S Restoration (A.D. 1660) pleased the Roman Catholics very much; for as they had fought and suffered for his father and for himself, they naturally expected to be reinstated, at least to a reasonable extent, in their lands, from which they had been expelled only six or seven years previously. Without any great difficulty, he could have repaired much of the injustice done to the old inhabitants while inflicting no very serious hardship on the new. But the faithless king, while rewarding several leading persons who had been his bitterest enemies, gave himself little concern about those who had befriended him in his time of need, either in England or in Ireland; and the Catholics received a scant measure of justice. The Irish parliament, having considered the claims of the old and of the new proprietors, passed what is called the Act of Settlement (A.D. 1661), which gave the new settlers, as a body, a title to their holdings. But those of the dispossessed Catholic owners who could prove that they were innocent of any connexion with the rising of 1641 were to be restored. The term "Nocent" was used to designate those who had been involved in the rebellion: "Innocent," those who proved themselves free of it. Any of the settlers whom this new arrangement displaced were to be "reprised" by getting land elsewhere.

To try these numerous cases a "Court of Claims" was established. But before this court had been long at work, it was found that almost all who came before it to be tried were able to prove themselves "Innocent"—a result quite unexpected; so that the settlers became greatly alarmed, and many threatened to rise in rebellion. Through their influence a stop was put to the proceedings, and a new act was passed, known as the "Act of Explanation" (1665), under which the settlers agreed to give up one-third of their possessions. But this did not afford nearly enough for all those who were able to make good their claim to be restored, and for those of the settlers who were to be reprised: and to make matters worse, the king gave immense grants to his relatives and to other favoured persons having no claim of any kind, which greatly lessened the available land.

After much wrangling, lasting over some years, matters were adjusted; and it came to this, that whereas before the Settlement the Catholics possessed two-thirds of all the arable land (the remaining third being held by Protestants of the plantation times of Elizabeth and James), after the time of this final arrangement they had only one-third, while two-thirds remained with the Protestants. There remained a large proportion of the Catholics who were not restored; most of them dispossessed persons whose cases were not heard at all, on account of the stoppage of the Court of Claims. Numbers of these held on in their poor homes in Connaught; and some, having no implements or stock or capital to start them in their new life, sank into hopeless poverty and perished of privation. It was quite usual to see, all over the country, gentlemen, only recently the possessors of large estates, going about, ragged, barefoot, and hungry, begging for food. As to the new settlers and their children, the majority, like those of earlier times, became gradually absorbed by intermarriage among the natives, and in half a century had to a great extent adopted their language, religion, and habits.

At the time of the Restoration the population of Ireland was about 1,100,000; of whom 800,000 were Roman Catholics—including the old English who were nearly all Catholics; 100,000 were Protestants of the Established Church; and 200,000 Non-conforming Protestants,[1] of whom one-half (100,000) were Presbyterians. All sections of Protestants were alike hostile to the Roman Catholics. During the Parliamentary sway the Non-conformists had the upper hand, and the Established Church was repressed, and its clergy removed, though beyond this neither clergy nor

---

[1] Non-conformists, as the term is generally applied, are those Protestants who do not conform to the doctrine, worship, or government of the Protestant Episcopal Church: such as Presbyterians, Methodists, &c. They have their own forms of worship, their own clergy, and their own churches.

people suffered much; while still stronger measures, as we have seen, were taken against the Roman Catholics. One of the first acts of Charles II was to restore the Established Church in Ireland; and the bishops and ministers returned to their dioceses and parishes, all being provided with good incomes. But as the lay members of this church were so few, most ministers had very small flocks, and very many none at all. This restoration of the church was bitterly resented by the Non-conformists, who greatly disliked government by bishops.

After this, the Act of Uniformity was brought to bear chiefly on the Presbyterians, although they had helped to restore the king; end they now suffered a sharp, though short, persecution: for nearly all determinedly refused to comply with the requirements of the act. They were forbidden to hold their customary kirk meetings or sessions; their clergy were fined or sent to jail for not conforming; and in the end, nearly all were expelled from their ministry and their homes, because they would not submit to be ordained by the bishop, while some were altogether banished from the country. But most held their ground, living in the old neighbourhood as best they could, and secretly kept religion alive among their flocks. A large number of the lay members—sober, industrious, and peaceful people—unwilling to live in a country where they were not permitted to practise their religion, sold their property and emigrated to the Puritan colonies of New England. But by unyielding firmness the Presbyterians at length obtained toleration and justice.

While the Presbyterians were suffering, the Catholics were treated with some leniency by Ormond, now lord lieutenant, through the interference of the king, who was at heart a Catholic. Ormond however soon resumed his severities; whereupon the king removed him in 1669, and appointed others more pliant. This was followed by renewed severities against the Non-conformists, and by further toleration for the Roman Catholics.

But the leniency experienced by the Catholics was of short duration. It was known that the king's brother James, duke of York (subsequently King James II), was a Catholic. It had become pretty generally believed too that the king himself was a Catholic; and reports went abroad that he was conspiring to restore the Catholic religion over the Three Kingdoms. Matters were brought to a crisis by the Titus Oates Plot in England, which was an evil turn for the Irish Roman Catholics; for now there were all sorts of wild unfounded rumours of their wicked intentions towards Protestants. Measures of extraordinary severity—proclamations in quick succession—were brought into play, and the Catholics now passed through a period of great suffering. Several innocent persons were arrested and imprisoned: and Dr. Oliver Plunkett archbishop of Armagh, a man of spotless character, respected equally by Protestants and Catholics, was brought to London, where in 1681, he was tried and executed on a false charge.

James II, who was a Roman Catholic, succeeded his brother Charles in 1685, and his accession gave great joy to the Catholics of Ireland, and corresponding alarm to the Protestants. He soon entered on the dangerous task of restoring the Catholic religion in both countries, and entered on it in a manner so openly offensive, harsh, and illegal, that the whole Protestant population rose up against him. Colonel Richard Talbot, a strict Catholic, of a disposition over-zealous and imprudent, was sent to Ireland as commander of the forces, and was created earl of Tirconnell. As a sort of set-off, the king appointed his own brother-in-law, Lord Clarendon, who was a Protestant, lord lieutenant in place of Ormond. But Clarendon was a mere shadow; Tirconnell was the real ruler; and one of his first acts was to disarm the militia, who were all Protestants. He disbanded thousands of Protestant soldiers and officers, and replaced them with Catholics. Most of the Protestant officers went to Holland, and were provided for by William prince of Orange, under whom they afterwards fought against King James in Ireland. Tirconnell also appointed Catholic judges, sheriffs, and magistrates, making room for them when necessary by the removal of Protestants. He made an attempt to have the Act of Settlement repealed: but in this he failed.

At length Clarendon was removed and Tirconnell was appointed lord lieutenant to rule Ireland (1687), which created quite a panic among the Protestants all over the country, so that hundreds fled from their homes to England and elsewhere. Ulster especially was in a miserable state of disquietude: Protestants and Catholics looked on each other with suspicion and fear; the memories of the mutual cruelties of 1641 were revived and exaggerated; and terrific rumours ran rife of intended murders and massacres. In the midst of all these alarms in Ireland, William prince of Orange, whose wife was King James's daughter Mary, landed in England on the 5th November to claim the throne; and King James, deserted by numbers of his officers, who went over to William's army, fled to France in December, in haste, secrecy, and abject terror.

Nearly all the people of England were Protestants, who, after the experience of James's recent proceedings, came to the determination to have a Protestant king; and they allowed William to take possession without opposition. In Ireland the vast majority of the people were Catholics, who did not want a Protestant king. They stood up for King James, so that William had to fight for Ireland; and thus began the war between the two kings, known as the War of the Revolution; which will be related in the next seven chapters.

Composed from the Book of Kells.

CHAPTER XLVIII
THE SIEGE OF DERRY—PART I
A.D. 1688–1689.—William and Mary.

EEING the turn things had taken in England, Tirconnell adopted immediate measures to secure Ireland for King James. He raised a large irregular untrained army of Catholics, and took possession of the most important places all through the country, garrisoning them with Jacobite[1] troops. In the south, where the Protestants were few, there was little or no resistance; but it was otherwise in Ulster, where the people of two important centres, Derry and Enniskillen, refused to admit his garrisons; and several other towns yielded only through force. Derry was then a small town, nearly in the form of an oblong half a mile in length, standing on a hill rising over the left or Donegal bank of the river Foyle, four miles from its mouth. It was encompassed by a wall, and communication was kept up with the opposite or eastern side by a ferry; for there was no bridge. It was, says one of the historians of that period, "a town of small importance, but made famous by the defence it made now, and the consequences which that defence had upon the future operations of the war."

The excitement among the Protestants of Ireland caused by the proceedings of Tirconnell, as described in the last chapter, continued to increase. But the terror was brought to a climax by an anonymous letter written by some mischievous person to a Protestant gentleman of the county Down, stating that the Catholics had arranged to fall on the Protestants and kill them, man, woman, and child, on the following Sunday the 9th December. Copies of this letter were instantly despatched all over the country, which set the poor people in a frenzy; for in their fright they believed everything, and they thought that the scenes of 1641 were now about to be repeated. Numbers fled on board ships. Many of those in the

---

[1]The adherents of the Stuarts were known as Jacobites, from *Jacobus,* the Latin form of *James.*

Leinster counties turned their steps towards Ulster, suffering incredible hardships on the journey; while those who could not leave home barricaded themselves in their houses, expecting in trembling anxiety to be attacked at any moment by their Catholic neighbours. The 9th of December came, and few Protestants in any part of Ireland went to bed on that miserable night. But it passed away without the least disturbance anywhere: even the most unprotected Protestant families experienced nothing but the usual neighbourly intercourse from the Catholics among whom they lived. For the letter was a wicked hoax, and the whole story was a pure invention. But it took several weeks to calm down the fears of the Protestant people.

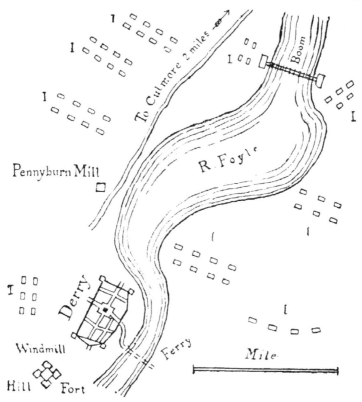

Plan of Derry and its neighbourhood during the siege. Constructed from contemporary plan in Harris's Life of William III. *I, I, I, Irish army.*

Let us now see how matters had been going on in Derry during this time of alarm. On the very day—Friday the 7th December—when the contents of the anonymous letter had been made known in the city, word was brought that Alexander Mac Donnell, earl of Antrim, with the Jacobite army, was approaching from Coleraine to demand possession. This news caused immense commotion. The aldermen and magistrates were in great doubt whether they should open the gates, or embark on a course of resistance that seemed desperate. But the humbler classes were in no doubt at all: they had their minds made up: for they believed the whole proceeding was merely a trap to secure their destruction all the more easily on the next day but one: and they clamoured to have the gates shut. At last the army appeared in view at Waterside on the far bank of the river; and a small party crossing in the ferryboat, presented themselves at the ferry gate and demanded admittance. While the authorities were debating excitedly what was best to be done, a few of the bolder young apprentices, seizing the keys, and arming themselves with swords, slammed and locked the gate and shut out the Jacobite party. They were joined by the crowd, and the authorities, sorely frightened at the grave and dangerous act of rebellion, were forced to yield: on which the party recrossed the ferry, and the Jacobite army marched back to Coleraine. Then, in order to make matters doubly safe in Derry for the next Sunday, all the Catholic inhabitants were sent away.

When Sunday had passed by harmlessly the citizens consented to negotiate; and they ultimately agreed, on condition of obtaining pardon for the rebellious shutting of the gates, to admit two companies of the Jacobite army, who, it was stipulated, were to be all Protestants to a man, and who were under the command of Colonel Lundy. Whereupon Lundy was appointed governor. But as Tirconnell continued openly to dismiss and disarm Protestants wherever he could, the Protestant gentry of Ulster began to arm and prepare for resistance. Not long afterwards came news from England, of William's successful progress, followed by a letter from himself, encouraging the northern people to continue their measures of resistance, and promising to send them help. And now the citizens of Derry, who had closed their gates through terror of being slaughtered, determined once for all to hold the city for William: and they renounced their allegiance to King James, and publicly proclaimed William and Mary as their sovereigns. Lundy took the oath of allegiance to William, with the others, but he did so with evident reluctance and not in public.

When King James heard of Tirconnell's active proceedings, and found that his cause had been taken up in the greater part of the country, he mustered up courage and sailed for Ireland, landing at Kinsale on the 12th March with a number of French officers and Irish refugees, and a supply of money, arms, and ammunition, furnished by King Louis of France: but beyond that, with no army properly so called. The commander of the expedition was a French general, Marshal Rosen. Among the Irish who accompanied the king, the most distinguished was Patrick Sarsfield, afterwards earl of Lucan: a great soldier and an honourable high-minded gentleman, who was quite as much respected by his opponents as by his own party. He was descended on his father's side from one of those nobles who had come to Ireland with Henry II, and on his mother's from the O'Moores of Leix: and he was at this time about thirty-eight years of age. His personal appearance corresponded with his character, for he had a noble countenance, and stood over six feet high, straight and well proportioned.

The king arrived in Dublin on the 24th March; and having created Tirconnell a duke, he came to the determination to proceed to Ulster; for he was told that he had only to present himself at Derry, and the gates would be thrown open to him. Some short time previously, General Hamilton had been sent northwards by Tirconnell to reduce Ulster to obedience: and as he advanced, the Protestant people retreated from point to point, breaking down the bridges, burning the ferryboats, and wasting and destroying everything as they went along, till they arrived at Derry, where they found refuge.

The king now set out for the North; and after a miserable journey through a desolated country, he joined his army under Hamilton a few miles south of Derry. Lundy, who was only half-hearted in the new cause, was all for surrendering the town: for he did not believe that it could be successfully defended. Moreover, although its governor, he remained quite passive; and any preparations for defence that were made, were made by others.

On the 14th April, while James and his army were approaching, some ships sent from England arrived in Lough Foyle, bringing two regiments under the command of Colonel Cunningham, to reinforce the garrison; but Lundy and some others persuaded them to withdraw, representing that the town could not possibly hold out. And most of the leading men of the city, and nearly all the officers of the garrison went on board the ships and sailed for England with Cunningham. When the report of these transactions got abroad, the citizens began to suspect that Lundy was dealing treacherously with them, and they became so enraged that they threatened to shoot or hang him.

Meantime the army appeared in view at the south of the town; and the inhabitants met to consider what was to be done. There was great hesitation and difference of opinion, with much uproar and confusion; and we are told that "while some were framing terms of surrender, others were placing guns on the wall for defence." Most of the authorities, with the governor at their head, were inclined to yield, while the populace, who had possession of the walls and gates, were all for fighting. The king approached the south gate with his staff, expecting to see it fly open;

but instead of a greeting he heard a fierce shout of "No surrender," and a volley was fired from one of the bastions which killed an officer by his side; on which he immediately retired out of range. But negotiations still went on, and Lundy and a section of the magistrates endeavoured to bring about a surrender. They probably would have succeeded but for the timely arrival of Adam Murray, well known as a brave and energetic man, with a small party of horse. The people at once chose him as their leader, and the project for surrender was instantly stopped. The popular rage against Lundy now became ungovernable, and he was obliged to hide himself till night came on, when he passed through the streets disguised as a porter, with a load on his back, and made his escape over the wall. Whereupon Major Baker and the Rev. George Walker were chosen as governors by the townsmen.

The die was now cast, and it was resolved to defend the city to the last. It was badly prepared to stand a siege; for Lundy had done all he could in a quiet sort of way to obstruct the preparations for defence. The walls were not very strong; the bastions had in many places fallen into ruin; and there was only a poor supply of artillery. Those who undertook the defence were merely the common working people; for with the connivance of Lundy and Cunningham the town had been deserted by most of the leading men. They were unaccustomed to discipline, and quite unused to fighting; and besides, they were not well supplied with arms. They had no military officers, no engineers to direct operations; for Murray, though able and daring, was unskilled in the art of siege defence. And what increased the difficulties tenfold was that there were crowded into the town thousands of refugees from the surrounding country, who had to be fed, while the stock of provisions was alarmingly small, and it was hard to obtain supplies.

But with all these discouragements, the determination of the Derry people remained unshaken. Under Murray's directions they formed themselves into companies and regiments, appointed officers to command them, took their turns at guarding and fighting, obeyed the orders of their newly appointed commanders, and faced dangers and hardships with the utmost docility and cheerfulness. When all arrangements had been completed it was found that there were about 7,000 fighting men, led by 340 officers—eight regiments in all, each under a colonel. The men worked incessantly strengthening the defences. Two guns were planted on the flat roof of the cathedral, which greatly annoyed the surrounding Jacobite detachments during the whole siege: and at every gate was placed a gun which commanded the approach.

As to King James: when he found all his proposals rejected he returned to Dublin, leaving the direction of the siege to the French General

Maumont, with Hamilton second in command. He summoned a parliament in Dublin, at which a number of measures were hastily passed. It was ordained that there should be full freedom of worship for all religious denominations; a measure, which though in a great degree dictated by mere prudence, was creditable in that period of religious intolerance. The Act of Settlement was repealed, which meant that the new settlers would have to restore the lands to the old owners, but with compensation when necessary. More than 2,000 persons were attainted, and their lands declared confiscated, for having joined the prince of Orange: an Act that has earned much blame for this parliament. But all this active legislation came to nothing; for before there was time to enforce it, King James and his government were superseded. To meet current expenses a tax was levied on estates. But as this was not enough, the king issued base coins to the amount of nearly £1,000,000, the real value of which was not more than about £60,000: the actual value of the £5 piece was only four pence. The issue of this "brass money," as it was called, greatly disarranged trade, and reduced many to poverty: and after about two years, Tirconnell, finding the measure a failure, recalled the coins.

A coin of James's base money. From *Kilkenny Archaeological Journal.*

Composed from the Book of Kells.

Chapter XLIX
The Siege of Derry—Part II
A.D. 1689.—William and Mary.

ET us now return to Derry. On the 18th April, 1689, the siege began in good earnest, and from that day forward was carried on with great energy. In the last chapter the disadvantages under which the besieged laboured have been set forth. But in one important respect the besiegers were much worse off: namely, in the supply of war materials. By some unaccountable negligence, a large part of the arms supplied to them were damaged and useless; the majority of the men had no swords or belts; and whole regiments had been sent from Dublin without ammunition. This fully explains the fact that in almost all the encounters during the siege, the Irish, though fighting with unfailing bravery, lost greater numbers than their opponents; and the wonder is that they had the spirit to fight at all under the circumstances. There were no sufficient means of moving the artillery from place to place; and the Jacobite army was scattered over so large a space as to weaken it greatly. Moreover, the greater part of the army consisted of men who had been recruited only within the last few months, wholly undisciplined and quite unused to arms and to fighting. Both parties were badly prepared, the one to carry on a siege, the other to resist it. But there was one all-important difference: the besiegers had a fair, though not a sufficient supply of food, while the defenders, towards the end of the siege, had to fight while starving.

Maumont and Hamilton felt assured that the town would yield to the first serious attack, and they began their work vigorously. The walls and town were battered, many houses were demolished, while others took fire, and everywhere in the streets people were struck down by balls or crushed by falling walls and chimneys. But the greater the danger and distress the higher seemed to rise the spirit of the people. Religious enthusiasm, too, came to their aid, animating them in fighting and helping to sustain them in their privations.

Derry in 1840. From Wright's Ireland Illustrated.

Anglicans and Dissenters attended at the same church at different hours of the day, when their turn off military duty came round; and the clergy of each denomination conducted divine service and preached to their respective congregations. Among the most active was the Rev. George Walker, who kept constantly exhorting the people during the siege, from both pulpit and rampart.

On the 21st April, Murray made a sally towards Pennyburn Mill with a party of horse and foot; but they were received with great determination by the Irish, and after a long and furious struggle had to withdraw, Murray barely escaping with his life. Yet the besiegers suffered severely in this fight; for they lost 200 men, and their general, Maumont, was killed by Murray in a personal encounter. Hamilton then took the chief command.

During May and June the fighting went on; sallies and attempts to storm; desperate conflicts and great loss of life; both parties fighting with equal obstinacy. There was an important fort at a place called Windmill Hill near the southern gate (the site of which is now occupied by the Casino); if that were taken it would help to open the way to the town; and Hamilton determined to attempt its capture, for which a large detachment of horse and foot were told off. On the 4th June the attacking party advanced with a great shout, each man bringing a faggot to fill up the outer ditch of the fort. The Derrymen, with as much military forethought as if they had been soldiers all their lives, had arranged themselves in three ranks on the walls: when the front rank discharged their muskets they filed to the rear, while the next rank stepped to the front and fired; and so on during the whole attack. Thus the assailants were met by a continuous fire, which greatly astonished and disconcerted them; for they had expected just a single volley, and intended then to make a dash for the wall. Yet they pressed on to the trench; but the wall was so high that they were unable to get to the top. Finding themselves foiled, some of them ran round to the back of the fort, and in the most daring manner attempted to enter; but here they met a like reception, some being shot down, while many were pulled over the walls by the hair of the head, and retained as prisoners. The horse, under Captain Butler, advanced boldly to the attack on the river side:

Bishop's Gate, Derry, from which the Garrison usually made their sallies.
From Mrs. Hall's Ireland.

but they were met just as boldly halfway on the strand—the tide being out—by a party issuing forth from the shelter of the redoubts, who, falling unexpectedly on them with muskets, pikes, and scythes, drove the main body back in spite of all efforts. A small party, however, with Captain Butler at their head, forced their way, with great determination, to the wall, which was low at that part, and putting spurs to their horses, attempted to leap over. The captain was the only one who succeeded in getting in, and he was at once taken prisoner: the others were either killed or driven back.

In the midst of all the din and danger of these several fights, the women assisted with great spirit and energy. "At this attack," says the Rev. John Mac Kenzie, a Presbyterian minister who was in the town during the siege, and who has left a diary of what he witnessed: "At this attack on the Windmill fort our women did good service, carrying ammunition, match [for the guns], bread, and drink to our men, and assisted to very good purpose at the bog side [of the fort] in beating off the grenadiers with stones who came so near to our lines." At length the assailants were forced to retire, after losing 400 men, with Captain Butler taken prisoner. This was the most important fight of the whole siege, and the Derrymen were greatly encouraged by the result.

After this repulse, a terrible fire of bombs, great and small, was kept up on the town for several days, doing immense damage. "They plowed up our streets," says the Rev. George Walker, who has left another diary of the siege, "and broke down our Houses, so that there was no passing the Streets nor staying within Doors, but all flock to the Walls and the remotest Parts of the Town, where we continued very safe, while many of our Sick were killed, being not able to leave their Houses." A great many of the women and children who were forced to sleep out in this manner, under shelter of walls, died from diseases brought on by exposure.

Seeing all active efforts foiled, Hamilton resolved to turn the siege into a blockade, and starve the garrison to surrender. On the land side he had the town quite surrounded, and every entrance strictly guarded; so that the townsmen found it impossible to hold any communication with the outside, or to obtain any supplies. Their hopes now lay in help from England—the help that William had promised. Every day watchmen took station on the church tower, anxiously looking out to sea for relief; and at length, in the middle of June, they shouted down the joyous news that thirty ships were sailing up Lough Foyle. Signals were made from masthead and steeple, but were not understood by either side; till at last a bold volunteer made his way, at great risk, through the Jacobite outposts, to Waterside on the eastern bank, and swam across the river, bringing news that deliverance was at hand, for that Major-General Kirke, the commander of the fleet, had come to relieve the town. But the hope was short-lived; for Kirke, having sailed as far as Culmore Fort at the mouth of the Foyle, which was held by the Jacobites, was afraid to enter the river, as he had heard of the forts bristling with guns that lined both banks all the way up; and the hearts of the townsmen sank when they beheld the whole fleet retiring and taking station outside the Lough. Yet, during all this time of miserable suspense and suffering, they never relaxed their vigilance, but kept working incessantly, repairing the old fortifications and constructing new ones; while the women everywhere encouraged the men and bore hardship and hunger uncomplainingly.

In order to make it impossible for the ships to bring relief, Hamilton now caused a great boom to be made of strong cables and timber logs, more than a quarter of a mile long, and stretched tightly across the river two miles below the town, strengthening it by huge stakes driven into the riverbed and by boats full of stones sunk to the bottom beside them. "This," says Walker, "did much trouble us, and scarce left us any hopes." The strict blockade told at last. Provisions began to run short among people of all classes. The weather was excessively hot, and hunger was followed by disease and many deaths. They buried fifteen officers in one day; and their governor Baker died, and was succeeded by another brave man, Captain Mitchelburn. They had no boats; for those persons who had left the town in the beginning carried them all away. They built up a rough one, however, and a little party of venturous rowers attempted to reach the fleet with an account of their sad condition; but the crew, not being able to endure the showers of shot from both sides, had to return.

Towards the end of June, King James, growing impatient at the length of the siege, sent Marshal Rosen to take command, with instructions to adopt more vigorous measures. This new commander invested the place still more closely and made many furious assaults: but all in vain; the defenders were as determined as ever, and repelled all his attacks. Becoming furious at last at the obstinate and prolonged defence, Rosen resorted to an inhuman plan to force surrender. Sending out a number of small military parties who traversed the country in all directions under officers, he had the Protestant inhabitants of the surrounding district, men, women, and children, to the number of more than a thousand, gathered together; and having driven them, on the 2nd July, to the open space between his army and the walls, he left them there huddled together in miserable plight, without food or shelter; and he sent word that there they should remain to die of starvation and exposure, or be admitted inside the gates to help to consume the small supply of provisions remaining, unless the town was surrendered.

But this savage device produced results the very reverse of what Rosen intended. These poor hunted people, far from craving relief, called out to the men on the bastions to continue their defence bravely, and not to think of yielding on account of those under the walls. The pitiful sight and the wailings of the women and children excited the townsmen to fury; instant death was denounced against anyone who should breathe the word "Surrender"; and they resolved on a terrible measure of retaliation. At this time there were in the town many Irish prisoners, some of them men of rank, who had been captured during the several conflicts: and the townsmen, erecting a great gallows on the ramparts in full view of the besiegers, sent back a message that they would hang their prisoners, every man, next day, unless the country people were set free. At the same time these condemned prisoners, being permitted to write to Hamilton, besought him to save them by inducing Rosen to let the poor people go:— "We are all willing to die," they say, "sword in hand for his majesty [King James]; but to suffer like malefactors is hard: nor can we lay our blood to the charge of the garrison, the governor and the rest having used and treated us with all civility imaginable." At last Rosen becoming alarmed, permitted the people to depart: and it is pleasant to have to record that he supplied them with food and some money. But numbers had died during their miserable sojourn of two days and two nights. The garrison gained somewhat by this piece of cruelty; for they managed to smuggle among the departing crowd several hundred old and useless people; while some strong men slipped into the town to recruit the fighting ranks. Yet some of those that came out were detected by their ragged clothes and hunger-pinched faces, and were sent back to the town.

It must in justice be recorded that Rosen alone was responsible for this barbarous proceeding. Hamilton was greatly pained, but could do nothing. King James, when he came to hear of it, expressed his strong disapproval and indignation, and recalled Rosen, leaving Hamilton in chief command. The Irish officers carried out the cruel orders with the utmost unwillingness, but they had to obey. Many wept at the sight of the miseries they were forced to inflict; and long afterwards some of them declared that the cries of the women and children still rang in their ears.[1]

Meantime Kirke made no move. For more than six weeks he lay idle, with abundance of food stowed away in his ships, though he could plainly see the signal of distress flying from the cathedral steeple; while the townspeople were famishing, driven to eat horseflesh, dogs, grease, and garbage of every kind. The garrison fared no better. Yet these brave

---

[1] In connexion with this, it is proper to remark that, though during the time of the siege the Catholic people and the Catholic armies had the whole of Ulster, except two or three small districts, at their mercy, they did not misuse their power by killing, or plundering, or otherwise ill-treating the Protestant people: and "in many instances the Jacobite army treated Protestants who fell into their hands with courtesy and kindness." (From *Derry and Enniskillen* by Witherow, who gives many instances—pp. 316–321.)

fellows—ragged and starving—stood resolutely to their posts, and uttered no word of complaint. But with all this constancy, hunger and disease were playing sad havoc with the cooped-up people, and must before many days bring about what force failed to accomplish. Walker gives a long list of the prices fetched by provisions towards the end of July. Horseflesh sold for 1*s*. 8*d*. a pound (about 10*s*. of our money): a dog's head, 2*s*. 6*d*. (15*s*. now): a pound of tallow, 4*s*. (24*s*. now): and so on. Pancakes made of starch and tallow were a favourite luxury; for they were not only food, but were found to be medicine against some diseases. Walker tells, by way of a grim joke, how a certain very fat gentleman, as he walked one day near the bastions, fancying that several of the garrison were looking at him intently with hungry eyes, got so frightened that he made straight for home, and hid himself in his house for three days. Compare all this with the abundance of only three months before, when, as we are told, a salmon two feet long could be bought for two pence, 25 eggs for a penny, and a fat goose for three pence. To add to the trials of the besieged, there arose from time to time among a section of the people, a good deal of impatience and insubordination, and proposals for surrender: and scarce a day passed without some deserters escaping and bringing news of their condition to the Irish camp.

At last, as matters seemed hopeless, for a large proportion of the fighting men had perished, and numbers of women and children were dying daily, the townspeople consented to negotiate. The garrison offered to yield the town on certain conditions, one of which was that they should be permitted to depart in any direction they pleased, every man fully armed; but Hamilton lost his chance by refusing, and the struggle was re-commenced. The walls were again battered and the assaults were delivered if possible more vigorously than before; but the defenders, though tottering with weakness, and sometimes falling with the mere effort of striking, successfully repelled every attack. Their cannonballs ran out, and to supply the want, they made balls of brick covered with lead, which answered the purpose very well.

On the evening of Sunday the 28th July, when silence, gloom, and despair had settled down on the town, the watchers, as they gazed despondingly over the waters, saw three ships from the fleet approaching the mouth of the river. For Kirke, having, as some say, received a peremptory order from England, had at last taken heart and sent relief. A tremendous fire was opened from the fort of Culmore, and from both banks all the way up, which the ships vigorously returned as they sailed along. When the townspeople heard the roar of artillery, a hungry crowd rushed to the battlements; and while they strained their eyes, breathless and anxious, the foremost ship, the *Mountjoy,* struck the boom, but rebounded from it and ran aground. Instantly the besiegers, with a mighty shout, sprang to their boats or plunged into the water to board her; and the multitude on the walls, who could see nothing for the smoke and darkness, heard the soldiers beneath them shouting that the ship was taken; whereupon, says an eyewitness, "a shrill cry of misery like the wailings of women was heard from the walls"; and men, in tatters, with faces all blackened with hunger, smoke, and powder, looked despairingly in each other's eyes. But only for a few moments. The vessel, freeing herself by the rebound of a broadside fired landward from her guns, was seen emerging from the smoke. A second time she struck the boom full force and broke it: and the whole three ships sailed up to the town amid frantic cries of joy. Great heaps of luxurious food—beef, bacon, cheese, oatmeal, butter, biscuits— gladdened the eyes of the famishing crowd, and the town was relieved. Hamilton, having continued to ply his batteries for the next day or two, at last gave up all further attempts and marched away: and thus came to an end, on the 31st of July 1689, a siege of a hundred and five days, one of the most famous in Irish or British history.

Walker's Monument, Derry, in 1840. From Wright's Ireland Illustrated.

Of the 7,000 fighting men of Derry, only 4,300 survived; and the mortality among the non-combatants was still greater: probably 10,000 altogether perished during the siege, chiefly of hunger and disease. The Irish army, though not so badly off for food, suffered almost as much as the defenders from want of camping and sleeping accommodation, from exposure and hardship night and day, and from unwholesome food and sickness: while, on account of the deficient supply of arms and ammunition, more of them fell in the several conflicts than of their opponents: so that the mortality among them was almost as great as it was in the town.

The ancient walls of Derry are still perfect, though the town has extended far beyond them; some of the old guns are reverently preserved; and on the site of one of the bastions, rises a lofty pillar surmounted by a statue of the Rev. George Walker.

Enniskillen, the other Williamite stronghold, was threatened by the approach of an Irish army; but the Enniskilleners, not waiting for a siege, marched forth on the day before the relief of Derry, and intercepted and utterly defeated them at Newtownbutler. It is stated that the Irish defeat here was due to a mistake in a word of command. The general ordered a detachment to face to the right in order to relieve another party that were hard pressed; but the next in command delivered the order, "Right *about* face and march," which in fact meant a retreat. This order was obeyed; on seeing which, the rest of the army, thinking the order was a general one, threw down their arms and fled. This mistake brought rout followed by merciless slaughter on the Irish, with little loss to the Enniskillen men.

Sarsfield was not present at Derry; he commanded a detachment at Sligo; but on hearing of these disasters, he retired to Athlone; and now Ulster was nearly all in the hands of the Williamites.

Chapter L
The Battle of the Boyne
A.D. 1689–1690.—William and Mary.

HE siege of Derry was only the beginning of the struggle. King William had now leisure to look to Ireland; and he sent over the duke of Schomberg—then above eighty years of age—who landed, in August 1689, at Bangor, with an army of about 15,000 men. After a siege of eight days, Carrickfergus Castle was surrendered to him; and he settled down for some time near Dundalk, in an unhealthy position, entrenching himself in a fortified camp, which soon became a vast hospital, where he lost fully half of his army by sickness.

In the following year King William came over to conduct the campaign in person. He landed at Carrickfergus on June 14th 1690, and immediately joined Schomberg. About half of the united army were foreigners, excellent soldiers, a mixture of French, Dutch, Danes, Swedes, and Prussians or Brandenburghers.

The Duke of Schomberg.

James had advanced from Dublin to Dundalk, but fell back on the south bank of the Boyne, with his centre at the village of Oldbridge, three miles above Drogheda, whither William followed and took up his position on the north bank. The two banks rise on both sides, forming low hills, on which were placed the camps, and the river flowed peacefully in the valley beneath. The Irish army, consisting of about 26,000 men, was largely composed of recruits, badly drilled and badly armed, having only twelve French field guns as their sole supply of artillery, with the crowning ill-fortune of being led by King James. They were opposed by a more numerous army—about 40,000 men—well trained and well supplied with all necessaries, including a fine artillery train of fifty field guns, and commanded by William, a man full of energy and determination, and one of the best generals of his time.

On the evening of the 30th June, King William, riding down to the river with some officers to observe the opposite lines, had a narrow escape. The Irish, observing the party, at once brought two field guns to bear on them. The first shot killed a man and two horses, and the second struck the king on the right shoulder, tearing away skin and flesh: but the wound was only slight. The Irish, thinking he was killed, raised a great shout, and alarming rumours went among the English lines: but William, having got the wound dressed, and making very little of it, rode all through his own camp to assure the army of his safety.

The conduct of James on this same evening—the evening before the battle—was enough to damp the spirits of any army. He was flighty and undecided. One time he seemed to contemplate a general retreat and gave orders to raise the camp; but in a few moments came a countermand, and he appeared determined to risk a battle. Finally he sent off towards Dublin his baggage and six of his twelve field pieces, which were badly needed on the battlefield; and this movement, which was a plain preparation for a retreat, presently became known through the army. His whole anxiety seemed to be to secure his own safety in case of defeat.

Early in the morning of the 1st July, William's army began to move: by his order each man wore a sprig of green in his cap, while the Jacobites wore little strips of white paper. "The day," says Story, the army chaplain, who was present, "was very clear, as if the sun itself had a mind to see what would happen." The river was low, for the tide was at ebb and the weather had been dry, and there were several fords so shallow as to be passable without much difficulty. The task to be accomplished was to force the passage of these fords in spite of the opposition of the Irish. One division of more than 10,000 men under Lieutenant-General Douglas, with young Count Schomberg, and others, had set out at sunrise for Slane, five miles, up the river, where there was a bridge, which James, though warned, had left unguarded, thereby leaving his left unprotected. Now, when too late—for the English had got a considerable start—he attempted to repair the error by sending a large part of his army, horse and foot, towards Slane to oppose them. In the upward march the Williamites found a ford at Rossnaree, two miles below Slane, where several regiments forced their way across. After some hard fighting the small Jacobite detachment that had first arrived at the ford to oppose them was routed, and their commander, Sir Neil O'Neill, was mortally wounded. The rest of the Williamite forces continued their march and crossed at Slane. The object of all this movement was, partly to take the Irish army in the rear, and partly to occupy the pass at Duleek, so as to intercept them in case they should retreat towards Dublin: for the only open road in that direction to Dublin was this narrow pass across the Nanny Water river and through a morass. But Douglas and the other commanders, though they succeeded in crossing the Boyne, were unable to effect much more on account of the difficulty of the ground: and there was very little fighting here beyond the hot skirmish at Rossnaree, so that the Irish were able to keep possession of the pass at Duleek till evening. Nevertheless, this movement materially contributed to the defeat at the Boyne: for the task of defending the fords near Oldbridge was unexpectedly thrown on a section of the Irish army under Tirconnell and Hamilton; who were outnumbered three to one.

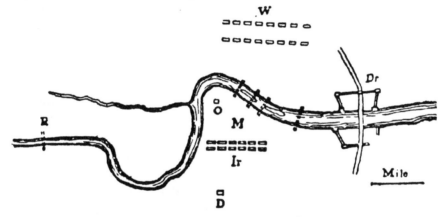

PLAN OF BATTLE ACCORDING TO STORY

W. William's army.	M. Main field of battle.
Ir. Irish army.	R. Rossnaree ford.
O. Village of Oldbridge.	The other fords where William's
D. Donore Hill and Church.	main army crossed are marked
Dr. Drogheda.	in dotted lines.

King William, having waited till an express messenger had come from Douglas to say he had succeeded in forcing a passage, issued his orders to cross the river at several fords, one near the village of Oldbridge straight between the two opposing camps, and the others lower down towards Drogheda. At the same time his batteries, which were placed on the high banks on the north of the river, opened fire on the Irish, who could not reply, as the six pieces King James had left them had been sent on towards Slane. In the midst of the roar of artillery, at a quarter past ten, the famous

Blue Dutch guards and the French Huguenots, all on foot, dashed in ten abreast, at the Oldbridge ford opposite James's centre, and were followed by a body of English and Danes, all up to their middle in the water. They were met by a volley, and as they were landing they were charged by the Irish and French, horse and foot, but succeeded in gaining the other side, where, however, the Jacobites, especially the cavalry, though far outnumbered, continued to charge with great spirit, so that in some places the foreign troops were forced to turn right round and rush back across the river. But in spite of all, the Williamites held their ground. "Much about this time," says Story, "there was nothing to be seen but Smoak and Dust, nor anything to be heard but one continued fire for nigh half an Hour."

It was at this point, just beside the village of Oldbridge, that old Duke Schomberg, rallying a body of Huguenots who had been broken by the Irish and were rushing back towards the river, was killed by a musket bullet which struck him in the neck. His body was immediately carried across the river to the English camp. About the same time Walker of Derry was shot dead near the ford. While this fierce struggle was going on, the rest of William's army began to cross, the king himself galloping up and down between the two armies at his own side of the river, directing the movements. At last, seeing his men well engaged wading and fighting, he crossed with a troop of horse at the lowest ford of all, more than a mile below Oldbridge, and seems to have met with little or no opposition. Having got his men in order at the other side, he drew his sword, though with difficulty, on account of his wound, and advanced towards his foot, who were struggling with the Irish. But he found it very hard to reach them; for the ground was soft, and once his horse got bogged, so that he had to alight till the animal was extricated; after which he headed his men in the forward march to take the Irish army in flank, exposing himself without the least hesitation to the heavy fire. When the Irish saw their right flank thus threatened, they retreated a little to Donore hill, where they made a stand: and succeeded in driving back the Williamite cavalry. The king now headed the Dutch and Enniskilleners and charged straight in the line of the Irish fire. He was at first repulsed, but came on again, and the fighting went on more furiously than ever. In this manner, during the day, the Irish kept up the unequal struggle, first at the fords, and next at their own side of the river, after William's whole army had succeeded in crossing. There were continual charges, countercharges, advances, and retreats, on both sides; and for a time the battle seemed doubtful. But no amount of bravery could compensate for the disadvantages under which the Irish fought that day, so that late in the evening they were forced to give way, and still fighting, they began their retreat.

King James, after issuing his orders in the morning, retired to the little church on the summit of the hill of Donore, from which he viewed the conflict in safety. He took no further part in the battle; and early in the evening, when he saw that the day was going against him, he fled in haste with a bodyguard of 200 horse, before the battle was over, leaving his men to take care of themselves, and reached Dublin a little after nine o'clock that same evening. The main body of the Irish army, making good the pass of Duleek, in spite of the attempts of the Williamite generals to intercept them, retreated southwards in good order to Dublin; and thence to Limerick. Drogheda, which was garrisoned by King James's troops, capitulated on honourable terms immediately after the battle.

Schomberg's Monument on the Boyne. From Wilde's Boyne and Blackwater.

Sarsfield was present at the Boyne, but he held a subordinate command, and was given no opportunity of taking any part in the battle: according to some he commanded the 200 horse that escorted James to Dublin. Conversing with a Williamite officer about the Boyne some time afterwards, he exactly pictured the true state of things when he exclaimed:—"Change kings with us and we will fight you over again!"

Having given the chief command to Tirconnell, James embarked at Kinsale and landed at Brest, the first bearer of the news of his own defeat. William arrived at Dublin and took possession of the city on Sunday the 6th of July. After this, Kilkenny, Duncannon, and Waterford surrendered in quick succession.

The body of the great old soldier Schomberg was brought to Dublin and interred in St. Patrick's Cathedral; and a tall obelisk to his memory now rises from a rock on the north bank of the Boyne.

Composed from the Book of Kells.

Chapter LI
The Siege of Limerick—Part I
Sarsfield and the Siege Train
A.D. 1690.—William and Mary.

ONCENTRATING their whole force at Limerick and Athlone, the Irish now determined to make the Shannon their line of defence, and to stand at bay in these two strongholds. On the 17th July, General Douglas, with 12,000 men, arrived before Athlone, which was the great important pass into Connaught. The town was divided in two, then as now, by the Shannon, the part on the Leinster or eastern side being called the English Town, and that on the Connaught side the Irish Town.

Colonel Richard Grace the Governor, a brave old soldier, one of the Confederates of half a century before, seeing that the English Town could not be defended, burned it and posted his whole army at the Connaught side, breaking down the bridge. Douglas, having taken possession of the ruins, sent a summons to surrender; but the Colonel, firing a pistol over the messenger's head, told him to return and say that these were the terms he was for. Douglas carried on the siege vigorously day after day, but was successfully kept at bay by the stout old governor. At the end of a week, news came that Sarsfield was approaching from the west: whereupon Douglas, fearing that his communication with Dublin might be cut off, suddenly raised the siege and marched away quietly in the middle of the night, not taking time even to demolish the walls. Turning southwards, he joined King William, who was at this time making his way leisurely towards Limerick. The king with the united army arrived before the walls on Saturday the 9th August, a little more than a month after the battle of the Boyne. He was not yet quite prepared for effective siege operations, as the whole of his artillery had not come up: but a great siege train was on its way from Dublin, guarded by a convoy of two troops

230

of horse, with heavy cannons, plenty of ammunition and provisions, tin boats or pontoons for crossing the river, and other necessary war materials.

While the citizens of Limerick were busily engaged preparing for defence, a French deserter from William's camp brought intelligence of the approach of the siege train: on which Sarsfield, who commanded the cavalry, instantly determined to intercept train and convoy: an uncertain and perilous venture, requiring courage, coolness, and dash. On the night of Sunday, August 10th, after a hasty preparation, he quietly crossed Thomond Bridge to the Clare side with 500 picked horsemen. Knowing that the fords near the city were all guarded by Williamite detachments, and wishing to escape observation lest he might be intercepted, he rode to Killaloe, fifteen miles above Limerick, keeping the river close on the right. Crossing at a ford a little above Killaloe, so deep and dangerous that it had not been thought necessary to place a guard on it—or perhaps it was not known—the party turned east and halted towards morning on the northern slope of Keeper Hill, in the neighbourhood of Silvermines. On Monday

Thomond Bridge in 1681, with King John's Castle and the Cathedral: from the Journal of Thomas Dineley. Kilkenny Archaeological Journal, *1864–6, p. 426. Key: A. King's Castle. B. Cathedral. C. The Watch-House. D. Thomond Bridge. E. Shannon River.*

morning they moved leisurely round the eastern base of the mountain, and rested quietly for the remainder of the day, hidden among the glens at the eastern extremity of the Slieve Felim mountains: while Sarsfield sent scouts southwards for intelligence. During the whole of his journey, from the time he left Limerick, he was guided by rapparees and peasants, who were devoted to him heart and soul, and who knew every hill, glen, and pass along the difficult route. According to a vivid local tradition, which is probably true, his chief guide was a celebrated rapparee captain of the time, often mentioned by Story, well known then, and remembered to this day, by the name of "Galloping O'Hogan."

On Monday a country gentleman of the neighbourhood of Limerick, named Manus O'Brien, came to William's camp and told the officers that Sarsfield had left on the night before on some enterprise of importance: but they only laughed at him, believing it a dream of his own. The cautious king however, having questioned him, took the matter more seriously. He at once ordered out a party of 500 horse under Sir John Lanyer, to meet and protect the siege train: but the preparations were slow, and the party did not start till an hour or two after midnight.

The convoy had set out with their charge on Monday morning from Cashel, and passing through the little village of Cullen, halted for the night at the base of a rocky eminence on the summit of which stood the ruined castle of Ballyneety, just two miles beyond the village, and about twelve miles from the rear outposts of William's encampment .[1] As no danger was apprehended, little precaution was taken. The tents were scattered over the sward: the horses were turned out to graze; sentinels were set on guard; and the men lay down to sleep in fancied security, "but some of them," observes Story, in his quaint way, "awoke in the next world." Oddly enough the password for the night was "Sarsfield."

In the evening of the same day, Sarsfield's scouts returned to Slieve Felim with intelligence of the convoy's camping place; and some time after nightfall he and his party, refreshed after their long day's rest, set out southwards, and after a hard midnight ride, found themselves about two o'clock in the morning at Cullen. Here, by a lucky accident, Sarsfield found out the password, which enabled the party to pass some outlying sentinels without exciting any suspicion. As they approached the camping ground they rode as cautiously and noiselessly as possible, till the sentinel just outside the encampment was startled by the appearance of horsemen through the dim moonlight, with one tall form looming at their head, and called out for the password. "Sarsfield is the word and Sarsfield is the man!" was the answer to the challenge; and the whole party dashed in on the encampment. Instantly the English bugles sounded the alarm, and the sleepers sprang up and hastily snatched their weapons. But all too late:

---

[1] All through this chapter and the next I have given the distances in English miles. The mile of Story and other contemporary authorities is equal to 1½ or 1¾ or sometimes 2 English miles. Story says that Ballyneety was "not seven miles from our camp, and directly in the rear of it." His "seven miles" means abut twelve.

those who stood on the defence were at once cut down; and the rest, seeing resistance hopeless, saved themselves by flight. One prisoner was taken, an officer who lay sick in a neighbouring house, whom Sarsfield treated with kindness, and to whom, according to Story, he stated that he would have gone to France if the enterprise had failed.

Patrick Sarsfield.

Sarsfield could not bring away the guns or any other heavy articles, knowing he was sure to be pursued; but the horses were captured, and all portable things were stowed away in pockets and saddlebags. There was not a moment to lose; and while some of the party smashed up the tin boats, others hastily filled the cannons with powder and buried their muzzles in the earth, piling over them the powder packets, waggons, ammunition, and provisions, in a great heap. A long fuse was fired when the party had got to a safe distance, and the whole train was blown up in one terrific explosion. Sir John Lanyer and his party, who were at this very time on their way towards Ballyneety, saw the heavens and all the surrounding landscape lighted up for a moment, and heard the ominous rumble in the distance. Divining but too well the meaning of what he saw and heard, he galloped forward and arrived just in time to see the last of Sarsfield's column disappearing through the darkness. He tried to overtake them; but Sarsfield wishing to get back as soon as possible without any more fighting, soon distanced the pursuing party, and crossing the Shannon, made his way safely to the city, where he was welcomed with a mighty cheer. The garrison, as we are told in the *Life of King James,* "was hugely encouraged by this advantage": and having before their minds the noble defence of Derry just a year before, all, both garrison and citizens, determined to emulate it.

Sarsfield's Rock: two miles west from Cullen, and five miles west from Limerick Junction. Space in front, where Siege Train was blown up. From a Photograph.

The very spot where the train was blown up is still well known; and the rocky eminence rising over it is now called Sarsfield's Rock; but the old castle has almost disappeared. The whole place abounds in traditions of the event; and the people tell how, some years ago, persons digging deeply came upon quantities of human bones.[1]

---

[1]There are half a dozen places called Ballyneety (White's Town) in Tipperary and Limerick; and attempts have been made, in the face of the plainest evidence, to identify the scene of Sarsfield's exploit with the little hamlet of Ballyneety near Cahirconlish, which *lay barely three English miles from the rear posts of William's camp,* though Story tells us the distance was about seven; *i.e.* about twelve English. This Ballyneety is fully thirteen miles from Cullen; whereas Story and Mullineux, both present at the siege, and White and Ferrar, who wrote some years afterwards, all tell us that the camping place was the Ballyneety near Cullen. Again, Story relates that Sir John Lanyer—with his troop of horse—had been *an*

Sculpture on Chancel Arch, Monastery Church, Glendalough, 1845.
From Petrie's *Round Towers.*

CHAPTER LII
THE SIEGE OF LIMERICK—PART II
A.D. 1690.—William and Mary.

T the opening of the last chapter it was stated that King William arrived with his army at Limerick on Saturday the 9th August 1690. He was attended by Ginkle, Douglas, and others of his best generals; and he encamped near Singland, within cannonshot of the walls, his lines extending in a curve east and south of the city. The place was so badly prepared for a siege that the French general Lauzun laughed at the idea of defending it, saying that "it could be taken with roasted apples." He refused, as he said, to sacrifice the lives of the Frenchmen entrusted to him in what he considered, or pretended to consider, a hopeless contest. But in truth he was sick of this Irish war, with all its hardships and privations, and he longed to get back to France. The Duke of Tirconnell, who was old and sickly and weary of turmoil, voted with him to surrender the city. But Sarsfield was of a different mind: he was for defence: and he was heartily seconded by a brave French captain named Boisseleau or Boileau. They infused their spirit into the native troops; and it was resolved at all hazards to defend the city; whereupon Lauzun and Tirconnell marched to Galway with all the French troops, bringing away a great quantity of ammunition sorely needed by the citizens. And thus the two chief men entrusted with the guardianship of Limerick deserted their posts, leaving the Irish to defend it as best they could. Boileau, having been appointed governor, set about repairing and strengthening the old

hour on the march from his own camp towards the camping place of the train at Ballyneety, when he saw the flash and heard the report *in the distance:* and yet it seems, according to this new identification, the place of the explosion was only three or four miles from Lanyer's starting-point! There are other evidences equally strong, showing this identification to be quite wrong: but the point need not be argued further. The place where William's train was blown up is known with as much certainty as the site of the Battle of the Boyne.

walls, towers, and forts: the citizens vied with the soldiers: and even the women and children assisted with the greatest spirit and cheerfulness.

At this time Limerick was the second city in Ireland. The principal part, called the English Town, stood upon the King's Island, which is enclosed by two branches of the Shannon, and is about a mile in length. Here also stood, as it still stands, the fine ruin of King John's Castle beside the main branch of the river, and near it the old Cathedral. Here were the dwellings of the nobility and gentry, and the principal buildings and houses of business. On the mainland, at the county Limerick or south side, was another and smaller part of the city called the Irish Town, which was connected with the English Town by Ball's Bridge, a large stone structure. The English Town was connected with Clare by Thomond Bridge, also of stone. Those two old bridges were removed about seventy years ago, but the new structures retain the old names. Each part of the city was encompassed by a stone wall, outside which was a trench and a weak palisade—"a toy of a palisade," as one of the old writers calls it. It was a handsome well-built city. Story tells us that the houses were "generally built very strong within the Walls, being made most of them Castleways, with Battlements." In modern times the Irish Town has far outgrown its former dimensions, and is now the principal part of the city.

King John's Castle, Limerick, in 1845. From Mrs. Hall's *Ireland.*

King William had an effective army of about 26,000 men, well supplied with arms and ammunition; while the Irish army of defence numbered about 25,000, scarcely half of them armed. The attack was to be directed against the Irish Town; for the King's Island and the English Town were beyond reach. King William had heard of the departure of the French troops; and when he and his officers viewed the crumbling old walls, they felt assured that from a greatly reduced garrison behind such feeble defences, no serious resistance would be encountered: the city would fall with the first vigorous assault.

Before beginning operations the king sent a summons to surrender; on the receipt of which a council of war was held, in which the line of action to be taken was unanimously agreed on; and the reply was a polite letter from the governor to the king's secretary, conveying the determination to defend the city for King James. And now began another famous siege.

During Sunday and Monday operations were carried on by William with such appliances as were to hand, pending the arrival of the heavy guns. But on Tuesday came the intelligence of the destruction of the siege train by Sarsfield, as has been related in the last chapter. "This News," says Story, the Williamite historian and army chaplain, who was present and has left us an account of the siege, "This News was very unwelcome to everybody in the Camp, the very private men shewing a greater concern at the loss than you would expect from such kind of people." Notwithstanding this disaster, the king, after a delay of about a week, pressed on the siege; for he had procured from Waterford two large guns and a mortar; and, in the wreck at Ballyneety, two of the great cannons were found uninjured. This week's breathing time was turned to good account by the citizens in pushing on the repair of their old defences by every possible contrivance.

On the 17th August the Williamite men began to dig trenches to enable them to get near the walls, and they worked in relays steadily day and night; while the Irish, on their part, did everything in their power to retard the work. The garrison sometimes made sallies, and then there were bitter conflicts, every inch of ground being obstinately contested. There were several high towers on the walls, in which were posted sharpshooters, who kept firing down into the trenches, killing numbers of the sappers. Once, in the darkness of night during a sally, two parties of the besiegers fired on one another, each mistaking the other for Irish: and for two full hours, while this misdirected combat was going on, the Irish kept up a fire on both, the king all the time looking on from a distance, hearing the firing and seeing the flashes, and not knowing what to make of it.

As soon as the artillery had been got into position, the heavy guns began to play; and in a short time the high towers on the walls were levelled, which freed those working in the trenches from the sharpshooters. After this the fire was mainly concentrated on a particular part of the wall near St. John's Gate, with the object of making a breach; while shells, red-hot shot, and a sort of destructive explosives called *carcasses,* which ran along the streets blazing and spitting out fragments of iron and glass, were poured in among the houses without intermission, so that the city was set on fire in several places, and a great store of hay was burned to ashes. "I remember," says Story, "we were all as well pleased to see the town flaming as could he, which made me reflect upon our profession of soldiery not to be overcharged with good nature."

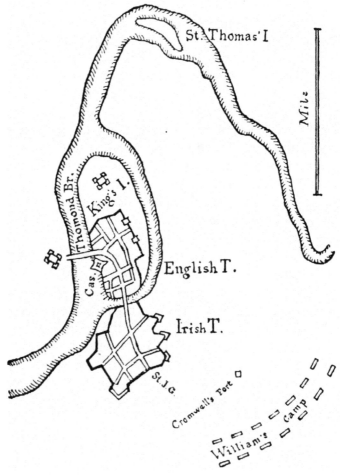

Plan of Limerick during the siege. Constructed mainly from Story's Plan.

An incident related by a gentleman from the county Meath, who happened to be in the city with his family during the siege, gives a vivid idea of the dangers to which the citizens were exposed. He had just got out of bed in the night to speak to one of the servants:—"But before I had time to return a Ball had beat down the Wall, a great Part of which had fallen in and demolished the Bed. It then passed through my Father's Bed-chamber, broke the Posts of the Bed where he and my Mother were asleep, but thank Heaven had no worse effect than putting the Family in a Consternation." Many soldiers and citizens were killed by the showers of missiles; but with danger and death all round them from balls and carcasses and fires, the spirits of the people never flagged, and neither soldier nor citizen called for surrender. Great numbers of women and children were sent for safety to the King's Island and to the Clare side of the river, where they encamped in such shelters as they were able to put up.

The defenders had a strong fort outside the wall, opposite St. John's Gate, from which they so harassed the besiegers that it was determined at all hazards to attempt its capture. A large party advanced to the attack, and after an obstinate hand-to-hand fight of several hours, the Irish were forced to retire and the English took possession; but both sides lost heavily in this prolonged encounter.

During the whole time, the king directed the siege operations, often exposing himself to great danger with the utmost coolness, and having one or two narrow escapes. On one occasion he was riding leisurely towards Cromwell's Fort, when he stopped for an instant to speak to a gentleman: but, as Story relates, "in the very moment there struck a twenty-four pounder in the very place, which would have struck His Majesty, and Horse too, all to pieces, if his usual good Angel had not defended him: it struck the Dust all about him however, though he took little notice of it, but alighting, came and laid him down on the Fort, amongst all the Dust." While the king worked with tireless energy on the outside, Sarsfield and Boileau were equally watchful and active in the city directing the defence.

The sappers, working without intermission, gradually advanced the trenches in spite of all opposition, till at last they were within a few yards of the wall; and it required only a sufficient breach to enable the besiegers to attempt a storm. When the old wall at last showed signs of yielding in one fated spot, under the tremendous cannonade, Boileau caused great sacks of wool, held by ropes from the inside, to be thrown over and hung down on the outside, to deaden the impact of the balls. But despite woolsacks, sallies, and resistance of every kind, a great breach thirty-six feet wide was made near St. John's Gate, after ten days' incessant battering: and through this it was determined to make an assault and storm the city.

At half past three in the afternoon of the 27th August, under a blazing sun and cloudless sky, a storming party of over 500 grenadiers, supported in the rear by 10,000 men, consisting of seven regiments of foot and a large body of horse, leaped up from the trenches at a signal of three guns fired from Cromwell's Fort, and made a rush for the breach, throwing their hand grenades and firing their muskets among the defenders. "This," says Story, "gave the Alarm to the Irish who had their Guns all ready and discharged great and small Shot upon us as fast as 'twas possible: Our men were not behind them in either: so that in less than two Minutes the Noise was so terrible, that one would have thought the very Skies to rent in sunder. This was seconded with Dust, Smoke, and all the terrors that the Art of Man could invent to ruin and undo one another; and to make it more uneasie, the day itself was excessive hot to the By-standers, and much more sure in all respects to those upon action."

The storming party succeeded in crossing the trench outside the broken wall; and, pushing on over the stones and rubbish that strewed the breach, after a desperate hand-to-hand conflict, drove the Irish before them, and rushed on for some distance inside. But here an unexpected obstacle met them. Some days before, when Boileau saw that it was likely a breach would be made, he caused to be thrown up a great rough rampart of earth and stones, about 60 yards from the wall inside, where the space happened to be free from houses, placing on it some light cannon, and having men armed ready to take their station behind it at the proper time. No sooner had the storming party reached the open space than they were met, front and flank, by a terrible fire of cartridge shot and bullets from cannon and muskets, so that they showed signs of wavering. But thousands of resolute men pressed on from behind, knowing they were fighting under the very eyes of their king, who surveyed the whole conflict from Cromwell's Fort at a little distance from the wall.

The Irish had planted two small field pieces on the Canons' Abbey near Ball's Bridge, which swept the space in front of the breach and killed great numbers of the closely-packed Williamites as they struggled on to gain the breach. But in spite of all, the party who had got inside the wall, being every moment reinforced by eager comrades from behind, still continued to gain ground, and the Limerick men continued to yield. The want of a sufficient supply of arms told heavily here; for it was observed that a whole regiment of 400 of the defenders, all Ulstermen under MacMahon, kept flinging stones at the front ranks of the Williamites, having no better weapons.

During all this time the citizens viewed the fight from every convenient standpoint—walls, windows, roofs, and streets—but could see little through the thick cloud of smoke and dust. When at last they became aware that the assailants were prevailing, they rushed down in multitudes by common impulse from their view places, and seizing every weapon they could lay their hands on, dashed into the midst of the uproar and joined eagerly in the fray. Even the women, like the women of Derry, forced their way in crowds to the front, right up to the solid advancing ranks, and regardless of danger and death, flung broken Bottles, stones, and all sorts of next-to-hand missiles in the very faces of the assailants. "The very women," as Story tells us, "who boldly stood in the trench, were nearer our men than their own."

Among William's foreign troops, the Brandenburgh or Prussian regiment had distinguished themselves for cool and determined bravery. They forced their way into the city with the others; and attacking the Black Battery, situated inside, not far from the breach, took it after a bloody contest; when suddenly, either by accident or design, the powder in the vaults beneath exploded with a mighty roar, and battery and Brandenburghers were blown into the air, men, stones, and fragments of timber mingled up in horrible confusion.

For four hours in the hot afternoon this dreadful conflict raged. The thickly-packed masses advanced and yielded in turn through the streets; a close and furious struggle, where all strained their utmost to force back the opposing ranks, and no one thought of personal danger. The rattle of small arms and the roar of cannon never ceased for an instant, and a cloud of smoke and dust that veiled the sunlight rose slowly over the city, and was wafted along by the gentle autumn breeze, till it disappeared behind a range of hills six or eight miles off.

At last the assailants, unable to withstand the tremendous and unexpected resistance, yielded, and turning round, rushed back through the breach in headlong confusion: and in a few moments the old city was cleared of every foreign soldier, except the killed and wounded. King William, having witnessed the repulse of his best troops, "Went to his Camp very much concerned," says Story, "as indeed was the whole army, for you might have seen a mixture of Anger and Sorrow in everybody's countenance." Over 2,000 of his men were killed, while the loss of the Irish was comparatively small. It was a matter of consideration whether another attempt should be made; but as the rainy season was coming on, which was sure to bring disease among his troops, the king thought it more prudent to raise the siege. He returned to England, leaving general Ginkle in command: and on the 31st August the army marched away from the city. The siege had lasted three weeks; and the heroic defenders of Limerick had, almost without ammunition, and with crumbling old walls for a defence, repulsed a well-equipped veteran army, directed by a great general celebrated all over Europe, who had never before been foiled by any fortress however strong.

Lauzun and Tirconnell, who were at this time in Galway, were no doubt ill-pleased to hear of the successful defence of Limerick, which they had deserted in its worst time of need: and fearing the displeasure of King Louis, they both embarked for France in order to have the first story.

In September 1690, Cork surrendered, after a fierce struggle, to the skilful generalship of John Churchill, afterwards the celebrated duke of Marlborough; and Kinsale followed. The capture of these two important places, which more than counter-balanced the successful defence of Limerick, ended the campaign of 1690.

Chapter LIII
Athlone and Aughrim
A.D. 1691.—William and Mary.

o military events of importance took place in Ireland for about ten months after the Siege of Limerick, except the capture of Cork and Kinsale. But the war was carried on without intermission all over the country, from Cavan southwards, by detached parties of Williamite forces, who were resisted everywhere, with varying success, partly by detachments of Irish regular troops, and partly by bands of rapparees, a sort of irregular volunteers, who were looked upon as mere robbers by the English captains and were hanged whenever caught. So long as the two armies had been kept together in large bodies, the men were under the usual discipline, outrage was repressed, and the ordinary laws of warfare were fairly observed. But when they got broken up into roving bands, discipline was all but abandoned, and they committed cruel outrages everywhere on the people. The account left us by the Williamite chaplain, Story, of the mode of warfare, of the numerous conflicts and daily executions by the Williamite captains, and of the general state of the country, is a fearful record of bloodshed and misery.

Tirconnell, who had sailed from Galway to France after the Siege of Limerick, as already related, returned with some money and stores in January 1691; and as he was King James's lord lieutenant, he resumed authority. In May a French fleet sailed up the Shannon, with provisions, clothing, and military stores, but no men or money: bringing Lieutenant-

General St. Ruth, a brave and experienced French officer, but cruel, haughty, and excessively conceited, to take command of the Irish army, by direction of King James, who was at this time in France. It would no doubt have been better if James had given command to Sarsfield, who was at least as good an officer, and who had a cooler head, as well as a perfect knowledge of the country and of the modes of warfare best suited to it. But James and his party treated Sarsfield exactly as the Anglo-Irish majority of the Confederation had treated Owen Roe O'Neill half a century before. Both these two great soldiers were kept in the background through jealousy; and in each case those responsible suffered for it in the end. Yet the Irish, though dissatisfied, obeyed the king's order and fought loyally under St. Ruth; while Sarsfield himself was too high-principled to endanger the cause by offering any opposition.

Castle of Athlone in 1845. From Mrs. Hall's Ireland.

After the failure at Limerick, the next attempt was to be made on Athlone, which was almost equally important; and on the 19th June, Ginkle appeared before it with an army of 18,000 men. The main body of the Irish was encamped at the Connaught side, about a mile west of the town. They were commanded, for the time being, by Sarsfield; for St. Ruth, the commander-in-chief, had not yet arrived; and Sarsfield could not undertake any important movement in his absence.

It will be remembered that when Douglas had hastily abandoned Athlone in the previous year, he left the walls of the English Town standing. The Irish were now again in possession, but the wall offered only a feeble resistance to Ginkle's heavy guns; and after some battering, a great breach was made. Four thousand men advanced to the assault. The breach was defended by about 400 Irish, who kept the assailants at bay for some time; but worn out at last with fatigue and want of sleep, they were forced to retire across the bridge, after losing half their number: and Ginkle took possession of the English Town. On the evening of that day St. Ruth arrived in the camp and took measures to defend the Irish Town. He had some earthworks thrown up along the banks of the river; and behind these, and in the castle, the Irish took their stand. They still held possession of the greater part of the bridge. But the English cannon, firing night and day, battered to pieces the earthworks and part of the castle; and the numerous thatched houses were set on fire by *carcasses,* so that this part of the town was reduced to a mere heap of rubbish; and the Irish had hardly any protection, and no means of answering the heavy continuous fire from the other side. Ginkle now sent a party to attempt to cross the Shannon at Lanesborough near the northern end of Lough Ree, thinking that to be an easier plan than forcing the bridge: but the Irish becoming aware of the movement, successfully resisted the passage, and the party had to return. Meantime the defenders raised some batteries in the nighttime, from which they greatly annoyed the English. At last Ginkle, foiled at Lanesborough, tried to force his way across the bridge, and for several days there was desperate fighting in the narrow roadway, so that the English, though greatly outnumbering their opponents, were, as Story tells us, only able to advance inch by inch. On the bridge, towards the Connaught side, stood a mill, worked in the peaceful days of the past by the current beneath. In this building 64 Irish were stationed: but it was set on fire by hand grenades from the English lines, and the little garrison, being unable to escape, were burned to death, all but two who leaped into the river and swam to land. At length by mere pressure of numbers the besiegers obtained possession of the greater part of the bridge, though not till very many of them had been killed: whereupon the defenders abandoned it, but broke down one arch at the Connaught side.

To cross that broken arch was now Ginkle's task. His cannon having been turned on the farther bank, so that as one of the spectators, Colonel Felix O'Neill of the Irish army, tells us, "a cat could scarce appear without being knocked on the head by great or small shot," a party, under cover of a rude wooden shelter, dragged a number of planks along the bridge, and succeeded in throwing them across the chasm; and Ginkle's men were preparing to step forward on the perilous journey. At that moment a volunteer party of eleven Irish, encasing themselves in armour and helmets—for they were fully aware of the deadly danger—rushed forward and began to pull down the planks and hurl them into the stream beneath; but they were met by a volley from the English lines; and when the smoke had cleared away every man of the little band was seen lying dead or wounded. On the instant another party of eleven, unterrified by the fate of their comrades, stepped forward, and dashing in, succeeded in tearing down all the remaining planks: but again the deadly fire did its work, and nine of the eleven fell. Thus foiled, Ginkle made another attempt by constructing a sort of long wooden shed or gallery, which was filled with men and pushed across the narrow bridge way; but the Irish contrived to set it on fire, and the men had to run back for their lives: after which he gave up all idea of forcing his way across the bridge.

A tremendous cannonade had been kept up incessantly for ten days, during which 12,000 cannonballs, 500 bombs, and many tons of stones had been discharged, and 50 tons of powder had been consumed; yet the capture of the town seemed as far off as ever. An anxious council of war was held; and Ginkle, in despair, proposed to raise the siege, for provisions were running short; but his generals prevailed on him to try another plan. The season had been unusually dry, and it was found that the river could be forded, though at great risk, at a point about sixty yards below the bridge. Here it was resolved to make an attempt to cross. St. Ruth had, on the day before, received warning of the intended attack from a deserter. But in his overweening confidence he scoffed at it; feeling quite assured that after the successful defence of the bridge, no other attempt need be feared. From the beginning he believed the passage of the river impossible: "Ginkle deserves to be hanged," said he, "for attempting to take Athlone, while I am here with so great an army to defend it; and I shall deserve to be hanged if I lose it." He was earnestly urged by Sarsfield and others to take precautions; but he met their suggestions with insults, and having sent a small party of untrained recruits to guard the deep ford, he sat down in his tent to enjoy himself. Ginkle was told all this by deserters, so that even Story is able to record how matters stood on the Irish side:—"Three of the most indifferent regiments in the Irish army were on guard," he says, "the rest being all very secure in their camp."

On the 30th June 1691, a volunteer party of Grenadiers was told off for the perilous attempt, "and for the greater encouragement of the Soldiers"—

Story goes on to say—"the General distributed a sum of Guineas amongst them." They plunged into the deep and rapid river twenty abreast, and with great resolution made their way across through fire and smoke; and landing with hardly any opposition, some of them laid planks over the bridge, while others fixed some boats that had been kept ready, so as to form another complete bridge across. The small party of Irish had been taken quite by surprise, and in less than half an hour Ginkle was master of the town. Thus Athlone was captured almost within sight of the whole Irish army, when a little care and vigilance would have rendered the passage of the river impossible; and the heroism of the noble fellows who had sacrificed their lives to tear down the planks went for nothing. After the fight was over the body of the veteran, Colonel Richard Grace, was found under the ruins of the castle: a heroic ending to a heroic life.

The Irish officers bitterly reproached St. Ruth for the loss of Athlone, so that with good reason he became alarmed; and fearing the displeasure of his master King Louis, he now resolved to stake all on the result of a single battle. Falling back on the village of Aughrim in Galway, four miles from Ballinasloe, he determined to make a stand there; and with great judgment he selected an excellent position along the ridge of Kilcommedan Hill, beside the village, with a sluggish stream and a morass in the low ground in front, which was impassable for horse, but might be crossed by foot. At both ends were two narrow passes through the bog, both well guarded; one an old causeway to the Irish left, near the ruined castle of Aughrim, the other on the right, near a ford over a little stream at a place called Uraghree. The slope of the hill in front, down to the morass, was intersected by fences, which were all lined by Irish marksmen.

At six o'clock on the morning of the 12th July, Ginkle's army, consisting of English, Scotch, and Irish, with French, Danes, and Dutch, set out from their encampment at Ballinasloe: but as the morning was foggy, there was a pause till near midday, when an advance was made, and the army drew up in battle array on the heights at the far side of the marsh. There were about 20,000 men on each side. It is proper to remark that the army led by St. Ruth, both here and at Athlone, was purely Irish, as he brought no French soldiers to Ireland.

Ginkle attempted to force the Pass of Uraghree, but was resisted with great spirit, the numbers engaged at this point increasing by accessions every moment, so that what was at first a skirmish became almost a battle. The assailants, after several repulses, came on doggedly again and again, and at last gained their way through the pass, but were set upon with such fury that they were driven back in confusion. At this dangerous juncture Ginkle, after a hasty council of war with his chief officers, determined to draw off for the day, and defer the battle till next morning. Orders were actually given to this effect, when, observing what he believed to be some disorderly movements on the Irish side, he resolved to renew the attempt. A more numerous body was now sent to Uraghree with the object of drawing St. Ruth's forces from the pass at Aughrim; and at half-past four the battle began afresh.

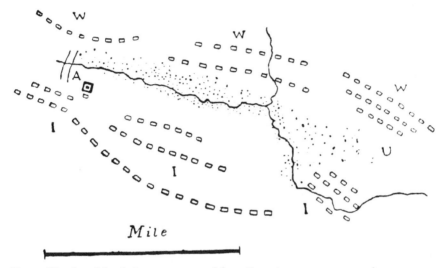

Plan of Battle of Aughrim: constructed from Story's contemporary plan.
A. Castle and Pass, near the present village of Aughrim, U. Pass of Uraghree. W,
W. Ginkle's army. I, I. Irish army.

The plan succeeded, for large bodies of Irish were withdrawn from the Aughrim Pass to help to defend Uraghree; on which Ginkle gave an order for a general advance, one body on his right through the causeway at the castle, and the main body of infantry through the marsh in the middle, in front of St. Ruth's main army. The castle pass was defended with great determination, and while the fight was hottest here, Ginkle's main body succeeded in crossing the stream and marsh, though up to their middle in water and bog. They fought their way steadily up the hill, but at last a terrible onslaught from the fences forced them to recoil. Again and again they advanced, and each time they were driven back, so that a general rout seemed imminent. St. Ruth, all elated, waved his hat and exclaimed: "The day is ours, my boys! We shall now drive them back to the gates of Dublin." But immediately after, while riding down the hill to give some orders about the pass at the castle, he was struck by a cannonball which took off his head. This changed the whole fortunes of the day. No one knew what orders to give, for St. Ruth had let none of his officers into his confidence. There was one man who might have retrieved the disaster—Sarsfield. But St. Ruth, who hated and feared him, took good care to keep him in a subordinate position at the head of some horse, far in the rear, with directions not to move without express orders; and it was only after some time that he was made aware of St. Ruth's fall and of the success of the English. After this, the only service he was able to render was to help to cover the retreat of the Irish infantry after the battle.

General Ginkle. From an old print in the National Gallery, Dublin.

Even after the death of St. Ruth, the contest was obstinately maintained for some time; but without aim or method. At last, late in the evening, the Irish gave way. A great number who had taken refuge in a bog were massacred; and they lost altogether probably 5,000 men. Only about 500 prisoners were taken, and in proportion to the numbers engaged, this was the most destructive battle in the whole war.

Galway submitted on the 21st of July, and Sligo in September, both on favourable terms, their garrisons being allowed to march to Limerick.

———————◆◇◆———————

CHAPTER LIV
THE SECOND SIEGE AND TREATY OF LIMERICK
A.D. 1691–1693.—William and Mary.

ENERAL GINKLE, after his victory at Aughrim, marched southwards for another attempt on Limerick. Tirconnell proceeded to put the city in a state of defence: but he died of apoplexy on the 14th August; on which the chief command devolved on Sarsfield. On the 30th August, just a year after the memorable defence, the second siege began. Ginkle's first operation was a bombardment with sixty cannon and nineteen mortars, from which were poured bombshells, red-hot balls, and carcasses; and soon the city was on fire in several places; so that many of the citizens, muffling themselves in their bedclothes, left and formed an encampment in the open country at the Clare side, beyond the reach of the missiles.

By some extraordinary negligence on the part of a Jacobite officer named Clifford—some say by treachery—Ginkle was able to construct a pontoon bridge of tin boats across the river, above the city, near St. Thomas' Island, and to send a detachment to occupy the Clare side. On the 22nd September an attack was made on the fort that stood at the Clare end of Thomond Bridge, which was for a time obstinately defended; till the Irish at last, overpowered by numbers, had to retreat across the bridge. The town-major, a Frenchman, raised the drawbridge too soon and shut out 600 of them, who, being caught between the drawbridge and their enemies, could make no defence, and though holding up their handkerchiefs, in token of surrender, and calling out for quarter, were all massacred.

There was now a short truce, and negotiations were set on foot for capitulation. Both sides were anxious to end the war. Ginkle saw no prospect of being able to take the city in reasonable time. To capture it at once by storm he considered impracticable—having probably the experience of last year in his mind: and he was in great distress for provisions, so that if

Thomond Bridge in 1840. From Wright's Ireland Illustrated.

there was any further delay, he must, as he said in one of his letters, either starve or begone. We have Story (*Continuation,* p. 214) expressing himself to the same effect:—"Indeavouring to reduce the Town by Force with such a little Army as we had seeming dangerous, considering the very great Strength of their Works which were still intire though the Town was much shattered: these and other reasons were like to render it a Work of longer time than at first we hoped for, and the Winter [was] now drawing on apace." And further on (page 279) he says:—"And though we had passed the river, yet we were as far from entering the Town as ever." The cold and rainy season was sure to bring pestilence among the troops; at the same time it was rumoured that aid was coming from France. The arrival of the French might prolong the struggle indefinitely, the consequence of which no man could foresee; for William and his government were at this time in a very unsettled position. For all these weighty reasons, Ginkle was very anxious to end the war, and willing to grant any reasonable terms as the price of surrender.

Sarsfield on his part, saw no hope in further unaided resistance. Accordingly, on the 3rd October, a Treaty of Peace was signed by Ginkle and the English lords justices on the one hand, and on the other by Sarsfield, now earl of Lucan, and by others; and it was confirmed by King William a short time afterwards. The stone on which it was signed is still to be seen on a pedestal beside Thomond Bridge. We shall see that the Treaty was not kept by the government; but for this violation King William was not to blame. This ended the War of the Revolution; and William and Mary were acknowledged sovereigns of Ireland. A few days afterwards a French fleet sailed up the Shannon: 18 ships of the line and 20 transports, with 3,000 soldiers, 200 officers, and arms and ammunition for 10,000 men; but Sarsfield refused to receive them, and honourably stood by the treaty.

The Treaty of Limerick consisted of two parts, one Civil, the other Military; containing altogether forty-two articles. The most important of the civil articles were these:—The Irish Roman Catholics were to have the same religious liberty as was consistent with the existing law of the land, or as they enjoyed in the reign of Charles II (which was the one period since the Reformation when they had most liberty):[1] and "the oath to be administred to such Roman Catholicks as submit to Their Majesties Government, shall be the Oath [of Allegiance] afore-said, and no other" (Ninth Article). Those in arms for King James to retain the estates they possessed in the time of Charles II, and to be permitted to freely exercise their callings and professions.

Treaty Stone as it appeared half a century ago recently placed on a pedestal.
From Mrs. Hall's Ireland.

---

[1] Here are the very words of this portion of the Treaty, which is the first article of the Civil part, indicating the importance attached to it:—"The Roman Catholicks of this Kingdom shall enjoy such Privileges in the exercise of their Religion as are consistent with the Laws of Ireland, or as they did enjoy in the Reign of King Charles the Second; and Their Majesties (as soon as their Affairs will permit them to summon a Parliament in this Kingdom) will endeavour to procure the said Roman Catholicks such further Security in that Particular, as may preserve them from any disturbance upon the account of their said Religion."

The principal military articles were:—The garrison to be permitted to march out of the city with arms and baggage, drums beating and colours flying. Those officers and soldiers who wished might go to any foreign country, the government to provide them with ships; those who chose might join the army of William and Mary. Ginkle was anxious to keep these

Medal struck to commemorate the surrender of Limerick. King and Queen on obverse. Fame sounding trumpet on reverse, with city in distance. From Ferrar's History of Limerick, 1787.

soldiers in the king's army; but only 1,000 joined; and 2,000 got passes for their homes. More than 20,000 sad exiles—among them Sarsfield—went to Brest and entered the French service. These formed the nucleus of the famous Irish Brigade, who afterwards distinguished themselves in many a battlefield—Fontenoy, Ramillies, Blenheim, Landen, and others; always led by Irish officers, voluntary exiles like themselves. Sarsfield, after brilliant service, fell mortally wounded, in the moment of victory, at the battle of Landen in 1693, where he commanded the left wing of the French army. It is stated that while lying on the ground, seeing his hand stained with his own blood, he exclaimed, "Oh, that this was for Ireland!" There was at this time and for long after, a vast exodus of the very flower of the Irish people to the Continent. Between 1691 and 1745 it is reckoned that 450,000 Irishmen died in the service of France; and many, who if they had remained at home would have lived in obscurity and degradation, attained positions of influence and power in every country on the Continent. The war had cost the English about seven millions, representing probably fifty millions of our money, besides vast destruction of houses, cattle, and other kinds of property.

King William was kindly disposed towards the Irish; and taking advantage of the Treaty, he restored a good part of their estates, and granted many pardons. But he rewarded his followers with vast tracts of land. He created Ginkle earl of Athlone, and gave him 26,000 acres; and to others he gave much larger estates. Altogether he made seventy-six land grants to his own people.

Lord Sydney, the lord lieutenant, summoned a parliament, which met in Dublin on the 5th October, a year after the conclusion of the war: the first held since 1665, with the exception of that of King James. It was exclusively Protestant; for the good reason that almost the first thing done was to frame an oath, to be taken by all members of both houses, that the chief Doctrines of the Catholic church were false; though the Ninth Article of the Treaty had, just a year before, provided that the Catholics were to be required to take only the Oath of Allegiance. Sydney, as representing the king, opposed the measure; but it was carried in spite of him; whereupon all the Catholics present in both houses walked out.

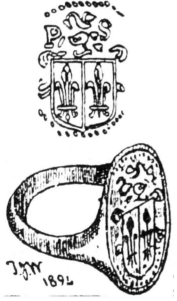

Sarsfield's ring. From the Journal of the Royal Society of Antiquaries of Ireland, vol. iv., 5th ser. 1894, p. 296.

In the course of its proceedings this parliament declared that it was independent of that of England; and though granting a supply of money to the king, it rejected a money bill sent from England, on the ground that it had not been originated in the Irish Commons. This may be regarded as the beginning of the long contest between the English and Irish parliaments, to be related in subsequent chapters. Sydney was so indignant at this refractory proceeding that he twice prorogued this parliament, which was finally dissolved on the 5th November 1693.

There was now another confiscation, as will be further related in next chapter. In less than a century there had been three great confiscations in Ireland, the old proprietors being in all cases dispossessed:—the first after the Geraldine and O'Neill rebellions; the second in the time of Cromwell; and the third after the conquest by King William. These three comprised the whole island, except the estates of about half a dozen families of English blood. Moreover, the three confiscations sometimes overlapped; so that large portions were confiscated twice, and some three times over, within that period. As the result of all, only about a seventh of the land of all

Ireland was left in the hands of the Catholics. The Catholics of old English blood were involved in this general ruin, so far as their numbers went, as well as those of the native Celtic race.

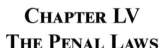

Chapter LV
The Penal Laws

BEFORE resuming our regular narrative, it is necessary that we here turn aside to describe the penal and repressive legislation that followed the capitulation of Limerick, which will be done in this chapter and the next.

The Irish Catholics were now crushed and dispirited; they were quite helpless, for their best men had gone to France; and all hope of resistance was at an end. Yet the Treaty of Limerick remained; and they had the consolation of feeling that in that agreement they had secured tolerable conditions. But here they were doomed to a woeful disappointment. The Irish parliament, with the full concurrence of the English authorities, refused to carry out the treaty in its most important parts; though, as we have seen, it was purchased by most valuable concessions on the part of the Irish commanders, and had been solemnly guaranteed, first by Ginkle and the Irish lords justices, and next by King William himself. "Since the *Irish,*" says Story (*Continuation,* p. 279), "had it still in their power [before the treaty was made] to give us the Town or to keep it to themselves, I see no Reason why they ought not to make a Bargain for it, and expect the performance of their Contract, which Their Majesties have been graciously pleased to ratifie under the Great Seal of England." We may fairly conjecture that when Story (who, it will be remembered, was one of King William's chaplains) wrote these remarkable words in 1691, he had some suspicions and fears that the treaty would not be kept: and that he wrote them in a generous spirit to advocate its faithful fulfilment.

The violation of the treaty greatly displeased King William, who would have honourably kept to his part of the agreement, as Sarsfield did on his side when he refused to admit the French fleet. For William was not disposed to oppress anyone on account of religion; and he was often heard to declare that he came over *to deliver the Protestants but not to persecute the Catholics.* It does not appear, indeed, that he ever redeemed his pledge, made in the first article of the treaty, to try to procure further religious security for the Catholics: but, no doubt, he thought it would be useless—as it certainly would have been—to attempt to move either the Irish or the English parliament in that direction.

After the conclusion of the War of the Revolution, the government of Ireland was completely in the hands of the small Protestant minority, who also possessed almost the whole of the land of the country; and they held nearly all the offices of trust and emolument. And now, not only did they refuse to carry out the treaty, but they went much farther by passing a number of Penal Laws, which, so long as they remained in force, would keep down the Catholics, who formed four-fifths of the population, and would secure for the Protestant minority the great possessions and privileges they already enjoyed.

Before 1695 there were many penal enactments against Irish Catholics, with the main object of compelling them to abandon their own religion and to adopt the doctrines and forms of worship of the Reformation; but they were passed only at long intervals, and the authorities, for various reasons, were not always anxious, or were not able, to have them carried out. But after that date they came in quick succession, growing more and more severe as time went on; till they reached their worst phases chiefly in the first years of the reign of Queen Anne, and partly in the reign of George II; and they were generally enforced, so far as lay in the power of the authorities. These repressive laws were mostly the work of the Irish parliament, but the English parliament sometimes stepped in and lent its aid. The Code remained in full force for about three-quarters of a century, when it began to be relaxed, though by very small degrees at first. Gradually, and very slowly, the worst of the enactments were repealed, one by one, as will be noticed in the proper places as we go along, till, with the exception of some particulars, the Emancipation Act of 1829 put an end to the disabilities of Irish Catholics. It will be convenient to bring the leading enactments of the whole Penal Code into this chapter, though it will oblige us to run a little in advance in point of time.

The parliament of 1692, as related in the last chapter, led the way by framing an oath to exclude Catholics from parliament, contrary to the ninth article of the treaty. But the really active penal legislation was entered upon by the parliament which met in Dublin in 1695. Their first proceeding was to introduce a bill "for the confirmation of Articles made at the Treaty of Limerick": and thereupon they confirmed all the minor provisions of the treaty and omitted all the important ones. This bill passed easily through the House of Commons; but it was vigorously resisted in the upper House by a powerful minority of Irish lords—all Protestants be it remembered—who vehemently condemned such breach of faith. And when, in spite of opposition, the bill was at length passed, a number of them, including seven Protestant bishops, signed a strong protest against it. Having thus secured what amounted to the rejection of the treaty, this parliament, during the sessions of 1695 and 1697, passed a number of penal laws, of which the following are the most important:

Catholic schoolmasters were forbidden to teach, either in schools or in private houses, and Catholic parents were forbidden to send their children to any foreign country to be educated; from which it will be seen that care was taken to deprive Catholics—as such—altogether of the means of education.

Although the treaty secured to the Catholic gentry of certain specified counties the possession of their estates, the parliament dispossessed them all, and seized their lands, which they gave to others.

Catholics were to deliver up their arms; and if a magistrate suspected that there were any in the house of a Catholic, he might make a search, and if refused admission, might break open the door. If a Catholic had a valuable horse, any Protestant might take possession of it by offering £5—which answers to about £30 of our present money.

The existing parish priests were not to be disturbed; but all had to be registered in a government book, and had to give security for good behaviour. About a thousand were registered; and these were allowed to celebrate Mass, but they could keep no curates. It was ordained that all other Catholic clergy—bishops, Jesuits, friars, monks, and the Regular clergy of every order—should, under penalties, quit the kingdom by the 1st May 1698; and any who returned were adjudged guilty of high treason, of which the punishment was death. This would of course, after some time, leave the people altogether without priests; for according as the existing clergy died out, there would be none to take their places, since a priest could not be ordained without a bishop. Several hundreds of those against whom the decree was directed left the country; but many remained, including some bishops, who disguised and concealed themselves as best they could. It was ordered that no Catholic chapel should have either steeple or bells. There were many other stringent measures passed by this parliament, which it would be tedious to enumerate.

This was the first instalment of the Penal Code; but it was followed by much worse. When, a few years later, the Duke of Ormond (grandson of Ormond of the Confederate times) came over as lord lieutenant, the House of Commons petitioned him for a further extension of the penal legislation; though the reason why is hard to make out; for the Catholic people had been quiet and submissive, and had given no provocation whatever. Yet

Ormond consented; and in 1704 an act was passed, of which the following were the most important provisions. If the eldest son of a Roman Catholic with landed property declared himself a Protestant, he became the owner of all his father's land, and the father sank to the position of life-tenant; and if any other child, no matter how young, professed that he was a Protestant, he was placed under a Protestant guardian, and the father had to pay all the expenses of separate maintenance and education. One very bad feature of these provisions was that they encouraged baseness, by tempting children to the unnatural course of turning against their own parents for the sake of mere gain. If the wife of a Catholic became a Protestant, she could claim separate support from his estate, and one-third of all his other property. No Catholic could be a guardian to a child: so that when a father who had young children felt himself dying, his last hours were troubled by the consciousness that his children were likely to be brought up Protestants.

No Catholic was permitted to purchase land, or even to take a lease of land for life (which was called a *freehold lease*), or for longer than 31 years: and if land descended to a Catholic as heir to some former owner, or if land was left to him by will; in neither case could he accept it. The profit of a Catholic's farm, over and above the rent, was never to exceed one-third of that rent; and if any Protestant proved that the profit realised was more than that, he could take possession of the farm. The intention of all these provisions was to make it impossible for Catholics ever again to own any part of the land of the country.

No person could vote at an election for a Member of Parliament without taking an oath that the Catholic religion was false. A Catholic could not hold any office either in the Civil or Military Service without taking the same oath and submitting to the "Sacramental Test," that is, receiving the Sacrament on Sundays in some Protestant place of worship, according to the rite of the Established Church. This last item of the Code is what is called the Test Act; and it applied to the Presbyterians and other Non-conformists as well as to the Catholics; for they have special rites of their own.

Later on—in the first year of the reign of George II—the Catholics were wholly disfranchised, that is, they were forbidden to vote at an election under any circumstances whatever. No Catholic was to be permitted to come to live in the cities of Limerick or Galway; but those who were residing in them at the time were allowed to remain, provided they gave security for good behaviour: but this law soon became a dead letter, for it was found impossible to have it carried out.

Rewards were offered for the discovery of bishops, Jesuits, unregistered priests, and schoolmasters: and whenever such a reward was earned, the Catholics had to pay it. Very determined measures were taken, moreover, to have this law enforced. In the last year of Queen Anne's reign (1714), the English parliament extended to Ireland the "Schism Act," which ordained that no person could teach a school unless he had a license from the Protestant bishop: and this license could not be granted unless the applicant submitted to the Sacramental Test.

In the foregoing sketch, only the main provisions of the Penal Code have been enumerated.

These laws were mainly intended to suppress the Catholic religion. But they had no effect whatever in making the people conform, as is shown by the fact that twenty years later, we find the Irish parliament complaining of the continued increase of Catholicity, and proposing other measures for its suppression of so violent a character that the English authorities refused to sanction them.

The Catholics were not the only people who suffered under this legislation. In a very little time the "Test Act" and the "Schism Act" were brought to bear against the Ulster Presbyterians, who were now subjected to bitter persecution: for they refused either to apply to the bishop for licenses to teach in schools, or to receive the Sacrament according to the English rite. They were expelled from Belfast and Derry, they were dismissed from the magistracy, prohibited from teaching school, their marriages were declared void, and the Regium Donum, an annual grant given by King William to their clergy, was stopped for the time. But they bore it all with steady resolution rather than violate their principles. Many, however, took another course. It will be related in the next chapter how the ruin of the wool trade, in 1698, drove numbers of Presbyterians to emigrate to New England: and as the distress continued, so also did the emigration. But it was greatly increased by these religious hardships; and now the Presbyterians went off in large numbers. This alarmed the government, as it increased the relative proportion of Catholics; yet they obstinately retained these two acts, though earnestly recommended to repeal them by successive lord lieutenants: and so the exodus continued. For a long period about the middle of the century, it is calculated that 12,000 emigrated every year from Ulster. The sufferings of the Presbyterians, however, though bitter for the time, were trifling and brief compared with those of the Catholics.

It would be unjust to view these laws as if they stood alone. In many parts of Europe at the time, there were stringent penal laws: of Protestants against Catholics in some countries: of Catholics against Protestants in others: a fact that must be carefully borne in mind in reviewing this legislation. But in at least two respects the Irish laws contrasted unfavourably with other penal codes. In all other countries it was the great majority persecuting a small sect, to force them into religious compliance, with the general body: in Ireland alone was the attempt made by a small minority to suppress the religion of the whole nation among whom they lived. But perhaps the worst feature of the Irish enactments was that they were made in open breach of public faith.

To us, looking back at those evil times from a distance of nearly two centuries, the picture is not wholly black. There are spots brightened by humanity, which, when well considered, should stir up feelings of mutual kindliness among the people of the present day. It will be good to point out a few of these relieving features.

It was the governing classes that made those terrible penal laws; the general body of the Protestant people, whether in England or Ireland, had no hand in them. And when the laws came into operation, a large proportion of Irish Protestants, all through the country, looked upon them with silent disapproval, and did a great deal in a quiet way to protect their Catholic neighbours; just as many Catholics—both clergy and laymen—in 1641, and subsequently in 1798, saved their Protestant friends from the fury of the mob. This was especially the case where property was concerned. A Catholic gentleman, when in danger of losing his land through some one of the means provided by law, told his story to his Protestant neighbour, who on the spot purchased the estate, or rather pretended to purchase it, drawing out a regular agreement and taking over the title deeds, but paying no purchase money. He was now the owner according to law, and received the rents, but secretly handed them over to his Catholic friend as they came in; and this continued generally during the lives of the two, and often during the lives of their children and grandchildren, till the repeal of the statute enabled land and deeds to be restored to the owners. Cases such as this were quite common all over the country: and among the Protestant gentry it was considered a special point of honour to keep and restore the property undiminished, faithfully, and without fee or reward. Many a Catholic gentleman holds his estate at this day through the kind feeling of the ancestors of his present Protestant neighbours.

So also it often happened that a dying Catholic, with young children, sent for his Protestant friend and complied outwardly with the law by leaving them to his guardianship, with the secret understanding that they should be educated by some Catholic selected by the family; and there is good reason to believe that guardians thus appointed were generally faithful to their trust: often at great risk to themselves. The enactment about the horse of more than £5 value was taken advantage of only in a very few cases; and Catholic gentlemen continued to hunt and race and drive equipages with valuable horses, among the Protestant gentry, without any molestation during the whole time the law remained in force.

While many magistrates were active in seeing the law carried out, there were others more under the influence of good feeling. One of these, suppose, received information that some banned priest or schoolmaster was hiding in the neighbourhood; but he intentionally delayed, or went to the wrong spot, or met with some trifling accident, or sent word secretly: and at last arrived at the hiding place, looking very wicked, only to find the culprit gone.

In other ways the operation of these cruel laws was mitigated, and it often turned out that matters were not quite so bad with Catholics as the lawmakers intended. Evasions were very often winked at, even where well-known. Catholic bishops remained all through in the country in spite of every effort to discover them, living in huts in remote places under various disguises, and meeting their congregations by night in wild glens and bogs. Young priests who had been educated abroad managed to return, and took up their duties though not registered. But such breaches and evasions were always very dangerous, and might at any moment end in detection and punishment. Then as to education. Many priests kept schoolmasters, who taught in sheds put up in remote glens, or they instructed individual scholars, in a scrappy kind of way, in fields or lanes; which however was only a flickering sort of education, that could not reach the general mass of the people.

In one very important particular the penal code failed to reach the Catholics. Though they were shut out from the ownership of land, and from the professions, many branches of business lay open to them; so that numbers of Catholics prospered in trade, and became rich, with no power to hinder them, especially in large towns and seaports.

Along with all this, it is well known that towards the middle of the eighteenth century, though the worst of the penal statutes remained in force, many of them were quietly suffered to fall into disuse, so that Catholics began to bestir themselves a little, and to hope for better times. In some parts of the country too, there was such an overwhelming preponderance of Catholics, that even in the worst of the penal times it was impossible to have the laws enforced.

But making every allowance for kindliness, protection, evasion, and non-enforcement of the law, the Catholic people underwent terrible sufferings for three or four generations; and no one who has not read the detailed history of those times can have any idea of the sort of life they led. Though the Penal Code quite failed to make them Protestants, it succeeded perfectly in crushing, impoverishing, and degrading them. Deprived of the means of education and advancement, the great body sank in the end into such a state of listless ignorance and poverty, and became so downtrodden and oppressed with a sense of inferiority, that after their disabilities had been removed and the way had been cleared for them, it took them many generations more to recover anything like the position of independence, self-respect, and influence, they had enjoyed before the penal times.

———◆◇◆———

CHAPTER LVI
LAWS TO REPRESS IRISH TRADE AND MANUFACTURE

HE Penal Laws described in the last chapter applied mainly to Catholics: but the repressive code now about to be described oppressed Irishmen of all creeds.

Ireland has a good climate, a fertile soil, and a fair supply of minerals; and towards the end of the seventeenth century, in spite of wars and other troubles, several branches of manufacture, trade, and commerce were flourishing. But the traders and merchants of England fancied that the prosperity of Ireland was a loss to them, by drawing away custom; and in their short-sighted and selfish jealousy, they persuaded the English parliament—which, indeed, needed little persuasion—to ruin almost the whole trade of Ireland. As in the case of the penal enactments touching religion, it will be convenient to bring all the main provisions of this code into one chapter.

This legislation was generally the work of the English parliament alone; but sometimes the Irish parliament followed in the same direction; and, in obedience to orders, passed acts impoverishing their own country. It must be borne in mind that religion had nothing to do with these proceedings, which are all the more to be wondered at, seeing that the blow fell chiefly on Irish Protestants; for at this time the general body of the Catholics were barely able to live, and could do very little as a body in the way of industries. But the English traders cared nothing for all this; they wanted to destroy Irish trade for their own gain; and whether the ruin fell on Protestants, Presbyterians, or Catholics, was a matter of indifference to them.

Down to 1663 Irish merchants had been in the habit of exporting goods of various kinds to different foreign countries, especially to the British colonies all over the world; and as Ireland is a good grazing country, a flourishing trade was also carried on by the export of Irish cattle to England. Now, an end was put to all this; for several acts were passed in the English parliament from 1663 to 1680 prohibiting Irish merchants from exporting or importing any goods to or from the colonies; and the export of cattle, sheep, pigs, beef, pork, mutton, butter, and cheese, to England, was altogether stopped. Thus the chief Irish industry was destroyed; and the people, being unable to find a market for the produce of their farms, fell at once into poverty.

Yet the Irish did not despair. Driven from cattle-rearing, they applied themselves to other industries, especially that of wool, for which the country is well suited. In those times Irish wool was considered the best in Europe; and, notwithstanding the measures of Wentworth to cripple this trade, it began to flourish again, and was rapidly rising to be a great national industry, which was carried on almost exclusively by the Protestant colonists. But this, too, was doomed. The English cloth dealers, taking the alarm, petitioned in 1698 to have it suppressed: and King William, in the speech from the throne, promised to discourage the Irish wool trade, to encourage the Irish linen trade, and to promote the trade of England.

It is worthy of remark that in their petitions and addresses, the English never made the least secret of what they wanted, namely, to destroy Irish trade for their own benefit. When the traders sent forward their petition about wool in 1698, the English House of Lords, in a petition to the king, say:—"The growing manufacture of cloth in Ireland, both by the cheapness of all sorts of necessaries of life, and goodness of materials for making all manner of cloth, . . . makes your loyal subjects in this kingdom very apprehensive that the further growth of it may greatly prejudice the said manufacture here." And, in the same year, the people of Aldborough and Folkstone petitioned that the inhabitants of the eastern coast of Ireland should be stopped from fishing and selling their fish, because of the injury done "by the Irish catching herrings at Waterford and Wexford and sending them to the Straits, and thereby forestalling and ruining petitioners' markets." And other such instances might be cited.

The upshot of the agitation against the wool trade was that, in 1699, the servile Irish parliament, acting on directions from the other side, put an export duty of four shillings per lb. on fine woollen cloths, and two shillings per lb. on frieze and flannel, knowing well that this was sure to ruin their Protestant fellow-countrymen. The English parliament followed up this measure by passing an act prohibiting the Irish from exporting either wool or woollen goods to any part of the world except a few specified seaport towns in England; and it was forbidden to ship woollens even to these except from Dublin, Cork, and four other Irish seaports.

These acts accomplished all that the English merchants looked for: they ruined the Irish wool trade. The heavy duty the Irish wool merchants had to pay obliged them to put such a price on their goods that they found it impossible to sell them in England; so the trade was stopped altogether, just as the lawmakers intended. The woollen mills ceased to work, the work-people were turned idle, and the buildings went to ruin. Forty thousand Irish Protestants—all prosperous working people—were immediately reduced to idleness and poverty by it; the Catholics, of course, sharing in the misery so far as they were employed; and 20,000 Presbyterians and other Nonconformists left Ireland for New England. Then began the emigration, from want of employment, that continues to this day. But the English parliament professed to encourage the Irish linen trade; for this could do no harm to English traders, as flax-growing and linen manufacture had not taken much hold in England.

As almost always happens when plenty of a commodity can be produced, on which there are prohibitive duties—that is, duties so heavy that it is impossible to pay them and afterwards sell the goods with reasonable profit—smuggling now increased enormously. Wool became so plentiful at home that it fetched only about five-pence a lb.; while three or four shillings could easily be got for it in France. This drove people to smuggle—to send out cargoes of woollen goods secretly, so as to avoid paying the customs duties; and the smugglers imported, in return, contraband goods—that is, those that ought to pay duty, but did not. Every returning vessel brought back quantities of brandy, wine, silks, and so forth, and landed them in remote places on the coast, so as to elude the customs officers and escape the duties. All these articles they bought cheaply in France, and either kept them for their own use, or more commonly sold them—cheaply, indeed, but still far beyond cost price; so that smuggling was, in those days, a very profitable business. None cared to interfere, for thousands of the Irish of all classes profited by it; and high and low, squires, magistrates, clergy, and peasants, Protestants and Catholics—almost the whole population in fact—were in active combination against the law. The Government were powerless to stop this trade; and for generations it flourished all round the coasts: one of the evil results of unjust and unwise legislation.

It would be tedious to describe in detail the various provisions for the ruin of Irish industries enacted by the English parliament. Gradually it came to pass that almost all branches of Irish trade and manufacture were destroyed—beer, malt, hats, cotton, silk, sailcloth, gunpowder, ironware, &c. And a little farther on, it will be related how the embargo in the time of the American war not only ruined the farmers, but ruined the trade in salted beef and other such commodities.

The destruction of all industry produced the natural results. During the first half of the eighteenth century Ireland was in an appalling state of misery: regularly recurring famines with their attendant diseases all over the country, and whole districts depopulated. A large proportion of the little capital left in the country was sent to England to absentee landlords by middlemen, who, in their turn, extracted the very last penny from the wretched cottiers; and this constant drain of money greatly aggravated the wretchedness brought on by want of employment. During the eighteenth century the peasantry of Ireland were the most miserable in Europe; and in the frequent famines, a large proportion of the inhabitants were quite as badly off as the people of Derry during the worst part of the siege.

But the evil consequences of those evil laws did not end with the eighteenth century: they have come down to the present day. For when, subsequently, the restrictions were removed and trade was partially relieved, the remedy came too late. Some branches of manufacture and trade had been killed downright, and others permanently injured. An industry once extinguished is not easily revived. The trade in wool, a chief staple of Ireland, which was kept down for nearly a century, never recovered its former state of prosperity. The consequence of all this is that Ireland has at this day comparatively little manufacture and commerce; and the people have to depend for subsistence chiefly on the land. And this again, by increasing the competition for land, has intensified the land troubles inherited from the older times of the plantations.

Chapter LVII
The Beginning of the
Parliamentary Struggle
William and Mary (to 1702).
A.D. 1698–1757. Anne (1702–1714).
George I (1714–1727).
George II (1727).

EADERS of Irish History should carefully bear in mind that the proceedings of the Irish Parliament, and the political history of the country during the eighteenth century, have reference almost solely to the Protestant portion of the community; and that the struggles of the Irish legislature for independence, to be related in this and the following chapters, were the struggles of Protestants alone. The Catholics had no power to take part in these contests: for no Catholic could be a member of parliament, or even vote at an election for one. They kept almost wholly silent—at least during the first half of the century—believing that the less attention they drew on themselves the better: for they cowered under the law, and knew not the moment they might be visited with further crushing enactments. The Protestants of the Irish Patriotic party strove for the rights of the Protestant people only. The Catholics never entered into their thoughts except for the purpose of keeping them down. Molyneux, Swift, Lucas, Flood, and many other patriots that will come before us as we go along, were all against granting any political liberty to Catholics. Burke and Grattan were almost the only two great Protestants of the first three-quarters of the eighteenth century who took a broader view, and advocated the right of the Irish Catholics to be placed on terms of equality with the Protestant people.

The position of the Irish parliament during the greater part of the century was this. The high government officials, from the lord lieutenant down, were nearly all Englishmen, with commonly a few Irishmen of English sympathies. These formed what may be called the Court Party. They were in favour of English ascendancy, being always ready to carry out the wishes of the king and the English council; and as, by the various means at their disposal described farther on—bribery, pensions, situations, titles, &c.—they were nearly always able to have a majority of members in their favour, the English interest was all-powerful in the Irish parliament. But among a thoughtful section of Irish Protestants, who had the interests of their own country, or at least of the Protestant part of it, at heart, the unjust laws that destroyed the industries of Ireland and ruined and impoverished its people to enrich English merchants and tradesmen, and the appointment of Englishmen to all the important posts to the exclusion of Irishmen, provoked feelings of resentment and distrust towards the English government akin to those produced in times of old by a similar course of ill-treatment, and kindled in them a sentiment of patriotism which became more intensified as time went on. They were always represented in parliament by a small opposition, who came to be called Patriots, or the Patriotic or Popular Party. Some of these were indeed selfish and corrupt, and made themselves troublesome merely to induce the government to buy them off by giving them good situations or pensions. But there was always a solid body of men of a different stamp, like Molyneux and Grattan, who, so far as lay in their power, resisted all dictation and all encroachment on the privileges of the Irish parliament, or on the rights and liberties of the country. They held steadily in view two main objects:—To remove the ruinous restrictions on trade and commerce, and to make their parliament as far as possible independent, so that it might have a free hand to manage the affairs of Ireland. It was the unjust trade laws, and the constant preferment of Englishmen over the heads of Irishmen that gave origin to the Irish Patriotic Party, and brought to the front their great leaders both in and out of parliament, from Molyneux to Swift and from Swift to Grattan. Gradually, year by year, they gained strength, and ultimately, as we shall see, carried their main points against the government: but it was a long and bitter struggle. Sometimes it happened in cases of unusual provocation, that, not only the small party of Patriots, but the great majority of the Irish members were roused to successful resistance in spite of the influence of the Court Party: of which we shall see instances as we go along. The struggle between these two parties forms the main feature in the political history of Ireland during the greater part of the eighteenth century.

The resistance began early. In 1698, some years before the time we are now treating of, William Molyneux, member of parliament for the University of Dublin, a man of great scientific eminence, published his famous book, *The Case of Ireland's being bound by Acts of parliament in England stated,* in which he denounced the commercial injustice done to Ireland, traced the growth of the Irish parliament, and maintained that it was independent of that of England, and had a right to make its own laws. This Essay was received in England with great indignation; and the parliament there, pronouncing it dangerous, ordered it to be burned publicly by the hangman. But the powerful statement of Molyneux, though it taught his countrymen a useful lesson, did not close up the road to ruin; for in the very year after its publication came the most crushing of all the restrictions, the act already described destroying the Irish wool industry.

A few years later on, the bitter feelings excited in Ireland by these and other such proceedings were greatly intensified by a notable event brought about by a lawsuit commonly known as the "Annesley case." A dispute about some property arose, in 1719, between two Irish persons, Hester Sherlock and Maurice Annesley, which the Dublin court of exchequer decided in favour of Annesley; but the Irish house of lords, on being appealed to, reversed this and gave judgment in favour of Hester Sherlock. Annesley appealed to the English house of lords, who affirmed the exchequer decision, reversing that of the Irish lords; and they fined Burrowes, the sheriff of Kildare, because he refused to put Annesley in possession in obedience to their decree. But the Irish peers remitted the fine, declaring the appeal to the English lords illegal, commended the sheriff for his action, and went farther by taking into custody the three barons of the court of exchequer who had given judgment for Annesley. The English parliament at last ended the dispute by passing a momentous act (known as "The Sixth of George I") deciding that the English parliament had the right to make laws for Ireland; and depriving the Irish house of lords of the right to hear appeals. It will be remembered that Poynings' Act did not give the English parliament the power of legislating for Ireland. The Sixth of George I now asserted this right for the first time, and thus took away whatever little independence Poynings' Law had left, and reduced the Irish parliament to a mere shadow.

The task of actively opposing the Court Party, by speech and pen, was not left solely in the hands of members of parliament: there were men equally able and active outside, of whom the most brilliant by far was Jonathan Swift, the celebrated dean of St. Patrick's in Dublin. He was indignant at the destruction of Irish industries for the benefit of English traders; and, in 1720, he wrote an essay encouraging the Irish people to retaliate by rejecting all clothing and furniture made in England, and using only their own home manufacture: an essay that so enraged the authorities of both countries that, although there was nothing illegal in the proposal, the Government prosecuted the printer, but failed to have him punished, notwithstanding the brow-beating efforts of the corrupt judge who tried the case.

It was however Swift's action in the case of "Wood's Halfpence" that brought him into the greatest notoriety. At this time much inconvenience was felt in Ireland from the want of small copper coins: and, in 1723, the English treasury, without consulting the Irish authorities, granted a patent for coining £108,000 in base-metal halfpence and farthings, to the king's favourite the Duchess of Kendal, who sold the patent to an English iron merchant named Wood, a transaction which would bring an immense profit to the duchess and to Wood. And what made the matter all the worse was that not more than about £15,000 in small coin was needed. This gross job created intense alarm and indignation in Ireland. The Patriots vehemently attacked and exposed it; the two Irish houses addressed the king, representing that this base coinage would diminish revenue and destroy commerce; and multitudes of pamphlets, songs, squibs, and coarse caricatures were written and circulated in Dublin attacking "Wood's Halfpence." But the scheme was pressed by powerful friends at court, and would have succeeded only for Swift. He wrote and printed five letters, one after another, with the signature "W. B. Drapier," pointing out in simple, homely, vigorous language that the most ignorant could understand the evils which, according to him, would result from the coinage. These coins were so bad, as he told his readers, that twenty-four of them were worth no more than one good penny; that if a lady went shopping she should have to bring with her a cart loaded with the new money; that a farmer

Jonathan Swift. From portrait in National Gallery, Dublin.

would have to employ three horses to bring his rent to his landlord; that a poor man would have to give thirty-six of the halfpence for a quart of ale; and that it would ruin all classes, even the very beggars; for, when a man gives a beggar one of these halfpence, it "will do him no more service than if I should give him three pins out of my sleeve." There had been great excitement; but it was increased tenfold by these letters. The Court Officials were greatly provoked; and the lord lieutenant offered a reward of £300 for the discovery of the author; but, though everyone knew who the author was, no one came forward to inform on him. At length matters looked so threatening that the patent had to be withdrawn, a victory that greatly strengthened the hands of the Patriots; and the dean became amazingly popular all through Ireland among both Protestants and Catholics.

In the middle of the century the Popular Party had for leaders, Councillor Anthony Malone, a member of the house of commons, a good statesman and a good orator; and Charles Lucas, a Dublin apothecary, not then in parliament, though he was subsequently elected: while their leader in the lords was the Earl of Kildare, afterwards Duke of Leinster. Under these three able men they boldly attacked the corrupt practices of the government, and triumphed on more than one occasion.

Charles O'Conor, of Bellanagar.

The feeling against Catholics had lately been growing somewhat less bitter; and they began to bestir themselves, hoping to obtain some little relief. The first timid movements were made by three Catholic gentlemen:— Dr. Curry, a physician of Dublin, historian of the civil wars in Ireland; Charles O'Conor of Bellanagar in Roscommon, a distinguished scholar and antiquarian, author of several books on Irish historical literature; and Mr. Wyse of Waterford. They endeavoured, in the first instance, to stir up the Catholic clergy and aristocracy to agitate for their rights; but here their efforts quite failed; for these classes, having already suffered so much, were fearful that any attempt to obtain justice might only make matters worse. At this time, however, a good many Catholics, driven from the professions, had, as already stated, taken to business and commerce in Dublin and other cities: and among these classes Curry and his colleagues were more successful; so that they founded the "Catholic Committee" to watch over the interests of Catholics. This body was to hold its meetings in Dublin. The association spread some enlightenment, and infused some faint life and hope among the Catholics; and it may be regarded as the feeble beginning of the movement for Catholic relief, which subsequently became so formidable and successful under O'Connell.

CHAPTER LVIII
DISCONTENT AND DANGER
A.D. 1761–1772.—George III.

IDDLEMEN, a class of persons well known in Ireland, had a great deal to do with the wretched condition of the Irish peasantry during the eighteenth century. These were men who took tracts of land from the absentee landlords at a moderate rent, and sublet it to cottiers and small farmers at rackrents that left hardly enough to support life. Sometimes there were two middlemen, the one who let the land to the farmers being himself the tenant of another over his head, who, in his turn, rented it from the great absentee; and not unfrequently there were three, each making a profit from the next below. But whether one, two, or three, the tillers of the soil were always kept in a state of the greatest poverty, being quite at the mercy of their immediate landlord. Those who had leases were indeed a little better off; but very few had; nearly all were tenants at will; and the landlord made them pay whatever he pleased. This state of things, which affected both Protestants and Catholics, existed in every part of Ireland during the whole of this century, and continued far into the next.

Other causes contributed to the prevailing depression. Towards the middle of the century, there was a very general movement among landlords, both great and small, to turn the land to pasture; for they found it more profitable to graze and sell cattle than to let the land for tillage; and thousands of poor cottiers were turned off in order that the land might be converted into great grazing farms. Near many of the villages in various parts of Ireland were "Commons," stretches of grassy upland or bog which were free to the people to use for grazing or for cutting turf, and formed one of their chief ways of living. These had belonged to them time out of mind, being in fact the remains of the Commons Land of ancient days; but about this period the landlords had begun to enclose them as private property, chiefly for grazing. The people had other reasons for discontent too. They complained that the landlords charged excessive rents for bogs; and the gentry everywhere managed to evade the tithes payable to the ministers of the Established Church, which in consequence fell chiefly on the very poorest of the people. In addition to all these was the general want of employment due to the loss of trade of every kind, already referred to, which drove the peasantry to depend on land as almost their sole means of subsistence.

At last the people, with some wild notions of redressing their grievances, began to combine in various secret oath-bound societies, by which the country was for many years greatly disturbed. Of these the most noteworthy were the Whiteboys—so called because they wore white shirts over their coats when out on their nightly excursions—who were confined chiefly to the counties of Waterford, Cork, Limerick, and Tipperary. The movement was not sectarian; and it was not directed against the government, but against the oppression of individuals. The Whiteboys rose up in the first instance (in 1761) against the enclosure of commons, and persons of different religions joined them; for all suffered equally from the encroachments of the landlords: and Catholics as well as Protestants fell under their vengeance. They traversed the country at night, levelling all the new fences that enclosed the commons, and digging up pasture land to force tillage: whence they at first got the name of Levellers. But they soon went beyond their original designs, setting themselves up as redressers of all sorts of grievances; and they committed terrible outrages on those who became obnoxious to them. Sometimes they took people out of their beds in winter, and immersed them naked up to the chin in a pit of water full of briars. At length they became so troublesome that a large force was sent, in 1762, to suppress them, under the marquis of Drogheda, who fixed his headquarters at Clogheen in Tipperary. The parish priest, Father Nicholas Sheehy, was accused of enrolling Whiteboys, and a reward was offered for his arrest; but he, earnestly denying the charge, surrendered, and was tried in Dublin and acquitted. He was immediately re-arrested on a charge of murdering one of his accusers, and put on his trial this time in Clonmel; and on the evidence of the self-same witnesses, who had been disbelieved in Dublin, as persons well known to be of bad character, he was convicted and hanged. Father Sheehy asserted his innocence to the last; the people considered him a martyr, and his execution caused fearful excitement.

In Ulster there were similar secret associations among the Protestant peasantry, brought about by causes of much the same kind as those of the south. One main ground of complaint was that every man was forced to give six days' work in the year, and six days' work of a horse, in the making or repairing of roads, which the gentry made full use of, while they themselves contributed nothing. Those who banded together against this were called "Hearts of Oak." Another association, the "Hearts of Steel," rose in 1769, against unjust and exorbitant rents; for the people of Ulster were as much oppressed as those of Munster by middlemen, who were here commonly known as "Forestallers." These "Oakboys" and "Steelboys," not content with their original objects, set themselves to redress various abuses about land, like their brethren in the south; and they also opposed the payment of tithes, which had been lately very much increased in Ulster. The oppression of the northern peasantry by the gentry caused a great emigration of the best of the people to New England, or rather increased the emigration begun more than half a century before; and when, a little later, the war broke out between England and the United States, the most determined and dangerous of the troops who fought against the English were the sturdy expatriated Presbyterians of Ulster, and the descendants of those who had emigrated on account of religious persecution and the destruction of the wool trade. There were many other secret societies at this time and for long afterwards, culminating later on in the most celebrated of all, the United Irishmen.

Meantime, through all this trouble, the contest of the two parties in parliament went on without the least cessation. The Court Party were strong, and continued to purchase members to their side by various corrupt means; but the Patriots were sleepless and vigilant, and never gave the government a day's rest. Pensions constituted one of the principal forms of bribery. Large pensions were given to numbers of persons who had done nothing to earn them; and some were bestowed on favourites by the English privy council and charged to Ireland without any reference to the Irish government; so that the Pension List had grown to enormous proportions. This corrupt and ruinous pension list was vehemently attacked by the Patriots under the lead of a great man, Henry Flood,[1] who was aided

---

[1]At this time three great Irishmen, who for years played an important part in Irish affairs, began their career:—Henry Flood, born near Kilkenny, 1732, died 1791; Henry Grattan, born in Dublin, 1746, the son of the recorder, died 1820; Edmund Burke, born in Dublin in 1730, died 1797.

Burke, who figured in the English parliament, was one of the greatest political philosophers that ever lived. He began his public life in 1765, as private secretary to Lord Rockingham, the English prime minister, and in the following year he was elected member for Wendover. In 1774 he became member for Bristol. He opposed the American war; and on this question, as well as on those of the French revolution, and the Stamp Act, he wrote powerful pamphlets, and made a series of

by the growing eloquence of a still more celebrated patriot, Henry Grattan, then a very young man, and not yet in parliament. But, although they fully exposed the corruption of the pension list, the government proved too strong for them, and the evil, so far from abating, continued to increase year by year.

Henry Flood.

Another question arose about this time which excited great interest— that of the duration of parliament. In England the utmost limit was seven years; at the end of which the parliament, if it lasted so long, had to be dissolved, and there was a general election. This was a good plan; for if a

splendid speeches. He lifted himself above the prejudices of the times, and all his life advocated the emancipation of the Catholics.

Grattan was, perhaps, Ireland's most brilliant orator and one of her purest and greatest patriots. He began his parliamentary life in 1775, at twenty-nine years of age, as member for Charlemont; and his very first speech was in opposition to the pensions of two absentees. In oratorical power, Flood was second only to Grattan.

member acted wrong the electors could put another in his place without much delay. But, in Ireland, parliament lasted as long as the king wished; and the preceding one had continued during the entire reign of George II: thirty-three years.

This state of things led to great abuses; and several times the Patriots brought in a Septennial or seven years' bill, and the majority of the Irish parliament agreed to send over the heads of the bill for approval by the English council, in accordance with Poynings' Law. But, in each case, no notice was taken of the communication. Now, once more, the patriots, under the leadership of Charles Lucas, did the same thing; and this time the document was returned, approved, from England, but with the seven years changed to eight, which was accepted by the Irish parliament. The passing of this Octennial bill was the occasion of much popular rejoicing in Ireland.

After this bill had become law there was a dissolution, and a new parliament was elected. During the election, Lord Townshend—the same lord lieutenant under whom the Octennial bill had been passed—made use of every possible form of bribery, and with much success, to have members returned favourable to his side. But, with all his corrupt practices, he failed to bring this new house of commons with him on one important point. Both in England and in Ireland the commons have always jealously preserved to themselves the power to originate money bills—that is, the power to raise money by taxation and to apply it to the expenses of the country; justly holding that the representatives of the people have alone the right to tax the people.

On the present occasion the English privy council sent over a money bill for Ireland, with directions to have it passed by the Irish parliament; but it was rejected "because it did not originate in the house of commons"—the very phrase used in Sydney's parliament in 1692—which greatly incensed Lord Townshend. Keeping his mind to himself, however, he first got parliament to pass the usual money supplies to the government; and when these were safe, he had the commons summoned to the bar of the house of lords, where he lectured them severely for their conduct about the money bill, and prorogued parliament for fourteen months. He entered a protest in the books of the house of lords against the rejection of the bill; but the commons, who were more firm than the lords, forbade their clerk to enter the same protest on their books. These proceedings of Townshend, which were felt to be a mixture of trickery and tyranny, caused great indignation, and gave renewed strength to the popular party.

All this time the Catholics were almost wholly silent, taking no part in political questions: their only desire being to avoid the sharp fangs of the law. Yet there were signs of some faint desire to indulge them a little;

but how little may be judged from one small concession, and the difficulty of having even that granted. Lord Townshend had an act passed (1771), which had been previously often rejected, enabling a Catholic to take on long lease, and reclaim as best he could, fifty acres of bog; and, if it were too deep or marshy for building on, he was permitted to have half an acre of solid land on which to build a house. But these precautions were inserted:—that the bog should be at least four feet deep, and that it should not be nearer than a mile to any market town.

Townshend at last growing tired of the ceaseless opposition of the Patriots, and of the everlasting deluge of hostile literature in newspapers, pamphlets, ballads, and all sorts of witty squibs, with ugly caricatures, resigned in 1772. During his term of office, he had done more to corrupt parliament than any of his predecessors, by dismissing all opposed to him, and by giving pensions, places, and titles; all to secure a majority for the Court or English Party. By this open and perpetual corruption he managed to keep up a majority and to have most of his measures passed. But, on the other hand, these proceedings had the effect of consolidating the Patriotic Party, and of strengthening their determination to break down the purely English influence, and to have Irish affairs managed mainly for the benefit of Ireland, and not solely for that of England, as had hitherto been the case.

Chapter LIX
The Volunteers
A.D. 1775–1779.—George III.

N 1775 began the war between England and her North American colonies, which in more ways than one had much influence on the affairs of Ireland, mostly favourable, but sometimes the reverse.

Notwithstanding all the disastrous restrictions, some channels for commerce still remained open to Ireland; and a brisk trade was carried on by the export of provisions of different kinds, especially salted meat, to various countries. But even this industry did not escape; for in the very year after the breaking out of the war, an embargo was laid on the exportation of Irish provisions, in order to cheapen food for the British army, as well as to prevent supplies reaching America: in other words, all export of provisions from Ireland was prohibited. This nearly ruined the farmers and all others employed in the trade, and caused instant distress everywhere. As might be expected, it gave rise to a flourishing smuggling trade, which was extensively carried on, especially round the intricate coasts of the south and west, but which went no way in alleviating the distress. The embargo was ordered by the English authorities of their own motion, without consulting Ireland; and this fact, with the sight of the misery that had been suddenly brought on the country, caused such dangerous discontent in the Irish parliament, that it was considered desirable to dissolve it, and have a new set of more pliable members elected. The general election accordingly came, and as usual there was extensive bribery to secure a government majority.

In Ireland the people generally sympathised with America; for they felt that the grievances from which they had so long suffered were much the same as those against which the Americans had risen in revolt; and they began to entertain a hope that one outcome of the war might be free trade for their own country, the only possible remedy for the prevailing misery.

In England the feeling of the Irish people was well understood; and some discussions regarding the injustice done to Irish trade were originated in the English parliament by Edmund Burke and other friends of Ireland; but a great cry was instantly raised by English manufacturers and traders—an outburst of mere selfishness—against any movement that threatened their own privileges by relieving the Irish people; and the end of the matter was that only a few trifling concessions were made.

The war in America had gone steadily against the English; and great consternation was caused when news came that General Burgoyne with 6,000 men had surrendered to the American General Gage at Saratoga. But there was greater alarm still in the following year, when France acknowledged the independence of the United States. This was immediately followed by a measure carried in the English parliament, partially relieving English Catholics from their disabilities: and with this example to follow, Mr. Luke Gardiner, afterwards Lord Mountjoy, brought in a bill in the Irish parliament to grant considerable relief to Irish Catholics and dissenters.

At this time indeed much of the Penal Code had fallen into disuse; but still it hung over the heads of the Catholics, and might be brought down at any time. Yet there was considerable opposition to Gardiner's proposal; but the government favoured it, and the bill was carried by a small majority. At the same time the embargo was removed; but during the two or three years of its continuance it had done irreparable damage by causing the trade in salted meat to be transferred to other countries.

The act of relief repealed those enactments which prohibited the purchase of freehold property by Catholics, and which gave the whole property to the eldest son, and the right of separate maintenance at the father's expense, to any other child who became a Protestant. Catholics could now take land on freehold lease, *i.e.* on lease for life. Instead of the right to purchase land in perpetuity, they got what was much the same thing, the right to lease for 999 years. The Test Act was also abolished, which relieved Presbyterians as well as Catholics.

Edmund Burke.

All this time Ireland was in a very defenceless state. For in the very year of the opening of the war, 4,000 Irish troops had been sent away at the request of the king, for service in America, leaving only three or four thousand in the country: and though the English government proposed to send to Ireland 4,000 Protestant soldiers from Germany in place of those who had been drafted away, the Irish House of Commons declined to admit them, saying that the loyal people of Ireland were well able to protect themselves, without the aid of any foreign troops. Now, however, things began to look very threatening, and people feared foreign invasion. For not only was the war going on badly, but France and Spain were both hostile; and the English and Irish coasts swarmed with American privateers which captured British merchant vessels and did immense damage.

In the north of Ireland the people had good reason for apprehension. Only about eighteen years before (in 1760), Captain Thurot—an Irishman whose real name was O'Farrell—had landed at Carrickfergus with 1,000 men from three French vessels, and laid the people under heavy contribution for provisions. He was forced however to re-embark, and in an action a little north of the Isle of Man the three vessels were captured, and Thurot was killed. All this was vividly remembered; and now the celebrated privateer Paul Jones, a Scotchman in the service of the United States, with his vessel the *Ranger,* was committing great depredations round the Irish coast. Outside Carrickfergus he captured an English brig, and got safely off with her to Brest.

The Irish saw that if they were to be protected at all they must protect themselves; and this conviction gave origin to the Volunteer movement, which was begun towards the end of 1778. The first Volunteer companies were raised in Belfast, after which the movement rapidly spread; the country gentlemen armed and drilled their tenants; and by May of the following year nearly 4,000 were enrolled in the counties of Down and Antrim. The authorities did not look on this movement with favour, knowing well that it would strengthen the opposition; for it was got up by the people and their leaders, quite independent of the government; but the feeling of the country was too strong for them. The formation of Volunteer companies extended to other parts of Ireland: and before the end of the year, 42,000 volunteers were enrolled.

James Caulfield, earl of Charlemont, a man universally respected, of refined tastes and scholarly attainments, and moderate in his views, was in command of the northern Volunteers; the Duke of Leinster, of those of Leinster; and other gentlemen of influence took the lead in other parts of Ireland.

We must remember two things in regard to these Volunteers. First, the rank and file were the very people who most severely felt the prevailing distress caused by the suppression of Irish trade; and who, without being in any sense disloyal, were bitterly hostile to the government, while their sympathies were entirely with the Patriotic Party. Of all this the government were well aware: but they dared not attempt to keep down the movement. They were obliged even to go so far as to supply arms, though much against their will: but all other expenses, including uniforms, were borne by the people themselves. The second matter to be borne in mind is that this was a Protestant movement, the Catholics not yet being permitted to take any positions of trust: but as time went on Catholics gradually joined the ranks in considerable numbers.

Lord Charlemont.

Parliament met in October (1779). The Patriotic Party had now the Volunteers at their back, and just as the government had feared, assumed a bolder tone; and what gave their demands tenfold strength was that they were known to be thoroughly loyal, and wanted nothing more than the redress of admitted grievances. Flood had been their leader down to 1774 when he took office under the government, having been appointed vice-treasurer with a salary of £3,500 a year. This obliged him to keep silent on most of the great questions in dispute between the two parties; and he lost the confidence of the people, which was now transferred to Grattan.

Though the embargo had been removed, all the older restrictions on Irish trade still remained, under which it was impossible for the country to prosper, or even to emerge from poverty. On the assembling of parliament, Grattan, in an amendment to the Address, brought in a motion demanding free trade, which, after some discussion, was carried unanimously. Even the members in government employment voted for this: it was proposed by Walter Hussey Burgh the Prime Sergeant, and was supported by Flood, Hely Hutchinson, Ponsonby, and Gardiner, all holding offices. Dublin was in a state of great excitement, and the parliament house was surrounded by an immense crowd shouting for free trade; for now, at last, they saw some prospect of relief. The Address, with Grattan's amendment, was borne through Dame Street by the speaker and the commons in procession, from the parliament house to the castle, to be presented to Lord Buckinghamshire,

A Member of the Dublin Volunteer Corps, From The Universal Magazine: Dublin, 1792, p. 545.

the lord lieutenant. The streets were lined both sides with Volunteers under the Duke of Leinster: as the members walked along they were received with acclamation by an immense multitude; and the Volunteers presented arms in honour of the speaker and members.

It was in the debates on this question that Hussey Burgh made his reputation as an orator. In one of them he used a sentence that has become famous. Someone had remarked that Ireland was at peace: "Talk not to me of peace," said he: "Ireland is not at peace; it is smothered war. England has sown her laws as dragons' teeth: they have sprung up in armed men."[1] This sentence produced unparalleled excitement; and, when it had calmed down so that he could be heard, he announced that he resigned his office under the crown. "The gates of promotion are shut," exclaimed Grattan: "the gates of glory are opened!"

But to the British parliament alone, which had laid on the restrictions, belonged the task of removing them. In November (1779) the English prime minister, Lord North, introduced three propositions to relieve Irish trade: the first permitted free export of Irish wool and woollen goods; the second free export of Irish glass manufactures; the third allowed free trade with the British colonies. The first two were passed immediately; the third after a little time. The news of this was received with great joy in Dublin.

---

[1]Alluding to a classical fable:—Cadmus, the founder of Thebes, having killed a great dragon, sowed its teeth in the earth by the advice of Minerva: and the crop that sprang up from them was a party of mighty men all fully armed.

Sculpture on Window: Cathedral Church, Glendalough: Beranger, 1779.
From Petrie's *Round Towers*.

CHAPTER LX
LEGISLATIVE INDEPENDENCE
A.D. 1780–1783.—George III.

VERY important demand made so far by the popular party in Ireland had been conceded; and the more they forced the government to restore, the more they were determined to have. They had obtained some relief for trade: they now resolved that their parliament, which was bound down by Poynings' Law and by the Sixth of George I, should also be free. On the 19th of April, in a magnificent speech, Grattan moved his memorable resolutions:

That the king, with the lords and commons of Ireland, are the only power on earth competent to enact laws to bind Ireland.

That Great Britain and Ireland are inseparably united under one sovereign.

The question, however, was not put directly to a division: for, though it was obvious that the sense of the house was on the side of Grattan, he and his party might have been outvoted if a vote had been taken.

The next debate arose on a mutiny bill—that is, a bill to maintain and pay the army. In England the Mutiny Act is not permanent: it is passed from year to year, lest the army might be used by the king or government as an instrument of oppression, as it was often used in days gone by, when kings, with an army at their back, did what they pleased in defiance of parliament and people. The Mutiny Bill for Ireland was passed by the Irish parliament after a long contest; but, having been transmitted to the English authorities, it was returned changed to a perpetual bill—the very thing they took good care to avoid in England. The Irish government, following their directions as usual, proposed this measure in the parliament in 1780; but it was most resolutely opposed, and created great irritation and excitement all over the country. Nevertheless the Court Party carried it in spite of all expostulation; and carried it by wholesale bribery, especially by selling peerages and peerage promotions. In this, as in many other instances, the action of the government, both in England and Ireland, appears to have been singularly ill-judged and short-sighted, in exasperating the Irish people at the very time of wars with America, France, Spain, and other countries. Their proceedings, instead of suppressing the spirit now abroad through the country, or allaying excitement, intensified the discontent and spread the agitation.

Grattan. From the portrait in the National Gallery, Dublin.

Meantime the enthusiasm for home government was spreading and intensifying; and the opposition, led by Grattan, gained strength and confidence by the great increase of the Volunteers, who, much against the wish of the government, continued to be enrolled in the four provinces, till at last they numbered 100,000 men. The country was now all ablaze with excitement, though perfectly peaceable; and people scarcely thought or talked of anything but the question of a free parliament. During the early months of 1781 innumerable meetings were held all over Ireland; and what was more significant, there were reviews of the Volunteers everywhere in the four provinces, with the great question always in their thoughts and speech. In Belfast Lord Charlemont rode through the crowded streets at the head of his splendid corps, and issued an address, in which he hailed the spirit of freedom that had enabled them, without help from outside, to provide against foreign invasion, and looked forward to the accomplishment of legislative independence.

In the session of 1781, which did not open till October, Grattan was the great leader of the popular party. He was seconded with almost equal ability by Flood, who, towards the end of the preceding year, finding his position of enforced silence unendurable, had thrown up his government appointment, and had been removed by the king from his seat on the Privy Council. Though holding office, he had never worked well with the government; and he now joined his old friends, and thereby regained much of his former popularity. They had at their back a number of able and brilliant men—Hely Hutchinson, John Fitzgibbon (afterwards, when in office, a bitter enemy of the cause he now advocated), Hussey Burgh, Barry Yelverton, and others. Barry Yelverton had given notice of motion for the 5th of December, 1781, for the repeal of Poynings' Act; but on that day news came of a great disaster—the surrender of Lord Cornwallis and his whole army in America, which ruined the cause of England in the war. Whereupon Yelverton, abandoning his motion for the time, moved an address of loyalty and attachment to the king, which was carried. The repeal of Poynings' Law was, however, again moved in the same month by Flood, but the motion was defeated by government.

During all this session the government authorities were able to secure a majority by a plentiful distribution of patronage; so that it would have been quite useless to bring forward a motion for legislative independence. At last Grattan, hopeless of being able to contend in parliament against the forces of corruption, determined to let the empire hear the voice of even a more powerful pleader. A convention of delegates from the Ulster Volunteers was summoned for the 15th February at Dungannon, the old home of Hugh O'Neill. Two hundred and forty-two delegates from 143 Volunteer corps of Ulster, most of them men of wealth and station, assembled in the Dissenting Meeting House of Dungannon. The proceedings were managed chiefly by Grattan, Flood, and Lord Charlemont; and thirteen resolutions were adopted, of which the most important were:

That the king, lords, and commons of Ireland have alone the right to legislate for the country;

That Poynings' Law is unconstitutional and a grievance, and should be revoked;

That the ports of Ireland should be open to all nations not at war with the king;

That a permanent mutiny bill is unconstitutional;

And "That as men and Irishmen, as Christians and as Protestants, we rejoice in the relaxation of the penal laws against our Roman Catholic fellow-subjects; and we conceive the measure to be fraught with the happiest consequences to the Union and prosperity to the inhabitants of Ireland." This last was inserted at the instance of Grattan; and, among its most ardent supporters were three clergymen delegates—one belonging to the Established Church, the other two Presbyterians. The resolutions of the Dungannon Convention were adopted by all the Volunteer corps of Ireland; and they formed the basis of the momentous legislation that followed. These spirit-stirring proceedings were altogether the work of Protestants, for the Catholics were still shut out from taking any part in them.

Dungannon Meeting-House at the time of the Convention.
From The Anthologia Hibernica, *1793, II, 321.*

On the day that the Dungannon resolutions were passed, Mr. Luke Gardiner introduced a measure for the further relief of Catholics, which, after some opposition and delay, was adopted. They were allowed to buy, sell, and otherwise dispose of lands the same as their Protestant neighbours. The statute against celebrating and hearing Mass, and those requiring the registration of priests, and forbidding the residence of bishops and other clergy, were all repealed. Catholic schoolmasters could teach schools, and Catholics could be guardians of children; the law prohibiting a Catholic from having a horse worth more than £5 was repealed, as well as those which made Catholics pay for losses by robberies, and which forbade them to come to live in Limerick and Galway.

The next meeting of parliament was on the 16th April 1782. The citizens of Dublin, believing that what they had long hoped for was coming, were all abroad: and among them, the Volunteers were conspicuous with their bands, banners, and bright uniforms. The usual address was moved, to which Grattan moved an amendment. He was very ill at the time, and when he rose he was pale and trembling; but, as he went on, he gathered strength and energy; and his splendid speech moved the whole house to uncontrollable excitement. The amendment comprised all the chief demands of the Protestant Irish people; ending with the declaration that the king and Irish parliament alone had the right to make laws for Ireland. These were merely a repetition of the Dungannon resolutions, with the exception of that relating to Catholic emancipation, which was not expressly mentioned. The amendment was unanimously agreed to. The next part of the proceedings was in the English parliament. On the 17th of May, a resolution for the repeal of the Sixth of George I was proposed in the lords by the earl of Shelburne, and in the commons by Charles James Fox; to which both houses agreed.

This concession, known as the "Act of Repeal," was communicated by the viceroy to the Irish parliament at its meeting of the 27th of May. It was interpreted to mean that England gave Ireland an independent parliament, over which it renounced all authority, annulled Poynings' Law, restored to the Irish lords the right to hear appeals, abolished the right of appeal to the English lords, and in general yielded all the demands of Grattan's amendments. The news was received in Ireland with a tremendous outburst of joy, both in the House and among the people all over the country; and as an evidence of gratitude, the parliament voted to the British navy 20,000 men and £100,000.

It was felt and acknowledged that this consummation was mainly due to Grattan. "The man who, during the last anxious years, had stood forth from his countrymen, beyond all rivalry and all comparison, was Henry Grattan. His splendid eloquence, the perfect confidence which was felt in his honour and in his disinterestedness, the signal skill, energy, and moderation with which he had at once animated and controlled the patriotic party were universally acknowledged, and at this time almost universally admired."[1] The Irish parliament voted him a grant of £100,000. But he

[1]Lecky, *History of Ireland in the 18th century,* II, 315.

accepted only £50,000, and even that after much persuasion. With this he bought an estate in Queen's County: and he took up his permanent residence in a beautiful spot that he loved: Tinnehinch, near Enniskerry in Wicklow, twelve miles from Dublin.

Flood was of opinion that the English parliament should have gone farther by formally renouncing the right to make laws for Ireland: and, as confirming his view, the English parliament, in January of the following year—1783—when Lord Shelburne was prime minister, actually passed the "Act of Renunciation," declaring that Ireland's right to be bound only by the laws made by the king and the Irish parliament was "established and ascertained for ever, and shall at no time hereafter be questioned or questionable."

Chapter LXI
Grattan's Parliament
A.D. 1783–1785.—George III.

FTER 1782 the only connexion between the two parliaments of England and Ireland was that the king was head of both. Beyond this they were, at least in theory, quite independent of one another. The English parliament was free to legislate for England, but not for Ireland; and the Irish parliament could make any laws it pleased for Ireland, subject only, by the constitution, to the veto of the king, to which the English parliament was also subject. But now this free Irish parliament stood sadly in need of reform; for it was, unhappily, as bad a type of parliament as could well be conceived. Bad as it was, however, Grattan and his followers were only too glad to accept it, believing that reform would come in due course. With all its shortcomings, it encouraged trade and manufacture, and developed the natural resources of the country; so that Ireland prospered under its administration, as will be further noticed in the next chapter. Let us look at some of the worst features of this parliament.

Of the 300 members more than 100 were pensioners of the government, or held government situations, all of whom voted just as they were directed by the authorities. Nearly all the boroughs were in the hands of a few lords and rich men, most of them on the side of the government; so that any man might get to be a member of parliament by paying a sum of money to some borough owner, who then ordered the people to elect him: all which was a very moneymaking business; for sometimes a person who wanted to be elected paid as much as £10,000 for his seat. A parliament ought to consist of members elected by the free votes of those who have the franchise—the right to vote: but, of the 300 members of this parliament, not more than 70 or 80 were returned by the free votes of the people. All this was a bad state of things: but it was hard to remedy; for these placemen and borough owners, and those whom they got elected, were the very men who had the making, altering, and repealing of the laws in their hands. Then, again, the spurious boroughs formed in the time of the Stuarts still existed, many of which contained only about a dozen electors; so that it was always easy, by merely spending a little money in bribery, to have persons elected who would back up the government in everything. But, perhaps, the worst feature was that the Roman Catholics, who formed four-fifths of the population, were totally shut out: a Catholic could neither be a member nor vote for a member. The parliament did not represent the nation; and it did not represent even the Protestant people. Though it had the name of being, after 1782, independent of the English government, it really was not so; for the Irish authorities were directly under the influence of the English Council, and could almost always secure a majority in parliament. The government of Ireland was, in fact, a sort of oligarchy, in which the people of the country had hardly any voice; and the ministry might do almost what they pleased. There never was a parliament more in need of reform: and reform would have saved it, and saved the country, the horrors of 1798.

Two great questions now lay before the country:—Parliamentary reform and the removal of the restrictions which still remained on Irish commerce. A third question was Catholic emancipation; but people's minds were so occupied with the other two, that this was for the present left very much in the background. The Volunteers took up the question of parliamentary reform—the all important reform to put an end to bribery and corruption—to secure that all the members of parliament should be elected by the free votes of the people. Several meetings were held, at which the subject was discussed; and a general convention in Dublin of delegates from all the Volunteer corps of Ireland was arranged for the 10th of November, 1783; all which proceedings were very alarming to the government, who wanted no reform of any kind in the parliamentary representation. The parliament met in October. The necessity for retrenchment in the civil administration, which had grown costly mainly through the corruption of government, was before men's minds, and was strongly advocated by Grattan; but Flood proposed a reduction in the army, in which the sense of the house was against him; and Grattan opposed the proposal with much vehemence. Between those two great men an estrangement had been gradually growing up: and, in one of the debates on Flood's motion, there occurred a bitter and very lamentable altercation between them, which terminated their friendship for ever. Yet, subsequently, each bore generous testimony to the greatness of the other.

The 10th November came, and 160 Volunteer delegates assembled in the Rotunda, in Dublin. They elected as chairman the Earl of Charlemont, the commander of the whole force. The meeting was held while the parliament was sitting close by; and, after much discussion, certain reforms were agreed to, which were introduced immediately afterwards into parliament by Flood in the form of a bill. The debate was a stormy one, and the scene in the old parliament house is described as "almost terrific." Barry Yelverton, afterwards Lord Avonmore, now attorney-general, and of course on the government side, led the opposition to the bill, at the same time denouncing vehemently the attempt to coerce the parliament by an armed body of men; and John Fitzgibbon, now the leading opponent of reform, and others, followed in the same strain. Flood, in a powerful speech, advocated the bill and defended the action of the Volunteers. Grattan supported it, but not very earnestly, for he maintained it was not the right time to bring it forward; and John Philpot Curran, who had been elected for Kilbeggan this same year—1783—made his first parliamentary speech in favour of it. But the government party were too strong, and the bill was rejected by a large majority. Thus the efforts of the Popular Party to reform a corrupt parliament ended, for the present, in failure through government opposition. The result produced great indignation, and there were serious fears of a collision between the Volunteers and the government: but the counsels of Lord Charlemont prevailed; and on the 2nd of December the Volunteer convention was adjourned without any day being fixed for next meeting. This was the death blow to the influence of the Volunteers; and, though they held together and continued to be enrolled for years, they never afterwards played any important part in the political affairs of the country. But they broke away from the influence of Lord Charlemont and became more revolutionary in their ideas, after the example of France. In the following year (1784) Flood made another effort at reform, but the Irish government successfully resisted all attempts to improve the representation.

The Volunteers, deserted by their leaders, now formed themselves into clubs and associations, and held secret meetings. In Dublin, Belfast, and elsewhere, they began to drill men in the use of arms, Catholics as well as Protestants; whereupon the government increased the army to 15,000 men, and took measures to revive the militia, a force in the service of the crown. But the people hated the militia, and the country became greatly disturbed. Scenes of violence occurred everywhere. Even in Dublin the mobs paraded the streets, attacked and maimed soldiers, broke into shops, and ill-used the shopkeepers for selling English goods. It was a time of great trouble and alarm.

The commercial arrangements between England and Ireland needed reform as much as did the parliamentary representation; for the regulations for the export and import of goods between the two countries were all unfair to Ireland. There were prohibitory duties on many kinds of Irish goods exported to England, but little or none on English goods brought to Ireland; so that while English manufacturers and traders had free scope to sell their goods in Ireland, the Irish could not sell theirs in England, which repressed the little that remained of Irish commerce and manufactures, and helped to keep the country in a state of poverty.

A movement was now made to remedy this state of things; and here the Irish government were on the side of reform, though their ideas fell very short of those of the opposition. Mr. Thomas Orde, chief secretary, on the suggestion of William Pitt, then Chancellor of the Exchequer in England, brought down from the castle, on the part of the government, a scheme designed by Pitt, embodied in eleven propositions, which would go far to remedy the injustice, all of which were agreed to and passed through parliament in the shape of resolutions (in 1785). They were forthwith transmitted to England for adoption there; for as the restrictions had been the work of the English parliament, it was only in England they could be removed. But when they were proposed by Pitt, there arose violent opposition; petitions against them poured in from companies, manufacturers, and merchants, in all parts of England, who insisted on maintaining the arrangements which were for the advantage of themselves and for the disadvantage of Ireland. Whereupon Pitt, fearing to face the storm, abandoned Orde's bill, and brought down to the English parliament twenty propositions of his own, much less favourable to Ireland—containing several injurious restrictions—and had them passed. These, on being transmitted to the Irish government, and introduced by them to the Irish house in August 1785, were received by the opposition with an outburst of indignation. Flood led the opposition with all his old fire and energy. Grattan denounced the propositions in one of his finest speeches; and after an all-night stormy debate, the government had so small a majority—only 19—that they thought it more prudent to withdraw the bill; which caused great rejoicings in Dublin. Thus the whole scheme of reform, both parliamentary and commercial, fell through, and matters remained much as they were till the time of the Union.

Sculpture on a Capital: Priests House, Glendalough: Beranger, 1779.
From Petrie's *Round Towers*.

CHAPTER LXII
REVIVAL OF SECRET SOCIETIES
A.D. 1785–1791.—George III.

URING the year 1785, discontent prevailed everywhere in Ireland; for which there were various sufficient causes. The Catholics were still oppressed by the penal laws; and the farmers of all religions were harassed by middlemen. But tithes and tithe-proctors were perhaps the most potent influence for disturbance about this time. All householders, Catholics and Dissenters as well as Anglican Protestants, had to pay "tithes" for the support of the clergy of the Established Church. These would no doubt have been generally paid quietly enough but for the action of persons called "tithe-proctors," or "tithe-farmers," who collected them for absentee clergymen, or for those who were resident, but who for various reasons were not willing to enter personally on the business of collection. These proctors, some of them Catholics, some Protestants, commonly received a fixed proportion of the tithes—a third or a fourth—to pay for collection, so that it was their interest to raise as much money as possible; and they extorted from the very poorest of the peasantry contributions far beyond what the law contemplated. Moreover, grazing lands were exempt, so that the impost fell chiefly on poor cottiers. A rich grazier with two or three thousand a year paid no tithes, while a half starved cottier had to pay them for his little plot; and this again discouraged tillage and tended to make grassland of the whole country. The people also of all denominations had to pay "Church-rate," or "Church-cess," a tax to keep the Protestant churches in repair. The payment of tithes and church-rate was resented by the Presbyterians even more bitterly than by the Roman Catholics. Although it would have been quite easy to provide a remedy for tithes—something like the measure adopted half a century later (in 1838)—and though any reasonable proposal of the kind would have been approved by the authorities in England, the Irish government obstinately resisted every attempt to settle the matter, in spite of the earnest representations of Grattan and his party.

All through 1785 and 1786 the country was fearfully disturbed, and the peasantry formed themselves into illegal secret societies. In the south there was a revival of the Whiteboys, now calling themselves "Rightboys," led by an imaginary "Captain Right." These misguided men, like the Whiteboys, committed outrages on agents, middlemen, tithe-proctors, and others. The tithe-proctors especially, who had rendered themselves intensely odious by their cruel extortions, were pursued mercilessly, often mutilated, and sometimes killed. Another class, who were mostly blameless, the Protestant curates, always present to bear the odium, and striving to live on poor incomes of £40 or £50 a year, often suffered grievous ill-treatment. The Rightboys were denounced by the Catholic clergy, especially by Dr. Butler, archbishop of Cashel, and Dr. Troy, bishop of Ossory; but they still continued their evil courses.

In the north—in Armagh, Tyrone, and Down—another secret society had grown up among Protestants and Presbyterians, called "Peep-o'-day boys," and afterwards known as "Protestant boys" and "Wreckers." These directed their hostilities against Catholics, who again in self-defence formed themselves into bands called "Defenders." These two parties, who belonged generally to the lowest class of the peasantry, did immense damage—fought, maimed and killed each other, and otherwise caused great disorder.

The authorities were very much alarmed at the state of the country; and there were long and anxious discussions as to the best means of restoring quiet. So far as Dublin was concerned—for the city was as much troubled as the north and south—a plan was adopted, though after some opposition, which ultimately turned out an excellent and successful one:—the government had a bill passed for the appointment of a number of constables to aid the city watchmen. This small body of men originated the present splendid force of the Dublin metropolitan police.

Fitzgibbon, who was now the leading influence against remedial measures of every kind, attempted to put down the disturbances by causing the government to pass a crushing Crimes bill, that is, a bill to give more power to the authorities to apprehend and punish the disturbers. Grattan was convinced of the necessity of some bill of the kind; but he wished for one much less severe; and he succeeded in having struck out some very violent and dangerous clauses inserted by Fitzgibbon, and in limiting the duration of the bill to three years. He endeavoured also to have a parliamentary inquiry to ascertain the causes of the discontent and disorders, with a view to their removal; but here he was overruled; and this "Engine of Redress," as he called it, was rejected.

The Popular Party in parliament continued as vigilant and active as ever, and gave the government great trouble. The usual means were employed to break down their influence: but though the country had long been accustomed to this, probably at no previous period was there so much gross political corruption as during the lord lieutenancy of the Marquess of Buckingham from 1787 to 1790. He bribed openly and unsparingly, wherever he thought it would purchase supporters for the Court Party; and he dismissed all holders of government offices who showed any disposition to oppose him. Numbers of persons were made peers and baronets, and many peers were promoted; and he added £13,000 a year to the pension list, which before his time had grown to the yearly sum of £100,000. He became at last so intensely unpopular, that when he retired he had to steal away from Dublin by night.

During the year 1790 the north was far more disturbed than the south; and the Peep-o'-day boys and the Defenders increased and multiplied, continued their outrages, and fought their battles. Among the better educated classes, who saw no hope of reform by parliamentary and constitutional means, the doctrines of the French Revolution found many supporters. Committees were formed, partly to stem the tide of political corruption, and partly to discuss the best methods of government. The members of the Popular Party, who had been the leading men in the old Volunteers, formed themselves into clubs which greatly influenced public opinion; of which the Whig Club in Dublin, and the Northern Whig Club in Belfast, were specially prominent. Both of them included among their members many historic personages:—Lord Charlemont, Lord Moira, the Duke of Leinster, Grattan, Napper Tandy, John Philpot Curran, Wolfe Tone, and others. These clubs unsparingly exposed the evil system of the government; but the government, safe in its pensioned and corrupt majority, continued its course unchanged.

The Ulster Presbyterians were specially active and earnest in these movements. The anniversary of the taking of the Bastille, the great government prison in Paris, by the Revolutionists two years before, was celebrated in Belfast in July by the Northern Whig Club, joined by all the Volunteers of the neighbourhood, in a great procession, with drums, banners, and flags, on which were depicted various scenes enacted at the Revolution. The celebration ended with a banquet, where such toasts were drunk as "The National Assembly of France," "The Rights of Man," &c., and where proper representation in parliament, and the complete emancipation of the Catholics were demanded. There was nothing illegal in these proceedings, but they gave great uneasiness to the government, who, with the example of France before them, looked on all such movements with apprehension.

Theobald Wolfe Tone, a man of great determination, quite unselfish, and of remarkable persuasive power, was one of the most prominent leaders of public opinion in those times. Though a Protestant, he was appointed Secretary to the Catholic Committee in Dublin, which brought the Catholics into closer connexion with the Presbyterians. In the same year (1791) he visited Belfast, and thinking the Northern Whig Club not sufficiently advanced, he founded, in October, the society of United Irishmen, the members of which were chiefly Presbyterians. The objects of this society, which were quite legal, were:—to unite people of all classes and religions in one great organisation, this main idea being indicated in the very name—United Irishmen; to reform parliament so as to break down the corrupting influence of the government; and to remove the grievances of all Irishmen of every religious persuasion. This last chiefly aimed at the repeal of the penal laws against Catholics: for the leaders believed that if all the people of the country were united, their demand for reform could not be resisted. Tone next formed a branch of the society in Dublin under the auspices of the Catholic Committee: James Napper Tandy, a Protestant shopkeeper in Dublin, was its secretary.

Yet with all this unrest and disturbance, business of every kind was extending, and the country was rapidly advancing in prosperity. This was due to several causes, of which the principal were: the removal of the most ruinous of the restrictions on trade; the relief of Roman Catholics from their worst disabilities, which enabled them to take a part, and invest their capital, in industries; and the restoration of the freedom of Parliament, which gave the authorities a free hand to develop the resources of the country.

Let us now interrupt the purely political history, in order to trace the advances made, and the checks suffered, by the Catholics, in their efforts to free themselves from their remaining hardships.

Sculpture on a Capital: Priests House, Glendalough: Beranger, 1779.
From Petrie's *Round Towers*.

CHAPTER LXIII

CATHOLIC PROGRESS TOWARDS EMANCIPATION
A.D. 1792–1793.—George III.

ORE than thirty years had elapsed since the Catholic Committee had been founded. Its original purpose, as we have seen, was to look after Catholic interests in general, and especially to obtain a relaxation or repeal of the Penal Laws. The members felt that this business gave them quite enough to do, and as a body they did not mix themselves up much in other political movements. They had no wish to come in conflict with the government, and they were not much influenced by the revolutionary ideas so prevalent at this time among the Presbyterians. Indeed it was only among the prosperous business Catholics of the towns that there appeared much political life of any kind. The great body of Catholics through the country had been, during the whole of the century, so depressed, and had been reduced to such a state of ignorance, that they had hardly a thought or an opinion on anything beyond the necessaries of life, with a vague consciousness that they were suffering under wrongs which ought to be removed.

There were two parties in the Catholic Committee, the Aristocratic and the Democratic. The former included the Catholic nobility and the Catholic bishops: they looked with horror on the French Revolution and its excesses, and were inclined to be timid in agitating for their own emancipation. The Democratic party consisted chiefly of businessmen, of whom the ablest and most far-seeing was John Keogh, a Dublin merchant. These were for pressing their claims boldly, including the right to vote at elections, which the Aristocratic party wished to postpone to some future time. This question was eagerly and warmly discussed; and in order to clear themselves from even the suspicion of sympathy with revolutionary principles, sixty-four timid members of the Aristocratic party seceded from the committee.

The action of the democratic section had the approval of the general body of outside Catholics; and they carried their point, notwithstanding the defection of the aristocratic members.

On the 2nd December they convened a meeting of Catholic delegates from different parts of Ireland in the Tailors' Hall, a spacious building in Back Lane, Dublin—whence this assemblage is sometimes called the "Back Lane Parliament"—at which a petition to the king was prepared, asking for admission to all the rights of the constitution. It was signed by Dr. Troy, Catholic archbishop of Dublin, by Dr. Moylan, bishop of Cork, and by all the country delegates. As they believed, with good reason, that the English government was better disposed towards them than the Irish, they commissioned John Keogh and four other delegates to present the petition to the king direct, instead of following the usual course of sending it through the Irish authorities. On their way to England the delegates passed through Belfast, where they got a grand reception: the Presbyterian populace unyoked the horses from the carriage, and drew Keogh and his companions in triumph through the streets. On the 2nd January 1793, the petition was presented to his Majesty, who received it very graciously.

The wisdom of Keogh and his party was proved by what happened soon afterwards. In the dangerous and uncertain state of things on the Continent, with the rapid spread of sympathy in Ireland for the Revolution, and while a war with France was quite probable, it was considered of great consequence that the Roman Catholics should be well affected towards the government. Accordingly, on the 9th of April, mainly through the influence of the English ministers, aided by the powerful advocacy of Grattan and his party, but much against the wishes of the Irish government, a bill was passed through the Irish parliament which granted the Catholics a substantial measure of relief. The franchise was restored to them, so that all who were Forty-shilling Freeholders[1] had the right to vote for members of parliament; and as since 1778 these freeholders had grown very numerous, this measure gave the Irish Catholics great political influence. Besides this important concession, they were permitted by the Act to enter Trinity College, Dublin, and obtain degrees; almost all civil and military situations were opened to them; they could serve on juries and be justices of the peace; and the higher classes of Catholics were allowed to carry arms. They might open colleges to be affiliated to Trinity College, provided they were not exclusively for the education of Catholics. An attempt was made to insert a clause admitting them to parliament; but this wise provision the Irish government unhappily succeeded in defeating.

---

[1]A man who had a lease for life was called a Freeholder. A Forty-shilling Freeholder was one whose holding was worth at least forty shillings over and above the rent he was bound to pay by his lease. Nearly all the freeholds were up to that standard.

In order to have the benefit of the act it was necessary to take the Oath of Allegiance, which however any Catholic might take. But many disabilities still remained; the most serious of which was that no Catholic could sit in parliament: neither could a Catholic be lord lieutenant, or lord chancellor, or a privy councillor, or a fellow of Trinity College, or a sheriff or sub-sheriff. Still the measure was a great relief, and the Catholics were very grateful for it; but its conciliatory effect was much marred by the bitterness with which lord chancellor Fitzgibbon spoke of his Catholic fellow-countrymen, though he dared not oppose the bill. On the other hand, in the same session two coercion acts were passed:—the "Convention Act" against "Unlawful assemblies," intended to prevent meetings of delegates such as the "Back-lane parliament," as well as delegate meetings of the United Irishmen; and the "Gunpowder Act" to prevent the importation and sale of gunpowder and arms, and to give magistrates the power of searching for arms wherever and whenever they pleased; which applied to Protestants as well as Catholics. This last was intended as a precaution against the danger of disaffection in case of an invasion; for the French and English were by this time at war; and the dangerous sympathy of the United Irishmen for the French Revolutionary party was well known to the government.

Chapter LXIV

Catholic Disappointment
A.D. 1793–1795.—George III.

T the end of chapter LXII, it was related how Wolfe Tone had founded the Society of United Irishmen in Belfast and Dublin, a society which, so far, had nothing illegal in it. Still the government kept a strict watch on these United Irishmen, as well as on the Catholic Committee, and all such associations, so as to be ready for prosecutions in case they should be found to transgress the law as it then stood.

At a meeting of United Irishmen held in Dublin in February 1793, with the Hon. Simon Butler as chairman, and Oliver Bond, a Dublin merchant, as secretary, an address was adopted and circulated, boldly censuring the conduct of a committee of the house of lords for having in an illegal manner conducted a secret inquiry into the proceedings of the Defenders.

For this, Butler and Bond were sentenced by the committee, without any regular trial, to be imprisoned for six months and to pay a fine of £500 each.

Archibald Hamilton Rowan, the son of a landed proprietor of Ulster, who had been conspicuous as a volunteer, and was now a United Irishman, circulated an address to the Volunteers, written by Dr. Drennan, a well-known and very talented literary man, an Ulster Presbyterian, and the writer of many stirring national ballads and addresses. For this, Rowan was prosecuted, and was defended with great ability by Curran. He was convicted of a seditious libel, and sentenced to be imprisoned for two years, and to pay a fine of £500. While Rowan was in prison, an emissary from France, the Rev. William Jackson, a Protestant clergyman of Irish extraction, arrived in Ireland to sound the popular leaders about a French invasion. He had with him a London attorney named Cockayne, to whom he had confided the object of his mission: but Cockayne was really a spy paid by the English government. These two had interviews with the leading United Irishmen in Dublin—Wolfe Tone, Leonard Mac Nally, Hamilton Rowan then in the Dublin Newgate prison, and others. Mac Nally was a Dublin attorney, who managed the legal business of the United Irishmen: he was trusted by them with their innermost secrets, and lived and died in their friendship and confidence; but long after his death it was discovered that he was all the time a spy in government pay. Tone drew out a report on the state of Ireland for Jackson, who kept a copy of it in Rowan's handwriting.

When the government, who knew through Cockayne all that was going on, thought matters sufficiently ripe, they arrested Jackson on the 28th of April 1794. Rowan, knowing that his handwriting would betray him, contrived to escape on the 1st of May: and although a reward of £1,500 was offered for his arrest, he made his way to France and thence to America. On the 23rd of April in the following year Jackson was tried and convicted of treason on the evidence of Cockayne. He had managed however to take a dose of arsenic before coming into court, and dropped dead in the dock.

But now happened an event which gave the Catholics hopes of complete emancipation. Towards the end of 1794 people's minds became greatly excited in Ireland when it became known that Pitt had determined to adopt a policy of conciliation, to drop coercion, and to remove all the remaining restrictions against Catholics. With these objects in view Lord Westmoreland was recalled, and Earl Fitzwilliam, a just, liberal, and enlightened man, having large estates in Ireland, came over as lord lieutenant on the 4th of January, with full authority and with the firm determination, which he did not conceal, to completely emancipate the Catholics; and they gave him an enthusiastic reception, for his intentions had become known. The proposed measure would, as Pitt believed, attach the body of the Catholics to the empire, a thing of vital importance; for the French were at this time everywhere victorious on the Continent, and there were fears of an invasion.

Fitzwilliam at once applied himself to the work entrusted to him. He removed Edward Cooke from the post of under-secretary, on a pension of £1,200 a year; and also John Beresford, the commissioner of customs, whose relations held most of the lucrative offices of his department, and who retired on full pay. Both of these had been identified with the system Lord Fitzwilliam came to break up. In the joy of the good news, parliament, on the motion of Grattan, voted £200,000 for the expenses of the navy in the war now going on with France, and 20,000 men for the army. The whole country was in a state of excitement; innumerable petitions poured in from Catholics and Protestants alike; and it is interesting to note that one of the strongest addresses in favour of the intended measure came from the purely Protestant corporation of Derry, the descendants of the very men who had so valiantly defended the city a century before against the army of the Catholic King James.

As the first direct move, Grattan, having previously arranged the matter with the viceroy, brought in a bill, on the 12th of February, for the admission of Catholics to parliament; and there was almost perfect agreement on the question in the whole house. But an unexpected obstacle arose which disconcerted all the plans for reform, and dashed the hopes of the country. A small mischievous clique at the Castle, led by Fitzgibbon, Beresford, and Cooke, took determined steps to defeat the bill. Beresford went to England and had an interview with the king, to whom he made bitter complaints, while Fitzgibbon submitted an elaborate statement to show that his majesty could not consent to Emancipation without breaking the coronation oath. Between them they seem to have persuaded the king that the Protestant religion was in danger. On the other hand, it would appear that Pitt and the rest of the English Cabinet permitted themselves to be intimidated by Beresford and Cooke.

While all this was going on in England, Fitzwilliam was allowed to proceed openly with the measure in Dublin; and when the whole country was in a flutter of expectation, and after the large supplies mentioned above had been voted, the English minister turned right round; the king refused his consent, without which no measure could pass; orders were sent to stop the bill; and the whole matter came to an end. Emancipation was abandoned, Beresford was restored, and the old policy of hostility to

Catholics was resumed. Earl Fitzwilliam was recalled and left Ireland on the 25th March. He was escorted by sorrowing crowds to the water side, and his coach was drawn along by some of the leading citizens, while the shops were closed and the city put on the appearance of mourning: mourning and gloom with good reason, for by that fatal blow the joyous loyalty of the whole country was suddenly changed to sullen distrust, discontent, and disloyalty. And as if to show in the clearest way that the government approved of what had been done, Fitzgibbon, one of the chief agents in bringing about the withdrawal of the bill, was immediately afterwards made earl of Clare. That cruel disappointment spread sorrow and indignation all over the country, not only among the Catholics, but also among the Protestants of the two parties—the moderates led by Grattan and the more advanced represented by the United Irishmen; and from whatever causes it may have arisen, it was in a great measure answerable for the tremendous evils that followed. The king's objections are commonly put forward as the reason of the sudden change of policy. But some suppose that the whole scheme was planned by Pitt in order to obtain large supplies from the Irish parliament: at any rate it is certain he made no attempt to bring round the king by argument.

Later on in this same year, under Fitzwilliam's successor, Lord Camden, a measure was passed of great importance to the Catholics of Ireland. Catholic young men who wished to become priests had long been in the habit of going to France for their education, as they had no opportunity of getting educated at home. The government were well aware of this; and as they feared that the young priests, after so long a residence in France, might come back imbued with republican or revolutionary ideas, they founded the college of Maynooth for the education of the Catholic clergy, and endowed it with an annual grant of £8,000.

Maynooth College in 1820. From *Cromwell's Excursions*. Greatly enlarged since.

Sculpture on Window: Cathedral Church, Glendalough: Beranger, 1779.
From Petrie's *Round Towers*.

CHAPTER LXV

TOWARDS THE BRINK OF THE PRECIPICE
A.D. 1795–1797.—George III.

LOOM and silence had marked the departure of Lord Fitzwilliam. The arrival of his successor Lord Camden, on the 31st March 1795, was signalised by a furious riot in the streets of Dublin; several houses belonging to unpopular members of the government were attacked; the military had to be called out; and two of the mob were killed. The people all over the country became exasperated and desperate, and hoping for foreign aid, their leaders came to the fatal determination to attempt revolution and the establishment of a republic. The United Irishmen banded themselves as a secret, oath-bound, and of course illegal, society; and their republican principles were spreading fast among the Catholics; but the government were kept well informed of their proceedings, through Leonard Mac Nally and others within their body.

The great majority of the leaders of the United Irishmen were Protestants, who were all for Catholic Emancipation. But in many parts of Ulster there was, all along, bitter strife between the lower classes of Catholics and Protestants; strife and mutual hatred which had been kept up since the time of the Plantation nearly two centuries before. Tone, himself a Protestant, had done all in his power to bring them to friendly union and cooperation, but in vain: religious animosity was too strong for him. At last, on the 21st September 1795, the Defenders and the Peep-o'-day boys fought a regular battle at a village called the Diamond in Armagh. The Peep-o'-day boys, though inferior in number, were better armed, for the others could not keep arms unless by stealth, and the Defenders were routed with a loss of twenty or thirty killed.

The Protestants, chiefly of the Established Church, next, as a set-off against the Defenders, formed a new secret oath-bound society called

Orangemen, with the openly expressed intention to expel all Catholics from Ulster: but it is to be observed that the oath of this society was subsequently abolished. The Catholics were now, for some years, attacked and persecuted by the Protestant peasantry in many of the Ulster counties, and suffered terribly in person and property. The Protestant magistrates and gentry held meetings and endeavoured to protect them, but with little success: yet they gave some compensation to many Catholics whose houses were wrecked. Great numbers of inoffensive industrious Catholics were driven altogether out of the province, and took refuge in Connaught, which circumstance again extended the mischief: for they inspired the people among whom they settled with their own bitter feelings. Things became at last so intolerable that General Craddock was sent into Ulster with the military to restore order: but so close a watch was kept on his movements, that he found it almost impossible to arrest the bands of armed Orangemen and the evil work still went on. The more respectable members of the Orange body dissociated themselves from these proceedings, and declared that the worst of the outrages were committed by bodies of marauders who, though adopting the name, were not Orangemen at all.

The Defenders had spread rapidly from Ulster into various parts of the middle and west of Ireland: and now, like the Whiteboys, they applied themselves to redressing grievances of various kinds; and there were continual nightly disturbances, so that people's minds all over the country were kept in a state of painful anxiety General Henry Luttrell, Lord Carhampton, was sent to Connaught to repress them: but his action and the action of those who aided him held up an evil example to the people, for it was almost as lawless as the proceedings of the Defenders themselves. He seized all who were in the jails awaiting trial, and the magistrates, imitating him, arrested numbers of the peasants on the road sides: and all, both prisoners and peasants, were, without any trial, sent off to serve in the navy. Most of these men never saw their families again: and the transaction rankled fearfully among the people.

Meantime the society of United Irishmen spread, until finally it numbered 500,000. There were now many Catholics among them, for the Defenders, on the invitation of the United Irish leaders, joined the ranks in large numbers. But to the last the confederacy was mainly Protestant; and the members were far more numerous and active in Ulster than elsewhere. In 1795 Lord Edward Fitzgerald, a man of most estimable character, brother of the duke of Leinster, joined them. As a major in the British army he had served with credit in the American War; and on his return he entered the Irish parliament as an earnest supporter of Reform. The government dismissed him from his post in the army for openly expressing sympathy with the French revolution. In the end of 1796 the society was joined by

Thomas Addis Emmet, elder brother of Robert Emmet, by Arthur O'Connor formerly member of parliament for Philipstown, and by Dr. William J. Mac Nevin of Dublin, one of the few Catholics among the leaders.

Tone, who had been obliged to leave Ireland some time before, had been arranging in Paris for a French invasion, the object of which was to make Ireland an independent republic. In May 1796 Lord Edward Fitzgerald and Arthur O'Connor went to Hamburg, and O'Connor had an interview with General Hoche. The matter was at last arranged. On the 15th of December a fleet of 43 ships of war with 15,000 troops and 45,000 stand of arms, sailed from Brest for Ireland under General Hoche. General Grouchy was second in command, and with him sailed Theobald Wolfe Tone as adjutant-general. The authorities were badly prepared to repel the attack, but it was repelled without their intervention. The ships were dispersed by foul winds and fogs, and only sixteen that had kept together entered Bantry Bay. Here they waited in vain for General Hoche, whose vessel had been separated from the fleet by the storm. But the wild weather continued—tempest and snow—and at the end of a week, Roche not having come up, they cut their cables and returned to France.

Next came a stringent Insurrection act. The *Habeas Corpus* act was suspended, which suspension gave the magistrates the power to arrest anyone they pleased. General Lake got command of the army in Ulster, and he proclaimed martial law, which placed the people entirely at the mercy of the military. He arrested two committees of United Irishmen sitting in Belfast, and seized their papers, which disclosed secrets of great importance; and he attempted to disarm all Ulster, seizing great numbers of muskets, cannons, and pikes. But he did not succeed in taking all: in a little time not a gun or a pike was to be found in any house; for they were hidden in bogs and hedges where the owners could find them at any moment. For publishing a violent address, Arthur O'Connor was arrested and imprisoned in Dublin: and the jails all over the country were filled with people who had been taken up on suspicion on the evidence of spies.

The yeomanry were called out; militia regiments were sent over from England; and military, yeomanry, and militia were let loose on the people with little or no restraint. The soldiers were scattered through the country in small parties, billeted and living in free quarters on the peasantry; there was no discipline; and they did what they pleased without waiting for orders. Fearful brutalities were perpetrated, and thousands of peaceable people were driven in desperation to join the ranks of the United Irishmen.

For a good part of 1797, Ulster was really in rebellion, though no battles were fought: the United Irishmen spread everywhere, and practically had the whole province in subjection. Some, calling themselves by the name, committed many terrible outrages; but the perpetrators of these were individuals and small parties under no control; and they were denounced by the responsible United Irish leaders; just as the evildoers on the other side were denounced by the leaders of the Orange party. What greatly added to the horror of the situation in the North was the bitter animosity between the lower classes of Protestants and Catholics, each side committing frightful cruelties on the others at every opportunity. During the whole of this time assurances came from respectable classes of people all over the country, especially from Ulster, that the concession of Parliamentary Reform, Catholic Emancipation, and a satisfactory arrangement about tithes would restore quietness. In the month of May, Ponsonby and Grattan brought these matters before parliament, and Grattan produced a declaration of 900 representative Ulstermen of substance and position, a large proportion of them leading United Irishmen, that if these concessions were granted all agitation would cease. But though they earnestly urged the adoption of these reasonable healing measures, the government voted them down four to one. Whereupon Grattan and the other leading members of his party despairing of doing any good, and as a protest against the conduct of the government, withdrew from parliament.

There was yet another abortive attempt at invasion. A Dutch fleet with 15,000 men commanded by Admiral De Winter prepared to sail for Ireland in July, but again the weather interfered; they were delayed; and when at length they sailed, the fleet was utterly defeated at Camperdown by Admiral Duncan.

CHAPTER LXVI
THE REBELLION OF 1798
A.D. 1798.—George III.

ELIEVING it impossible to bring about reform of any kind by peaceable means, the United Irish leaders, in an evil hour, determined on open rebellion; but the government were kept well informed by spies of their secret proceedings, and bided their time till things were ripe for a swoop. They knew that the 23rd of May had been fixed as the day of rising. On the 12th of March 1798, Major Swan, a magistrate, acting on the information of Thomas Reynolds, arrested Oliver Bond and fourteen other delegates assembled in Bond's house in Bridge Street, Dublin, arranging the plan of rebellion, and seized all their papers. On the same day several other leaders were arrested in their homes.

A reward of £1,000 was offered for the apprehension of Lord Edward Fitzgerald, the moving spirit of the confederacy. After some time the authorities received information from Francis Higgins—commonly known as the "Sham Squire"—that he was concealed in the house of Nicholas Murphy, a feather merchant of Thomas Street, Dublin. Lord Edward was lying ill in bed, when Major Swan, yeomanry captain Ryan, and a soldier, entered the room; but he drew a dagger and struggled desperately, wounding Swan and Ryan. Major Sirr, who had accompanied the party, now rushed in with half-a-dozen soldiers, and taking aim, shot Lord Edward in the shoulder, who was then overpowered and taken prisoner. But on the 4th of June he died of his wound while in prison, at the age of thirty-two. On the 21st May two brothers Henry and John Sheares, barristers, members of the Dublin directory of the United Irishmen, were arrested. They were convicted on the 12th of July, and hanged two days afterwards. A reprieve for Henry came too late—five minutes after the execution.

Vinegar Hill.

The rising took place on the 24th of May. It was only partial: confined chiefly to the counties of Kildare, Wicklow, and Wexford; and there were some slight attempts in Carlow, Queen's Co., Meath, and county Dublin. But Dublin city did not rise, for it had been placed under martial law, and almost the whole of the leaders there had been arrested. The insurrection was quite premature; and the people were almost without arms, without discipline, plan, or leaders. On the 26th of May a body of 4,000 insurgents were defeated on the hill of Tara. On Whitsunday the 27th, the rising broke out in Wexford. There, as well as in some of the neighbouring counties, the rebellion assumed a sectarian character which it had not elsewhere: the rebels were nearly all Roman Catholics, though many of their leaders were Protestants. This Wexford rising was not the result of premeditation or of any concert with the Dublin directory of the United Irishmen; for the society had not made much headway among the quiet industrious peasants of that county, who were chiefly descendants of English colonists. Though there was a good deal of disaffection among them, chiefly caused by alarming rumours of intended massacres, they did not want to rise. They were driven to rebellion simply by the terrible barbarities of the military, the yeomen, and more especially the North Cork militia; they rose in desperation without any plan or any idea of what they were to do; and in their vengeful fury they committed many terrible outrages on the Protestant loyalist inhabitants, in blind retaliation for the far worse excesses of the militia.

Father John Murphy, parish priest of Kilcormick near Ferns, finding his little chapel of Boleyvogue burned by the yeomen, took the lead of the rebels, with another priest, Father Michael Murphy, whose chapel had also been burned; but although these and one or two other priests were among the insurgents of Ninety-eight, the Catholic ecclesiastical authorities were entirely opposed to the rebellion. On the 27th of May the peasantry, led by Father John Murphy, defeated and annihilated a large party of the North Cork militia on the Hill of Oulart, near Enniscorthy. Having captured 800 stand of arms, they marched next on Enniscorthy; and by the stratagem of driving a herd of bullocks before them to break the ranks of the military, they took the town after a struggle of four hours; on which the garrison and the Protestant inhabitants fled to Wexford—fifteen miles off. About the same time Gorey was abandoned by its garrison, who retreated to Arklow.

At the end of May the insurgents fixed their chief encampment on Vinegar Hill, an eminence rising over Enniscorthy, at the opposite side of the Slaney. While the camp lay here, a number of Protestants, brought in from the surrounding country, were confined in an old windmill on the summit of the hill, many of whom, after being subjected day by day to some sort of trial, were put to death. On the 30th of May a detachment of military was attacked and destroyed at the Three Rocks, four miles from the town of Wexford. The insurgents now advanced towards Wexford: but the garrison, consisting chiefly of the North Cork militia, did not wait to be attacked: they marched away; and while retreating they burned and pillaged the houses and shot the peasantry wherever they met them. The exultant rebels having taken possession of Wexford, drank and feasted and plundered; but beyond this there was little outrage: with one notable exception. While they occupied the town, a fellow named Dixon on the rebel side, the captain of a small coasting vessel, who had never taken any part in the real fighting—one of those cruel cowardly natures sure to turn up on such occasions—collected a rabble, not of the townspeople, but of others who were there from the surrounding districts, and plying them with whiskey, broke open the jail where many of the Protestant gentry and others were confined. In spite of the expostulations of the more respectable leaders, the mob brought a number of the prisoners to the bridge, and after a mock trial began to kill them one by one. A number, variously stated from forty to ninety, had been murdered, and another batch were brought out, when, according to contemporary accounts, a young priest, Father Corrin, returning from some parochial duties, and seeing how things stood, rushed in at the risk of his life and commanded the executioners to their knees. Down they knelt instinctively, when in a loud voice he dictated a prayer which they repeated after him—that God might show to them the same mercy that they were about to show to the prisoners; which so awed and terrified them that they immediately stopped the executions. Forty years afterwards, Captain Kellett of Clonard near Wexford, one of the Protestant gentlemen he had saved, followed, with sorrow and reverence, the remains of that good priest to the grave. Dixon probably escaped arrest, for he is not heard of again. All this time the Protestants of the town were in terror of their lives, and a great many of them sought and obtained the protection of the Catholic priests, who everywhere exerted themselves, and with success, to prevent outrage. A Protestant gentleman named Bagenal Harvey who had been seized by government on suspicion and imprisoned in Wexford jail, was released by the insurgent peasantry and made their general.

Besides the principal encampment on Vinegar Hill, the rebels had two others; one on Carrickbyrne Hill, between New Ross and Wexford: the other on Carrigroe Hill, near Ferns. From Carrigroe, on the 1st June, a large body of them marched on Gorey: but they were routed just as they approached the town, by a party of yeomen under Lieutenant Elliott. They fared better however in the next encounter. General Loftus with 1,500 men marched from Gorey in two divisions to attack Carrigroe. One of these under Colonel Walpole was surprised on the 4th June at Toberanierin near Gorey and defeated with great loss; Walpole himself being killed and three cannons left with the insurgents. This placed Gorey in their hands.

From Vinegar Hill they marched on Newtownbarry, on the 2nd of June and took the town: but dispersing to drink and to plunder, they were attacked in turn by the soldiers whom they had driven out, and routed with a loss of 400. The same thing, but on a much larger scale, happened at New Ross, on the 5th of June. The rebels marched from Carrickbyrne, and attacking the town with great bravery in the early morning, drove the military under General Johnson from the streets out over the bridge. But there was no discipline: they fell to drink; and the soldiers returned twice and were twice repulsed. But still the drinking went on; and late in the evening the military returned once more, and this time succeeded in expelling the rebels. The fighting had continued with little intermission for ten hours, during which the troops lost 300 killed, among whom was Lord Mountjoy, colonel of the Dublin militia, better known in this book as Luke Gardiner; while the loss of the peasantry was two or three thousand. Although the rebels ultimately lost the day at New Ross, through drink and disorder, the conspicuous bravery and determination they had shown caused great apprehension among the authorities in Dublin, and produced a feeling of grave doubt as to the ultimate result in case the rebellion should spread.

In the evening of the day of the battle of New Ross, some fugitive rebels from the town broke into Scullabogue House at the foot of Carrickbyrne Hill, where a crowd of loyalist prisoners, nearly all Protestants, but with some few Catholics, were confined, and pretending they had orders from Harvey, which they had not, brought forth thirty-seven of the prisoners and murdered them. Then setting fire to a barn in which the others were locked up—between one and two hundred—they burned them all to death. No recognised leader was present at this barbarous massacre: it was the work of an irresponsible rabble.

The rebels now prepared to march on Dublin; but Major-General Needham with 1,600 men garrisoned Arklow on the coast, through which the insurgent army would have to pass. On the 9th of June they attacked the town with great determination, and there was a desperate fight, in which the cavalry were at first driven back; so that Needham would have retreated but for the bravery and firmness of one of his officers, Colonel Skerrett. Late in the evening, the death of Father Michael Murphy, who was killed by a cannonball, so disheartened his men that they gave way and abandoned the march to Dublin.

The encampment on Vinegar Hill was now the chief rebel station, and General Lake, the commander in chief of the military, organised an attack on it with 20,000 men, who were to approach simultaneously in several divisions from different points. All the divisions arrived in proper time on the morning of the 21st of June, except that of General Needham, which for some reason did not come up till the fighting was all over. A heavy fire of grape and musketry did great execution on the insurgent army, who though almost without ammunition, maintained the fight for an hour and a half, when they had to give way. The space intended for General Needham's division lay open to the south, and through this opening—"Needham's Gap" as they called it—they escaped with comparatively trifling loss, and made their way to Wexford.

This was the last considerable action of the Wexford rebellion: in face of the overwhelming odds against them the rebels lost heart and there was very little more fighting. Wexford was evacuated and was at once occupied by General Lake. Many of the leaders were now arrested, tried by court martial, and hanged, among them Bagenal Harvey, Mr. Grogan of Johnstown, Matthew Keogh, and Father John Murphy, though Lake had been made aware that several of them had successfully exerted themselves to prevent outrage. The rebellion here was practically at an end; and the whole country was now at the mercy of the yeomanry and the militia, who, without any attempt being made to stop them by their leaders, perpetrated dreadful atrocities on the peasantry. They made hardly any distinction, killing everyone they met: guilty and innocent, rebel and loyalist, men and women, all alike were consigned to the same fate; while on the other side, straggling bands of rebels traversed the country free of all restraint, and committed many outrages in retaliation for those of the yeomanry. Within about two years, while the disturbances continued, sixty-five Catholic chapels and one Protestant church were burned or destroyed in Leinster, besides countless dwelling houses.

By some misunderstanding the outbreak of the rebellion in the north was delayed. The Antrim insurgents under Henry Joy M'Cracken attacked and took the town of Antrim on the 7th June; but the military returning with reinforcements, recovered the town after a stubborn fight. M'Cracken was taken and hanged on the 17th of the same month. In Down the rebels, under Henry Munro, captured Saintfield, and encamped in Lord Moira's demesne near Ballynahinch; but on the 14th of June they were attacked by generals Nugent and Barber, and defeated after a very obstinate fight—commonly known as the battle of Ballynahinch. Munro escaped, but was soon after captured, convicted in court martial, and hanged at his own door.

Lord Cornwallis, a humane and distinguished man, was appointed lord lieutenant on the 21st of June, with supreme military command. He endeavoured to restore quiet; and his first step was an attempt to stop the dreadful cruelties now committed by the soldiers and militia all over the country: but in spite of everything he could do these outrages continued for several months. Had he been in command from the beginning, instead of the harsh and injudicious General Lake, it is probable that the rebellion would have been suppressed with not a tithe of the bloodshed on either side.

After the rebellion had been crushed, a small French force of about a thousand men under General Humbert landed at Killala in Mayo on the 22nd of August 1798, and took possession of the town. Two Irishmen accompanied Humbert, Bartholomew Teeling and Matthew Tone, brother of Theobald Wolfe Tone. But as there was no sign of a popular rising, this little force, having first defeated the militia, and after some further skirmishing against vastly superior numbers, surrendered to Lord Cornwallis, and were sent back to France, all except Tone and Teeling, who were tried

John Philpot Curran. From an Engraving by S. Freeman: and that from original portrait.

and hanged. This partial expedition was followed by another under Admiral Bompart:—One 74 gun ship named the *Hoche,* with eight frigates and 3,000 men under General Hardi, among whom was Theobald Wolfe Tone, sailed from Brest on the 20th of September. The *Hoche* and three others arrived off Lough Swilly, where they were encountered by a British squadron under Sir John Borlase Warren. There was a terrible fight of six hours, during which the *Hoche* sustained the chief force of the attack till she became a helpless wreck and had to surrender. Tone fought with desperation: courting but escaping death. After the surrender, he was recognised and sent in irons to Dublin, where he was tried by court martial and condemned to be hanged. He earnestly begged to be shot, not hanged, on the plea that he was a French officer; but his petition was rejected. On the morning fixed for the execution he cut his throat with a penknife. Meantime Curran in a masterly speech, succeeded on legal grounds in staying the execution for further argument; but Tone died from his self-inflicted wound on the 19th of November, 1798. In the numerous trials during and after the rebellion, Curran was always engaged on the side of the prisoners; and though he did not often succeed in having them released, his brilliant and fearless speeches were wonderful efforts of genius.

CHAPTER LXVII
THE UNION
A.D. 1799–1803.—George III.

THE opinion of the English prime minister William Pitt, the course of events for the last few years in Ireland had rendered the time opportune for his long cherished project of a Legislative Union between Great Britain and Ireland:—that the Irish parliament should be abolished, and that there should be only one parliament for both countries. It was on all hands admitted that this could not be accomplished unless the Irish parliament willed it; and now that the rebellion was all over, he began to make carefully planned arrangements to secure a majority in favour of the Union: for he well knew that there would be determined opposition in Ireland. On the 22nd January, the marquis of Cornwallis being lord lieutenant and Lord Castlereagh chief secretary, the project of Union was, by Pitt's direction, indirectly referred to in the Irish parliament, in the speech from the throne; but the opposition at once took the matter up, and they were joined by many who had hitherto been supporters of the government, among others John Foster the speaker, Sir John Parnell chancellor of the exchequer, Prime Sergeant Fitzgerald, and Sir Jonah Barrington: all fearing the loss of their parliament. They moved "that the undoubted birthright of the people of Ireland, a resident and independent legislature, should be maintained"; and after an excited debate of twenty-two hours, the votes were equally divided, which was considered a defeat for the government. Subsequently the opposition succeeded in having the clause referring to the Union altogether struck out of the speech: which meant that they refused even to consider the question. Parnell and Fitzgerald were soon afterwards dismissed from their offices. It is to be observed that in these divisions nearly all those who voted for Union were office-holders or pensioners of the government; while the great majority of those who voted against it were persons who had been freely elected.

In February the scheme was brought forward in the English parliament by Pitt, and approved. In Ireland elaborate preparations were made to carry it in the next session. Persons holding offices who showed themselves adverse to the measure were dismissed, or brought round by threats of dismissal. The Irish government, as we have seen, had been all along corrupt; but now—still under outside orders—it went far beyond anything ever experienced before. Those who had the disposal of seats were in great alarm; for if the Union was carried the 300 members would have to be reduced to a third, so that about 200 constituencies would be disfranchised. The opposition of these proprietors was bought off by direct money payments; about £15,000 was paid for each seat; and several proprietors who had each a number of seats at their disposal, received very large sums. The entire amount paid for the whole of the "rotten" or "pocket" boroughs as they were called, was £1,260,000, which Ireland itself had to pay, for it was added to the Irish national debt.

To purchase the votes of individual members, and the favour of certain influential outsiders, twenty-eight persons were created peers, and thirty-two of those already peers were promoted; and there were besides, great numbers of bribes in the shape of pensions, judgeships, baronetcies, preferments, government situations, and direct cash. All this was done with scarcely an attempt at concealment. The chief managers of the whole business, under the inspiration of Pitt, were Lord Cornwallis, Lord Castlereagh, and Lord Clare (John Fitzgibbon); but Cornwallis, though quite in favour of the measure, expressed the utmost abhorrence at being forced to take a part in such transactions. So general was the feeling against the Union, and so deep was the indignation against the means employed to bring it about, that he expressed his belief that half the majority who voted for it would be delighted if they were defeated: yet he held on to his post till the measure was carried through. But though the majority in favour of

Union was secured by gross and illegal corruption, it must not be imagined that all who voted for it were corrupt; for there were some—though not many—who honestly believed it was the best course.

The country was now thoroughly roused: so that hundreds of petitions against Union came from all directions, and there was such exasperation everywhere, that dangerous riots were apprehended. The intense feeling against it extended even to the yeomanry, the very men who had taken such a prominent part in putting down the rebellion; and it was feared that they might turn out to resist it with arms in their hands. But the prime movers were determined: and in order to keep down the free expression of opinion, English soldiers were poured in by the thousand, so that the country was now occupied by an immense army. The session opened on the 15th of January: the last meeting of the Irish parliament. Grattan, knowing what was coming, had himself elected member for Wicklow; and though very ill, he rose from his bed and took his seat dressed in the uniform of the volunteers. Dublin was in a state of fearful excitement. The streets were filled with dismayed and sorrow-stricken crowds; but there were plenty of cavalry to keep them within bounds. Lord Castlereagh brought forward the motion in the commons. The anti-unionists opposed the project most determinedly; Grattan, worn with sickness, pleaded with all his old fiery eloquence. Sir John Parnell demanded that there should be a dissolution, and that a new parliament should be called to determine this great question, so that the opinion of the country might be obtained, as is usually done when measures of great importance are proposed; but the unionist leaders carried everything. There were many motions: on the first the government had 158 against 115: and in the others there were corresponding majorities; but the minority, who could not be bought over by bribes, stood firm and struggled vainly to the last. Despite all their efforts the bill was finally carried in the commons. It was next passed in the house of lords, by a majority of nearly three to one, after which the royal assent was given on the 1st August, and the Act came into force on the 1st January 1801.

The main provisions of the Act of Union were these. The two kingdoms to be henceforward one:—"the United Kingdom of Great Britain and Ireland." The Irish representation in the united Parliament to be one hundred members in the house of commons, and thirty-two peers (of whom four were to be spiritual peers, *i.e.* Protestant bishops) in the house of lords: the twenty-eight lay peers to be elected by all the Irish peers, and the four bishops to be selected in rotation. The same regulations as to trade and commerce to apply to all subjects of the United Kingdom. The Irish Established Church to be continued for ever, and to be united with that of England. Ireland to contribute two-seventeenths to the expenditure of the United Kingdom, for twenty years, when new arrangements would be made. Each of the two countries to retain its own national debt as then existing; but all future debts contracted to be joint debts.

Parliament House, Dublin: now the Bank of Ireland, From Wright's Ireland Illustrated. *Drawn by Petrie.*

Three years after the Union there was one other attempt at insurrection, which however was confined to Dublin. Several of the leaders of the United Irishmen were at this time in Paris; and as they had some reason to expect aid from Napoleon, they projected a general rising in Ireland. One of their body, Robert Emmet, a gifted, earnest, noble-minded young man, twenty-four years of age, returned to Dublin in 1802, to carry out the arrangements, and expended his whole private fortune in secretly manufacturing pikes and other arms.

His plan was to attack Dublin Castle and the Pigeon House Fort; and he had intended that the insurrection should take place in August 1803, by which time he calculated the invasion from France would come off; but an accidental explosion in one of his depots precipitated matters. News came in that the military were approaching; whereupon, in desperation, he sallied from his depot in Marshalsea Lane, into Thomas Street and towards the castle, with about 100 men. The city was soon in an uproar; disorderly crowds gathered in the streets, and some stragglers, bent on mischief and beyond all restraint, began outrages. Meeting the chief justice, Lord Kilwarden, a good man and a humane judge, they dragged him from his coach and murdered him. When news of this outrage and others was brought to Emmet, he was filled with horror, and attempted in vain to quell the mob. Seeing that the attempt on the castle was hopeless he fled to Rathfarnham, and might have escaped: but he insisted on remaining to take leave of Sarah Curran, daughter of John Philpot Curran, to whom he was secretly engaged to be married. He was arrested by Major Sirr on the 25th of August at a house in Harold's Cross; and soon after was tried and convicted, making a short speech of great power in the dock. On the next day, the 20th of September 1803, he was hanged in Thomas Street.

Chapter LXVIII
Catholic Emancipation
A.D. 1803–1829. George III (to 1820).
George IV (1820).

F the Irish Roman Catholics had actively opposed the Union, in all probability it could not have been carried; for as Lord Cornwallis afterwards declared, they "had it in their power to have frustrated the views of the government and throw the country into the utmost confusion." Accordingly Pitt had at first intended to include Catholic Emancipation in the articles of Union; an intention afterwards unhappily abandoned. But in order to lessen the hostility of the Catholics, they were led to believe, by the leading members of the Irish government, on Pitt's suggestion, that Emancipation would immediately follow the Union. Through these representations many of the leading Catholics, both lay and ecclesiastical, were induced to express themselves in favour of the measure, and the great body held back from active opposition. Thus the Catholics were kept out of the way and the Union was carried. And now they naturally looked for the fulfilment of the promise; but they looked in vain: for the government showed not the least disposition to move in the matter. It is known that on the appointment of Lord Cornwallis as lord lieutenant, the king had written to Pitt to say that he would not consent to Emancipation, as he considered it would be a breach of his coronation oath: and this is commonly assigned as the chief reason why the question was dropped. There is scarce a doubt however that if Pitt had been earnest in the matter he could have brought the king to yield: but he never made any real effort. For twenty-nine years emancipation was withheld; and when it came at last, the concession was brought about, as we shall see, by circumstances quite independent of representations and promises.

The Catholics, however, never abandoned their hope; and a few years after the Union a small section of them, including a few bishops, agreed, as an inducement for the government to grant Emancipation, that the crown should have a veto in the appointment of bishops: that is to say, when a person had been selected by the Irish ecclesiastical authorities, his name should be submitted to the king; and if the king objected another was to be chosen. The general body of Catholics, clergy and people, knew nothing of all this; but the matter was made public when, in 1808, a petition for Catholic Relief was presented to parliament by Grattan and some others, who, on the authority of two leading Irish Catholics, openly offered to accept the veto in case emancipation was granted. Whereupon the clergy and people generally repudiated it: the bishops formally condemned it; and besides all this, the government, even with this offer before them, refused to entertain the petition. Nevertheless the veto question continued to be discussed in Ireland for some years, and caused considerable divergence of opinion among Catholics; the Irish aristocracy were generally in favour of it; but those who opposed it, led by O'Connell, ultimately prevailed.

Soon after the Union, Grattan, the greatest and noblest of all the Protestant advocates of Catholic rights, entered the imperial parliament, and never lost an opportunity of pleading for Emancipation. Towards the end of 1819, while residing at Tinnehinch, his health rapidly declined; and he determined to make one last effort for his Catholic fellow-countrymen. He set out for the house of commons, but never reached it; and he died in London, speaking of Ireland with his last breath.

During the later years of Grattan's career, another great man was beginning to come to the front, before whose genius all the obstacles to Catholic emancipation ultimately went down. Daniel O'Connell, afterwards familiarly called "The Liberator," was born at Carhan beside Cahersiveen in Kerry on the 6th of August 1775, and was educated partly in Ireland and partly in France. He was called to the bar in 1798, and at once made his mark as a successful advocate. About the year 1810 he began to take a prominent part in public questions, and before long became the acknowledged leader of the Irish Catholics. Thenceforward, till the time of his death, he was the chief figure in Irish political history, and was one of the greatest popular leaders the world ever saw.

It may be said that O'Connell founded the system of peaceful, per-severing, popular agitation against political grievances—keeping strictly within the law. In all his labours, and more especially during the agitation for emancipation, he was ably seconded by Richard Lalor Sheil, who was almost as great an orator as O'Connell himself.

Richard Lalor Sheil. National Gallery, Dublin.

The old Catholic Committee had gradually died out; and O'Connell and Sheil founded the "Catholic Association," which was the principal agency that ultimately enabled them to achieve emancipation. The expenses were defrayed chiefly by a subscription from the people, of one penny a week, which was called "Catholic rent": and the association soon spread through all Ireland. This movement, of which O'Connell and Sheil were the mainsprings all through, was the means of spreading broadcast a free press and of creating healthful public opinion. The government viewed the new Association with jealousy and alarm; and an act of parliament was passed in 1825 to put it down; but O'Connell, who took great care never to have the law broken, contrived an ingenious plan by which the act was evaded; and the association went on as before. In Waterford and several other places, by means of the perfect organisation of this association,

Protestant members favourable to emancipation were returned, the forty-shilling freeholders voting for them; for as these tenants had leases for life they were in a great measure independent of the landlords, and successfully resisted their influence.

An oath similar to that framed in 1692 to exclude Irish Catholics from parliament, was at this period, and had been for a long time previously, in force in the parliament in England; so that although there was nothing to prevent a Catholic being elected, he could not enter the house as member, since no Catholic could take this oath. It had been recommended by the veteran John Keogh that some Catholic should be elected member, and should present himself at Westminster and be excluded by the oath; so that the absurdity and hardship of letting a constituency remain altogether without a member because the person elected refused to take an oath that his own religion was false, should be brought home to the people of the empire. Keogh believed that this would lead to emancipation. A vacancy now (1828) occurred in Clare, as the sitting member Mr. Vesey Fitzgerald, having accepted the office of president of the Board of Trade, had to seek re-election. O'Connell determined to oppose him, so as to bring the matter to a test. His address to the people of Clare aroused extraordinary enthusiasm, and notwithstanding the utmost efforts of the landlords, he was returned by an immense majority.

This election aroused sympathy everywhere in England for the Catholics, so that the government were alarmed; and they became still more so when they found that the branches of the association were preparing to return Catholic members all through Ireland. Wellington and Peel, forced by public opinion, gave way, being now convinced that emancipation could no longer be withheld with safety. Peel introduced into the commons a bill for the emancipation of the Catholics. After several days' stormy debate the third reading was carried on the 30th of March. The debate in the lords was even more violent than in the commons. But Wellington ended the matter by declaring that they should choose either of the two alternatives, emancipation or civil war. The bill passed the third reading, after a long debate and much bitter opposition, and received the royal assent on the 13th of April.

After the bill had become law O'Connell presented himself at the bar of the house for the first time since his election to claim his seat; knowing well what would happen. According to the terms of the Emancipation Act it was only those elected after the 13th of April that came under the new oath: a clause designedly inserted by Peel in order to put O'Connell to the trouble and expense of another election. The old oath was put into his hand; and looking at it for a few seconds he said:—"I see here one assertion as to a matter of fact which I know to be untrue: I see a second as to a matter of opinion which I believe to be untrue. I therefore refuse to take this oath": after which he withdrew. Another writ was issued for Clare, and he was returned unopposed.

By this Emancipation Act a new oath was framed which Catholics might take. The act therefore admitted Catholics to the right of being members of parliament in either house. It admitted them also to all civil and military offices, with three exceptions: those of regent, lord lieutenant, and lord chancellor.[1]

Thomas Moore. National Gallery, Dublin.

---

[1]The restriction regarding the last of these three offices was removed some years ago by act of parliament, when Lord O'Hagan, a Roman Catholic, became lord chancellor of Ireland.

The act contained one fatal provision which O'Connell had to submit to; it raised the franchise in Ireland to £10, though in England the qualification remained at the limit of forty shillings: this disfranchised all the forty-shilling freehold voters, who constituted the main strength of the Catholic party.

Several influences had been for years at work to soften the feelings of England towards Irish Roman Catholics, so as to prepare the way for emancipation; among the chief of which were the writings of Thomas Moore. Though Grattan's impassioned pleading had brought the claims of his country vividly before the English house of commons, Moore's Irish Melodies—beautiful words to beautiful music—were, it may be said, the first clear gentle voice heard across the sea directly from the Irish Catholics themselves. These songs were read and sung with delight all over England, and they sank deeply into the hearts of the English people. But there still remained, especially among the ruling classes, much hostility, and a widespread determination to resist further concession. To O'Connell is due the credit of breaking down the opposition of Parliament, and of carrying emancipation; but he was faithfully and ably seconded by Richard Lalor Sheil.

CHAPTER LXIX
FROM EMANCIPATION TO THE DEATH OF O'CONNELL
George IV (to 1830).
A.D. 1829–1847. William IV (1830–1837).
Victoria (1837).

FTER emancipation the way was opened to other reforms beneficial to the Catholics. For many years previous to this, the government had been giving money to support schools for elementary education all through Ireland. But they were suitable for Protestants only: Catholics could not conscientiously attend them, as they would have to be present at Protestant religious instruction, while no provision was made to give them instruction in their own religion. To remedy this state of things the National system of education was established, which afforded means of education to all, Catholics and Protestants alike. For this purpose it had—as it has still—two main rules: first, pupils of all religious denominations, who attended a school, were to be taught together in the ordinary school course, but to receive religious instruction separately: second, there was to be no interference with the religious principles of any child. From that time to the present both the number of schools and the money given by government to support them have gone on increasing.

The Catholic peasantry were still called on to pay tithes, and they continued to be harassed by the exactions of tithe-proctors and others, who, if the money was not forthcoming, seized the poor people's cows, furniture, beds, blankets, kettles, or anything else they could lay hands on.

At last about 1830 there arose a general movement against the payment of tithes: the people resisted all through the south of Ireland; and for many years there was a "tithe war." The military and police were constantly called out to support the collectors in making their seizures: and almost daily there were conflicts, often with great loss of life. At Newtownbarry in Wexford, in 1831, thirteen peasants were killed by the yeomanry and police; in 1832, eleven policemen and several peasants were killed in a tithe-conflict at Carrickshock near Knocktopher in Kilkenny: and many other such fatal encounters took place. There was determined resistance everywhere; and the cost of collection was far greater than the amount collected. Hundreds of Protestant clergymen received little or nothing and were reduced to poverty; and to relieve these temporarily, government advanced a large sum on loan. All this time O'Connell, seconded by Sheil, struggled vainly both in and out of parliament for the total abolition of tithes: or for some arrangement that would shift the burden from the shoulders of the tenants. The people continued to resist, and the tithe war went on, though an attempt was made to stop it by a Coercion act. Some years later (in 1838), the tithes, reduced by one-fourth to pay the cost of collection, were put on the landlords, which in a great measure put an end to the tithe war: an arrangement that would have saved endless trouble and much bloodshed if it had been adopted earlier.

In 1838, the Rev. Theobald Mathew, a young priest belonging to the order of Capuchin Friars, joined a temperance society that had been started in Cork by some Protestant gentlemen, chiefly Quakers. He took the total abstinence pledge, and soon became the leading spirit in the society. From that time forth he devoted himself almost exclusively to the cause of temperance, going all through Ireland, preaching to immense congregations, and administering the total abstinence pledge to vast numbers of people of all religious denominations. A wonderful change soon came over the country: for drunkenness with its attendant evils and miseries almost disappeared. The good effects were long felt, and are to some extent felt still. For though the evil of drink has in a great measure returned, it is not nearly so general as formerly; and drunkenness, which before Father Mathew's time was generally looked upon with a certain degree of indulgence, and by some was considered a thing to boast of, is now universally regarded as discreditable.

O'Connell and other Irish leaders had all along hoped to have the Act of Union repealed, that is, to get back for Ireland Grattan's parliament, with all its independence and all its privileges. But the struggle for emancipation absorbed so much of their energies that for about thirty years after the Repeal agitation was started in 1810, it was carried on only in a faint sort of way. In 1840 it was vigorously renewed, when O'Connell founded the

Daniel O'Connell. From an Engraving in National Gallery, Dublin: and that from an original portrait.

Repeal Association: and in 1843 he began to hold great public meetings in favour of Repeal, at which vast numbers of the people attended, eager to support the movement and to hear his magnificent addresses. At one meeting held on the Hill of Tara, the ancient seat of the Irish kings, it was computed that a quarter of a million of people were present. About thirty of these meetings—"Monster Meetings" as they came to be called—were held during 1843. At last the government took action, and "proclaimed," *i.e.* forbade, the meeting that was arranged to be held at Clontarf on the 8th October. After this O'Connell and several others were arrested, tried and convicted. But when they had spent three months in prison, they had to be released in September 1843; because the house of lords, before whom O'Connell brought the case, decided that the trial was not a fair one, inasmuch as the government had selected a one-sided jury. It may be said that this ended the agitation for Repeal.

In those days almost the whole population of Ireland subsisted on the potato. But in 1845 and 1846 the potato crop failed, and there was a great famine, the most calamitous the country had ever experienced. In 1846 and 1847 the people died by hundreds of thousands of starvation and fever. The preventive measures taken by government, in the shape of public works, were quite inadequate: but the English people individually made noble efforts to save the starving peasantry; and money in enormous amounts came pouring in. One sad feature of this great national catastrophe was that in each of those two years Ireland produced quite enough of corn to feed the people of the whole country; but day after day it was exported in shiploads, while the peasantry were dying of hunger. Notwithstanding the great efforts of benevolent individuals and associations, one-fourth of the people of Ireland died of famine and disease during 1846 and 1847. So tremendous a calamity had probably never been experienced by any other country of Europe.

After O'Connell's trial and conviction, a number of the younger men among his followers, losing faith in his method of peaceful and constitutional agitation, separated from him and formed what is called the "Young Ireland Party." They were educated men of the highest character, and many of them of great literary ability. O'Connell's various organisations from the very beginning of his career, had been almost exclusively Catholic; but the Young Ireland party included Catholics and Protestants; and one of their aims was to unite the whole people of Ireland of all religious denominations in one great organisation.

The *Nation* newspaper had been founded in 1842 by Charles Gavan Duffy, John Blake Dillon, and Thomas Davis; the first two Catholics, the third a Protestant; and they now used it to give expression to their views. It was very ably conducted, its pages abounding in brilliant writing, both prose and poetry: of which a large part has become permanently embodied in Irish national literature. The writers were much less guarded than O'Connell; their articles tended towards revolutionary doctrines; and they soon came in conflict with the law. Other papers with similar principles and objects were founded, with writers who were still more outspoken. Of these latter the most conspicuous for his brilliantly written and violent articles, was John Mitchel, an Ulster Unitarian, who openly advocated rebellion and total separation from England.

During all this time of disruption and trouble the whole of the Catholic clergy and the great body of the people, forming collectively the "Old Ireland Party," stood by O'Connell. The secession of the Young Irelanders was a cause of great grief to him; and he denounced them with unsparing bitterness; for he foresaw that they would bring trouble on themselves and on the country; which indeed came to pass soon after his death. Yet in many ways this brilliant band of young men exercised great influence for good, which remained after the trouble and the trials were all past and gone, and which remains to this day. They infused new life and energy into Irish national literature, spread among the people a knowledge of Irish history, Irish music, and Irish lore of all kinds, and taught them to admire what was good and noble among past generations of Irishmen of every creed and party.

In 1846, O'Connell, worn out by labour and anxiety began to decline in health: and he suffered intense anguish of mind at witnessing the calamities of the people he loved so well: for the famine was at this time making fearful havoc among them. In the following year his physicians, hoping that change of air and scene might benefit or restore him, advised him to go to the Continent. He set out on a journey to Rome, partly devotional and partly for health; but his strength failed on the way; and he died at Genoa on the 15th May 1847, at the age of seventy-one. In accordance with his latest wish, his heart was carried to Rome, and his body was brought back to Ireland and buried in Glasnevin, where a stately pillar-tower, after the model of the round towers of old, now marks his resting place.

The O'Connell Monument, Glasnevin.

Latin words fully written out.

Initium Aevangelii domini nostri ihesu christi filii dei sicut scriptum est in esaia profeta. Ecce mitto anguelum meum.

Translation.

The beginning of the Gospel of our Lord Jesus Christ Son of God as it is written in Esaia the prophet. Behold I send my angel.

Ornament on top of Devenish Round Tower. From Petrie's Round Towers, *400.*

INDEX

A

Abbey Knockmoy, Galway, 29.
Act of Explanation, 207.
—— of Renunciation, 286.
—— of Repeal, 285.
—— of Settlement, 206, 209, 215.
—— of Supremacy, 143, 186.
—— of Uniformity, 143, 186, 208.
Adamnan, St., 55, 56.
Adrian IV, Pope, 89.
Aedan, king of the Scottish Dalriada, 67.
Aed Mac Ainmirè, King, 55, 67–69.
Aengus mac Natfree, King, 52.
—— the Culdee, 63.
Aha-clee (Dublin), 75.
Aherlow, Glen of, at the Galtys, 151, 178.
Aidan, founder of Lindisfarne, 64.
Ailbè, St., 56.
Ailech, see Greenan Ely.
Aill-na-meeran, at Ushnagh, 41.
Alban or Scotland, 43, 44.
Albinus, 57.
Aldborough, 262.
Aldfrid, King, in Ireland, 62.
Aldhelm, Bishop, 62.
Allen, Archbishop, 133, 135, 140.
Alphabets, ancient Irish, 64.
Alps, the, 44.
Amalgaid, King, 52.
Amator, Bishop, 48.
Amergin, 38.
Amlaff, the Dane, 75.

Anglo-Irish Lords, chap. xix, 94, 95, 97.
Anglo-Normans, 31, 42, 86, 87, 93.
Angus, of Scotland, 67.
Animals, wild, 3, 4.
Annals, Irish, 7, 8.
Annaly, 102.
Anne, Queen, 255, 258, 264.
Annesley case, 266.
Anrad, the Dane, 79.
Antrim, 47, 66, 67, 103, 146, 153, 165, 205, 211, 278, 308.
Aran Island, 56.
Ardagh Chalice, 10.
Ardee, 71, 83, 107, 109, 111, 169.
Ardes in Down, 153.
Ardpatrick in Limerick, 178.
Ard-ri, the over-king, 29, 30, 38, 39, 41, 71, 82, 85, 104.
Ardscull near Athy, 107.
Arklow, 305, 307.
Armagh, 9, 14, 29, 39, 49, 52, 70, 80, 81, 86, 102, 133, 140, 159, 160, 164, 165, 167, 187, 198, 208, 291, 300.
Arms and armour, 30, 31, 129.
Art, 8–11, 65.
Artaine at Dublin, 136.
Ashton, Sir Arthur, 202.
Assaroe waterfall, at Ballyshannon, 35, 163.
Assemblies or Fairs, see Fes.
Athenry, Battle of, 108, 131.
Athlone, 224, 230, 242–247, 249, 253.
Athy, 81, 107.
Aughrim, 179, 242–247, 249.

326

H

I

T

U

CPSIA information can be obtained
at www.ICGtesting.com
Printed in the USA
BVHW09s2008020918
526266BV00015B/144/P